The US–India Nuclear Agreement

The US–India Nuclear Agreement

Accommodating the Anomaly?

Vandana Bhatia

LEXINGTON BOOKS
Lanham • Boulder • New York • London

Published by Lexington Books
An imprint of The Rowman & Littlefield Publishing Group, Inc.
4501 Forbes Boulevard, Suite 200, Lanham, Maryland 20706
www.rowman.com

Unit A, Whitacre Mews, 26-34 Stannary Street, London SE11 4AB

British Library Cataloguing in Publication Information Available

Library of Congress Cataloging-in-Publication Data

Names: Bhatia, Vandana, author.
Title: The US-India Nuclear Agreement : accommodating the anomaly? / Vandana Bhatia.
Other titles: U.S.-India Nuclear Agreement | United States-India Nuclear Agreement | India-US Nuclear Agreement
Description: Lanham : Lexington Books, [2017] | Includes bibliographical references and index.
Identifiers: LCCN 2017019003 (print) | LCCN 2017013133 (ebook) | ISBN 9781498506267 (Electronic) | ISBN 9781498506250 (cloth : alk. paper)
Subjects: LCSH: Agreement for Cooperation between the Government of India and the Government of the United States of America Concerning Peaceful Uses of Nuclear Energy (2008 October 8) | Nuclear energy--Law and legislation--United States. | Nuclear energy--Law and legislation--India. | Nuclear nonproliferation--Government policy--United States. | Nuclear nonproliferation--Government policy--India. | United States--Foreign relations--India. | India--Foreign relations--United States. | Nuclear nonproliferation--International cooperation.
Classification: LCC K3988.2.I4 (print) | LCC K3988.2.I4 B43 2017 (ebook) | DDC 327.1/7470954--dc23
LC record available at https://lccn.loc.gov/2017019003

∞™ The paper used in this publication meets the minimum requirements of American National Standard for Information Sciences Permanence of Paper for Printed Library Materials, ANSI/NISO Z39.48-1992.

Printed in the United States of America

Contents

Introduction

The dual nature of nuclear technology—its enormous technological benefits with substantial risks of annihilation—has created a paradox for the human race. Ever since the onset of the Atomic era, the world has been grappling with the challenge of proliferation of nuclear technology—illegitimate diversion of fissile materials and knowhow from civilian nuclear programs to weaponization.[1] The U.S. spearheaded the establishment of a global nonproliferation regime—a web of treaties, International Atomic Energy Agency (IAEA) safeguards, and export control arrangements—with the purpose of controlling the spread of nuclear technology. The Nuclear Nonproliferation Treaty (NPT), at the core of the nuclear nonproliferation regime, rests on a delicate balance of inequitable obligations and access to nuclear technology between nuclear weapon states (NWS) and nonnuclear weapon states (NNWS). The NPT is almost a universal treaty with 187 member states, yet it has faced considerable challenges. First, three states (India, Israel, and Pakistan) consistently refused to sign the treaty and subsequently, emerged as defacto nuclear weapon states. In addition, South Sudan, which became independent in 2011, has so far not acceded to the NPT. Second, the treaty has faced issues of non-compliance from the nonnuclear weapon member states. For instance, North Korea, despite being an NNWS member of the NPT, developed an advanced nuclear weapons program. In 2003, North Korea withdrew from the treaty and has since conducted five nuclear tests (2006, 2009, 2013, and twice in 2016). Proceeding on a somewhat similar path, Iran in pursuit of uranium enrichment capabilities refused mandatory inspections by the IAEA. Consequently, sanctions were imposed on Iran amidst apprehensions of Iran's withdrawal from the NPT or impending weaponization.[2] Libya, another member state, was diversifying civilian technologies toward the development of nuclear weapons, but discontinued this practice under international pressure. Similarly, Iraq under the Saddam Hussein regime was believed to be actively pursuing nuclear weapons program. Post-1991 Operation Desert Storm, Iraq was forced to verifiably dismantle its nuclear program under the supervision of IAEA inspectors from 1991–1997. Furthermore, post–9/11, the threat of proliferation of nuclear weapons assumed complex dimensions. There has been increasing focus on the nonstate actors, such as terrorist organizations and black market syndicates functioning in tandem to proliferate nuclear technology for aggressive purposes. Thus, the nuclear nonproliferation regime needs to be strengthened with additional measures to control the spread and use of sensitive technologies.

The gradual but inevitable economic growth and technological acumen in certain developing countries is creating an unprecedented demand for energy. With dwindling traditional sources of energy—oil, coal, forests—and concern that the use of fossil fuels is precipitating climate change, nuclear power is being increasingly touted as a clean, green, affordable energy solution for all nations. As of July 2016, there were a total of 446 nuclear reactors operating in 30 countries with 63 new nuclear plants under construction in 15 countries.[3] It is estimated that an electrical capacity of approximately 63 GW should be available by 2030.[4] In March 2011, the Fukushima Daiichi nuclear crisis in Japan exposed the potential dangers of nuclear reactors; yet, except for the strengthening of safety codes, it seems unlikely that this incident will thwart, or even slowdown, the voracious global quest for nuclear power. As William Potter argues:

> We cannot live with the paradox of [nuclear] proliferation and we cannot live without it. We can isolate its elements and analyse them, but we have not yet developed a political and social understanding sufficient to resolve it. Until we do, we will be like so many idiot savants, chasing the consequences of a global technological enterprise at once powerful, more, and more noxious than its creators can comprehend.

Since the spread of nuclear technology for civilian purposes, invariably, involves the risk of weaponization, this quest for nuclear materials necessitates international cooperation for equitable sharing of nuclear technology in a safeguarded environment.

In this context, India presents an interesting case study. Since the 1950s, India pursued civilian nuclear program to achieve its development objectives. In 1968, India vehemently opposed the NPT and refused to sign it; contending that the treaty was discriminatory and opposed to India's civilian nuclear energy needs. Subsequently, in 1974 India conducted the so-called "peaceful" nuclear explosion and was alleged to have diverted international nuclear technology intended for civilian purposes toward this nuclear test. In response to India's 1974 explosion, the United States established a web of technological cartels, primarily directed at prohibiting India's access to nuclear technology and materials unless it adhered to the NPT. Yet, in 1998, defying the technological sanctions, India carried out nuclear weapons tests, overtly declaring itself a nuclear weapon state. Through a series of five underground nuclear tests at Pokhran, in Rajasthan (hereafter Pokhran II), India challenged the credibility of the NPT-centric nuclear regime.

For three decades, the United States and India existed at extreme ends of a nuclear nonproliferation divide. Quite, unexpectedly, in 2005, U.S. President George W. Bush announced the plan to lift the technological embargoes on India; thereby, contradicting Washington's domestic legislation and the norms of global nuclear regime. President Bush's new framework for civilian nuclear cooperation with India came as a rude shock to the world. It seemed that the Bush administration was conveniently sidelining nonproliferation concerns to gain an ally in South Asia. India's nuclear weapons program is a spinoff of its civilian nuclear program; therefore, any nuclear agreement with India involved a risk of nuclear proliferation. However, the Bush administration hailed India as a "responsible" nuclear power and the U.S.-India nuclear cooperation agreement was signed into law by President Bush in December 2008.

RESEARCH QUESTION

This book investigates: Why did the United States, after three decades of nuclear estrangement, offer civilian nuclear cooperation to India, a defacto nuclear weapons state and non-NPT member? In other words, what factors influenced the transition in the U.S. policy, from nuclear estrangement to cooperation, toward India? Did the George Bush administration sideline the nuclear nonproliferation regime to sign the U.S.-India civilian nuclear deal with India? Does the U.S. nuclear cooperation agreement with India mark a transformation, or an accommodation, within the nuclear regime? To what extent, if any, did President Clinton, the predecessor of President George Bush, contribute to the transition in U.S. nonproliferation policy toward India?

RATIONALE FOR RESEARCH

It is pertinent to investigate and critically analyse the significance of the 2005 U.S. nuclear pact with India which marked a reversal of the decades-old Washington policy of restricting India's access to nuclear technologies, with significant implications on the nuclear nonproliferation. First, this policy shift is related to the proliferation of nuclear technology and weapons, which is a significant issue for international security. In the contemporary era, especially after September 11, 2001 (hereafter 9/11) terrorist attacks on America, nonproliferation of sensitive technologies has emerged as a topmost priority to curb the threat of Weapons of Mass Destruction (WMD) related terrorism. Second, this policy reversal impinges on the credibility of the United States as a leading promoter of the nuclear nonproliferation regime. Since the 1970s, successive U.S. administrations demonstrated commitment to the nuclear nonproliferation regime and strictly adhered to the technological embargoes launched in response to India's 1974 peaceful explosion. But, as Jay R. Kraemer and Frank Aum argue, "the U.S. which for decades has stood as exemplar of stringent nuclear export criteria . . . is now leading the way downhill."[5]

Third, the nuclear pact with India reflects a discrepancy in the United States's nonproliferation policy and impinges on the "legitimacy and fairness"[6] of the nuclear regime. The Bush administration through the 2005 nuclear pact agreed to provide dual-use technology to India, which never signed the NPT, "thus, not eligible for such cooperation under NPT auspices."[7] On the other hand, Washington vehemently opposed the nuclear advancements by Iran, a signatory of the NPT. Finally, for more than three decades, the United States and India shared an estranged relationship regarding nuclear technology. The United States was engaged in strengthening the NPT and building up export control regulations. India, on the other hand, had been opposed to all the major treaties of the nuclear nonproliferation regime. Despite decades of such nuclear divergence, the United States offered to sign a nuclear pact with India. This defies logic and encourages investigation into the motivations of the Bush administration.

THEORETICAL FRAMEWORK

Following the signing of the U.S.-India nuclear cooperation agreement, intense debates were sparked regarding the implications of the pact on the nuclear nonproliferation regime. Expectedly, a vast majority of policy analysts and scholars became wary that engaging India in nuclear commerce was detrimental to the regime. I argue that there was a considerable lack of objective assessment to understand this change vis-à-vis the nuclear nonproliferation regime. Toward this objective, this book employs regime theory to understand whether the U.S.-India nuclear agreement marked a transformation of or an adjustment within the global nuclear nonproliferation regime. Furthermore, there was considerable lack of comprehensive research regarding the motivations of the Bush administration to initiate the civilian nuclear trade with India, after three decades of nuclear estrangement. In this context, the book makes an important contribution to overcome this literature deficit, as well as provides a detailed analysis of the change in the U.S. nuclear policy toward India.

The concept of international regimes was first introduced by John Ruggie in the mid-1970s. He defined international regimes as "A set of mutual expectations, rules, and regulations, plans, organizational energies, and financial commitments which have been accepted by a group of states."[8] Since then, the concept of regimes has occupied the mainstream in international relations, and is employed in the subfields of international political economy and environmental politics with "particular vigor." The burgeoning literature reveals significant interest of the scholarly community in researching the monetary, trade, oceans, and environmental regimes.[9] Ironically, there has been "little scholarly analysis" in the field of security regimes.[10] In this context, Robert Jervis suggests that

> this dearth of scholarly study is not the result of neglect, but rather inherent in the nature of the subject. There is little security regime analysis because there are currently no security regimes; regimes are more difficult to establish in the security arena than in the economic realm because of the inherently competitive cast of security concerns, the unforgiving nature of the problems, and difficulty in determining how much security the state has or needs.[11]

Undoubtedly, there is a recognizable nuclear regime that regulates the behavior of states regarding the horizontal proliferation of nuclear technology and materials, and research on the nuclear nonproliferation regime abounds. Yet, there is a significant paucity of theoretical analysis, especially employing regime theory.

Scholars have differentiated between agreements and regimes. While agreements are based on promotion of short term interests, regimes encompass "not only norms and expectations that facilitate cooperation, but also a form of cooperation that is more than a following of short-run self-interest."[12] Trevor McTate observes that "an international regime is an authoritative arrangement among international actors (states) that facilitates the accomplishment of specific goals through a process involving coordination or expectations and modification of certain behavior patterns."[13] Puchala and Hopkins argue that "a regime exists in every substantive issue area in international relations where there is discernibly patterned behavior. Wherever there is regularity in behavior, some kinds of principles, norms, and rules must exist to account for it."[14] There is a considerable overlap in the scholarly definitions and certain common features of regime can be identified, such as multilateral agreements, patterned and regularized behavior, issue area, and injunctions.

Stephen Krasner's concept of regime is regarded as the standard explanation. Krasner defines regimes

> as sets of implicit or explicit principles, norms, rules, and decision-making procedures around which actor's expectations converge in a given area of international relations. Principles are beliefs of fact, causation, and rectitude. Norms are standards of behavior defined in terms of rights and obligations. Rules are specific prescriptions or proscriptions for action. Decision-making procedures are prevailing practices for making and implementing collective-choice."[15]

Nonetheless, critics argue that the elements of a regime—principles, norms, rules, and decision-making—overlap conceptually and are difficult to identify in the real world.[16] Robert Keohane, in an attempt to merge all the elements, posits that "regimes are institutions with explicit rules, agreed upon by governments, that pertain to particular sets of issues in international relations."[17] Rules, the most explicit element in

Keohane's definition, are concrete and useful in assessing compliance to the regime by participants. Nonetheless, singularly focusing on rules and eliminating other elements makes the definition of the regime conceptually thin. On the contrary, Krasner identifies several components—principles, norms, rules, and decision-making procedures—which impart "descriptive richness that is a major strength of regime analysis."[18] Futhermore, Krasner distinguishes between principles and norms on the one hand and rules and decision-making procedures on the other hand. According to him, principles and norms are the "basic defining characteristics of a regime" and thereby determine the rules and decision-making procedures.[19] He remarks, "There may be many rules and decision-making procedures that are consistent with the same principles and norms."[20] This "hierarchy of the regime elements," scholars opine, imparts a distinct advantage in regard to existing definitions, as it enables the assessment of regime effectiveness as well as regime change.[21]

Krasner's regime definition helps in identifying three kinds of regime change. First, "*Changes in rules and decision-making procedures are changes within regimes,* provided that principles and norms are unaltered."[22] Thus, alterations in rules and procedures consistent with the original principles and norms can be regarded as adjustment within the regime. These can occur in response to exogenous or endogenous factors, and thereby represent evolution of the regime to deal with emergent challenges. Second, on the other hand, when principles and norms—the fundamental defining elements of a regime—undergo change, this marks "*changes of the regime itself.*" This kind of change is transformative or revolutionary and leads to replacement of the original principles and norms. Krasner remarks, "When norms and principles are abandoned, there is change to a new regime or a disappearance of regimes from the given issue-area."[23] Revolutionary change, which includes replacement of the original principles and norms, leads to an entirely new regime.[24] Third, Krasner's definition can help in assessing the effectiveness of the regime—strengthening or weakening. He remarks, "*If the principles, norms, rules, and decision-making procedures of a regime become less coherent, or if actual practice is increasingly inconsistent with principles, norms, rules, and procedures, then a regime has weakened.*"[25]

There is an underlying consensus amongst scholars that regimes are complex social institutions, i.e., human artifacts, therefore, the process of change is inevitable in regimes. Oran Young avers that "international regimes do not become static constructs even after they are fully articulated. Rather, they undergo continuous transformations in response to their own inner dynamics as well as to changes in their political, economic, and social environments."[26] William Zartman, regards regimes as "a living organism par excellence," whose "stability is unlikely to be a steady-state endpoint."[27] He remarks, "Regimes, persist *as* regimes by maintaining their flexibility, their ability to change in response to varying needs for coordination and problem solving that gave them birth, and their adaptability to the shifting constellations of power and interests among their members."[28] Similarly, Daniel Bodansky and Elliot Diringer argue that "international regimes rarely emerge in a single step, fully formed"; rather, these "typically evolve over time." For instance, the General Agreement on Tariffs and Trade, emerging in the 1950s–1960s, was semi-institutionalized with provisional mandate, yet, today the World Trade Organization has emerged as an established international institution with a sound legal basis and an advanced dispute settlement mechanism.[29] Similarly, the European human rights concept began as a "relatively weak institution" and has now emerged "as a powerhouse" with compulsory jurisdiction and a strong centralized structure.[30]

Young laments that there are "few sustained efforts to describe and explain regime change or to account for the dynamics of regimes in the period following their initial establishment." This observation can especially be applied in the context of research on the nuclear nonproliferation regime. Despite significant attention and burgeoning literature on nuclear weapons, there is a paucity of theoretical analysis on the changes in the nuclear nonproliferation regime. In this context, this book employs the regime theory in an attempt to provide a theoretical understanding of the nuclear agreement. Using Krasner's definition, I investigate the significance of the change in U.S. nonproliferation policy toward India on the nuclear regime. I examine whether the U.S.-India nuclear pact caused a transformation (i.e., a change in principles and norms), or simply, an adjustment (i.e., a change in rules and procedures) within, the nuclear nonproliferation regime.

METHODOLOGY

Donald Polkinghorne specifies that research methods should be chosen in relation to the, "kinds of questions being addressed."[31] The research for this book integrates document analysis with semi-structured, elite interviews. I chose these methods for two reasons. First, to obtain an in depth understanding of the change in the U.S. nuclear nonproliferation policy, after three decades of technological isolation, to engage India in nuclear commerce. Thus, this is a qualitative research with emphasis, "on understanding and description, not on prediction."[32] Second, the issue under investigation was relatively uncharted, therefore, significant information was uncovered from primary documents. Besides, interviews with the former White House officials as well as policy experts were also conducted to gain an insight into the change in the U.S. policy toward India.

The field research for the book was conducted at several policy research centers and government institutions in the United States and India. I conducted field research in two stages. In the first stage, I traveled to Washington DC, New York, and Philadelphia in the United States. I visited the Carnegie Endowment for Research, the Brookings Institution, the Heritage Foundation, and the Council for Foreign Relations, *inter alia*. In the second stage, for the purposes of data collection, I visited New Delhi, India. I conducted research at several policy-research institutions and libraries, including the United Services Institution (USI), the Institute of Defence Studies and Analysis (IDSA), the Centre for Policy Research (CPR), and the Institute of Peace and Conflict Studies (IPCS). I also visited Nehru Memorial Library (also known as Teen Murti Library), the Parliament of India library, and the Jawaharlal Nehru University (JNU) library. During the research visits to these institutions and libraries, I collected data from primary documents such as policy papers, congressional testimonies, conference papers and reports, and policy proposals. In addition, I collected secondary data from published materials such as newspaper articles, journal articles, and books.

For the purposes of data collection, I employed theoretical sampling and purposeful sampling. Theoretical sampling is a focused data collection method and involves an ongoing sampling process.[33] As Merriam states, "the researcher begins with an initial sample chosen for its obvious relevance to the research problem. The data lead the investigator to the next document to be read, the next person to be interviewed, and so on."[34] Lincoln and Guba emphasize that data collection should continue until the researcher gets to a point of saturation or redundancy in sampling.[35] In a significant suggestion, Merriam states that during data collection or analysis, the researcher "might also look for exceptions (negative case selection) or variants (discrepant-case selection)."[36] Thus, I applied these principles in my research. I continued to collect data, from both primary and secondary documents, until redundancy was noticed, and resumed the research when the need for further information arose.

I conducted semi-structured interviews with scholars and policy experts (on nuclear nonproliferation, energy and related issues, South Asia and India) at U.S.-based policy research and academic institutions. Based on my initial research, I prepared a list of participants I intended to interview. Later, I employed a strategy related to purposeful sampling, that is, snowball or network sampling.[37] Patton remarks that this strategy involves identifying participants or "cases of interest from people who know . . . what cases are information-rich, that is, good examples for study, good interview subjects."[38] Since the shift in U.S. nuclear nonproliferation policy raised a storm of controversy, one purpose of the research was to arrive at an objective analysis of the genesis of this change. Therefore, the author carefully selected a pool of interviewees with knowledge of nuclear energy, South Asia, and India, and expertise with nonproliferation and foreign policy; individuals with nongovernmental and governmental experience were included. The inclusion of interviewees from a variety of backgrounds enabled the author to gain insight into different perspectives.

For the purpose of conducting interviews, I followed a semi-structured format. "This form of interviewing allows the researcher and participant to engage in a dialogue whereby initial questions are modified in the light of the participant's responses and the investigator is able to probe interesting and important areas which arise."[39] Prior to the interviews, I prepared a questionnaire of common questions, along with certain questions related to the specific knowledge and expertise of the interviewee. These questions were supplemented with questions that emerged during the course of the interview. I chose to conduct semi-structured interviews because they allow "greater flexibility of coverage" and tend "to produce richer data."[40]

Seventeen individuals who had substantial knowledge of U.S.-India, U.S.-South Asia, or nuclear energy and nonproliferation issues were available for interviews. Broadly, the questions were related to: factors that led to the major transformation in U.S. nuclear nonproliferation policy; the genesis of this transition; the motivations of the Bush administration to offer India access to nuclear technology; and implications of the U.S.-India nuclear rapprochement.

I wanted to understand the perspectives of key White House officials who were involved in crafting U.S. nuclear policy toward India, during the Clinton and Bush administrations. In this regard, I interacted with Strobe Talbott, deputy secretary of state in the Clinton administration, through email, and I read his memoir *Engaging India* based on the Strobe Talbott-Jaswant Singh dialogue in the Clinton era. Besides Strobe Talbott, I sought the opportunity to interview Philip Zelikow, Nicholas Burns, Kenneth Juster, and Thomas Pickering. Philip Zelikow, counsellor to the State Department (February 2005–January 2007) and a senior policy advisor to Condoleezza Rice, was central to decision-making with regard to the U.S.-India nuclear pact. Zelikow's interview gave me insight into the motivations of the Bush administration. Nicholas Burns at Belfer Center, Harvard University, served as undersecretary for political affairs (2005–2007) and, probably, had a tough job in the negotiations of the controversial nuclear deal with India. Kenneth Juster, undersecretary of the Department of Commerce during the Bush administration, chaired the High Technology Cooperation Group (HTCG) and was one of the key architects of the Next Steps in Strategic Partnership (NSSP) initiative. Thomas Pickering, known as the best diplomat of his generation, served as ambassador to India in 1992–1993 when India was reforming its economy and moving toward liberalization. He later served as undersecretary for political affairs in the Clinton administration and played an important role in setting up a strategic dialogue with India. Responses of the high-ranking officials of the Clinton and Bush administrations were correlated with the data collected from primary and secondary resources.

J. P. Rothe proposes two stages of data analysis. First, the researcher explores "for patterns that appear in the data, then interrelate them and link them to a context."[41] Second, the conceptual framework chosen by the researcher serves "as the vehicle for data analysis," which he calls, "deep-structure analysis."[42] Similarly, Polkinghorne submits that data analysis continues "with a movement between the proposed structural description and the examples until an account can be given which clarifies the data in the fullest manner."[43] Thus, I allowed the findings to emerge from the structure of the data and examined them within the proposed theoretical and conceptual framework.

LIMITATIONS AND SCOPE

Although this book is based on extensive research and analysis it is limited in scope. First, the research for this book is based on document analysis and semi-structured interviews, thus, the limitations inherent in these methods may be present in this book.[44] Second, there was a lack of comprehensive research studies, such as books, from which to obtain supporting information. Therefore, the research relied extensively on journal articles and interviews for information, and on newspaper articles to corroborate the facts.

Every research establishes certain reasonable boundaries so that the objectives of the research do not get confused or conflated with factors and issues of little relevance. Similarly, this book also set certain limits. First, the joint statement delivered by President Bush and Prime Minister Manmohan Singh on July 18, 2005, established the framework for U.S.-India nuclear cooperation and served as a basis for the March 2006 pact, and subsequently the August 2007 agreement (also known as 123 Agreement) which was signed into law by President Bush in December 2008. Similar to existing literature, this book considers the 2005 joint statement as the quintessential indicator of a change in the U.S. nuclear approach and reference throughout the book is to the 2005 nuclear pact, except where otherwise noted. Second, the July 2005 agreement traversed a tedious and complicated trajectory spread over forty months,[45] before being signed into law in December 2008. The technicalities and legalities of this process are beyond the scope of this book. Third, although, the nuclear agreement was signed during the George W. Bush administration, the book begins with an exploration of the nuclear issues that existed between the United States and India during the Clinton administration (1993–2001). This is so because: (i) Unlike previous administrations, the Clinton administration was intent on rolling back and eliminating India's nuclear capabilities; (ii) It was during the Clinton administration that India went overtly nuclear; (iii) The nuclear approach of the George W. Bush administration is often compared to that of the Clinton administration. Therefore, the book attempts to analyze the developments during these two presidential administrations.

SIGNIFICANCE OF THIS RESEARCH

This book makes significant contribution to the literature in several respects. First, the 2008 U.S.-India nuclear agreement, though almost a decade old, yet, there are few comprehensive studies to analyze the circumstances and factors that catalyzed this nuclear pact; this book overcomes this knowledge deficit. This book investigates the change in U.S. nuclear nonproliferation policy, during the Bush administration, that culminated in a U.S.-India nuclear agreement in July 2005; subsequently, the agreement came into force in 2008, after all the requirements for the agreement were successfully achieved. It also explores the role of the Clinton administration in changing Washington's nuclear nonproliferation stance toward New Delhi. Second, there was paucity of tools to objectively assess the impact of the shift in U.S. nuclear policy toward India on the nuclear nonproliferation regime. This book employs regime analysis to demonstrate that the shift in the U.S. nuclear policy toward India, marked an adjustment within, not a revolutionary transformation of, the nuclear nonproliferation regime. Third, rather than examining the U.S.-India nuclear cooperation agreement in a bilateral context, this book examines the triadic relationship among the United States, India, and the nuclear nonproliferation regime. It highlights how contending perspectives of a leading nuclear nonproliferation regime promoter (the United States) and a regime nonparticipant (India) impinge on the bilateral relations of the two countries. Last but not the least, the insight the book provides into the U.S.-India nuclear entente is especially relevant in dealing with current or potential defacto nuclear states.

ORGANIZATION OF THE BOOK

This book is divided into seven chapters. Chapter 1 reviews the literature related to the U.S.-India civil nuclear cooperation agreement. Although the U.S.-India nuclear agreement was viewed as having significant implications for the nuclear nonproliferation regime, the absence of concrete evidence and lack of theoretical analyses led to inconclusive scholarly debates regarding whether the agreement was detrimental or beneficial to the nuclear nonproliferation regime. I highlight the inherent discrepancies in the existing literature and establish how this book not only overcomes the knowledge deficit in the literature as well as employing the regime theory provides an objective understanding. Chapter 2 provides a historical background and highlights the contending perspectives of the United States and India regarding nuclear nonproliferation, which subsequently, led to estrangement with the establishment of the Nuclear Nonproliferation Treaty (1968). This chapter also describes how India transitioned from a supporter of international negotiations for a nuclear nonproliferation regime to a challenger of the NPT-centric regime. Chapter 3 demonstrates that the Clinton administration attempted to consolidate the nuclear nonproliferation regime at the global level, yet, simultaneously, failed to thwart the impending nuclearization of India. I discuss India's nuclear weapons tests in 1998 as strong defiance of the strengthening of the nuclear regime. In chapter 4, I analyze the failure of post-proliferation measures employed by the Clinton administration in response to the Indian Pokhran II nuclear tests. Despite changing its stance—from coercive to conciliatory—and considerable shifting of the nuclear goalposts, the Clinton administration failed to rein India within the nuclear nonproliferation regime. In chapter 5, I analyze how the reorientation of the nuclear nonproliferation regime during the Bush administration created space for engaging India in the regime. This chapter also shows that U.S.-India strategic trade measures—the High Technology Cooperation Group and the Next Steps in Strategic Partnership—based on the principle of reciprocal obligations, served as precursors for the U.S.-India nuclear cooperation. In chapter 6, based on regime analysis, I examine in depth the terms of the U.S.-India civil nuclear cooperation agreement and assess its implications for the nuclear nonproliferation regime. The analysis reflects that the U.S.-India nuclear agreement is consistent with the principles and norms of the NPT-centric nuclear regime focused on horizontal nonproliferation. It marked a mere adjustment to the criterion of nuclear trade adopted in the U.S.'s domestic legislation. The concluding chapter (seven) presents a quick summary of the findings; analyses the nuclear pact as progression rather than retrogression of the nuclear regime; discusses lessons for dealing with contemporary nuclear threshold states and defacto nuclear states; assesses the contribution of this book to theory and praxis, and; finally, provides some future directions for research. Thus, contrary to the general perception, that the U.S.-India nuclear agreement thwarts the nuclear nonproliferation regime, this book demonstrates that the Bush administration, in an attempt to strengthen the nuclear nonproliferation regime, brought India—an anomaly—within the global nuclear governance.

NOTES

1. Man-Sung Yim, "Nuclear Nonproliferation and the Future Expansion of Nuclear Power," *Progress in Nuclear Energy* 48 (2006): 506.

2. In 2015, P5+1 nuclear agreement was achieved with Iran to restrict its nuclear weapons capability.

3. The Database on Nuclear Power Reactors, Power Reactor Information System, PRIS, International Atomic Energy Agency, IAEA, updated July 13, 2016. Available at https://www.iaea.org/pris/ (accessed July 14, 2016).

4. International Atomic Energy Agency, *Number of Reactors Under Construction Worldwide*. China has a maximum of twenty-seven reactors under construction, followed by the Russian Federation at eleven and India at six, while U.S. has a single reactor being built. Available at http://www.iaea.org/cgi-bin/db.page.pl/pris.opercap.htm (accessed July 16, 2010).

5. Jay R. Kraemer and Frank Aum, "The U.S.-India Nuclear Agreement: Progress Toward Nuclear Cooperation with India and a New Paradigm in Non-proliferation Policy," *International Journal of Nuclear Law* 1, no. 4 (2007): 419.

6. T.V. Paul, "The US-India Nuclear Accord: Implications for the Nonproliferation Regime." *International Journal* (Autumn 2007): 846.

7. Michael Ruhle, "Enlightenment in the Second Nuclear Age," *International Affairs* 83, no. 3 (May 2007): 511. Also, see Dana R. Dillon and Baker Spring, "Nuclear India and the Nonproliferation Treaty," *Backgrounder*, no. 1935. Washington D.C.: The Heritage Foundation, May 18, 2006.

8. John Gerard Ruggie, "International Responses to Technology: Concepts and Trends," *International Organization* 34 (Summer 1975): 570.

9. Helmut Breitmeier, Oran R.Young and Michael Zurn, *Analysing International Environmental Regimes:From Case-Study to Database*, (MIT Press, September 2006), 1; Also see, Roger K. Smith, "Explaining the Non-proliferation Regime: Anomalies for Contemporary International Relations Theory," *International Organization* 41, no. 2 (Spring 1987): 253.

10. Smith, "Non-proliferation regime," 253.

11. Ibid.

12. Robert Jervis, "Security Regimes," *International Organization* 36, no. 2 (Spring 1982): 357.

13. Trevor McMorris Tate, "Regime-Building in the Non-proliferation System," *Journal of Peace Research* 27, no. 4 (1990): 402.

14. Donald J. Puchala and Raymond F. Hopkins, "International Regimes: Lessons from Inductive Analysis," *International Organization* 36, no. 2 (Spring 1982): 247.

15. Stephen D. Krasner, "Structural Causes and Regime Consequences: Regimes as Intervening Variables," *International Organization* 36, no. 2 (Spring 1982): 186.

16. Oran R. Young, "International Regimes: Toward a New Theory of Institutions" *World Politics*, (1986), 106; Also see, Marc A. Levy, Oran R. Young and Michael Zurn, "The Study of International Regimes," *European Journal of International Relations* 1, no. 3 (1995): 270.

17. Robert Keohane, *International Institutions and State Power: Essays in International Relations*, (Boulder, CO: Westview Press, 1989), 4.

18. Levy, et al., "International Regimes," 273; Also see, Andreas Hasenclever, Peter Mayer and Volker Rittberger, *Theories of International Regimes*, (Cambridge University Press: New York, 2002), 12.

19. Krasner, "Intervening Variables," 188.

20. Ibid.

21. Andreas Hasenclever, Peter Mayer and Volker Rittberger, *Theories of International Regimes*, (Cambridge University Press: New York, 2002), 12–13; Levy, et al., 273–74.

22. Krasner, "Intervening Variables," 188 (emphasis in original).

23. Ibid. (emphasis in original).

24. Ibid., 201

25. Ibid., 188 (emphasis in original).

26. Oran R. Young, "Regime Dynamics: The Rise and Fall of International Regimes," in Andrew Linklater, ed., *Critical Concepts in Political Science*, Volume 2, (New York: Routledge, 2000), 742.

27. I. William Zartman, "Negotiating the Rapids: The Dynamics of Regime Formation," in *Post-Agreement Negotiation and International Regimes*, edited by Bertram I.

Spector and I. William Zartman, (Washington D.C.: United States Institute of Peace, 2003), 17.

28. Ibid.

29. Daniel Bodansky and Elliot Diringer, *The Evolution of Multilateral Regimes: Implications for Climate Change*, (Prepared for the Pew Center on Global Climate Change, December 2010), 3.

30. Ibid.

31. Donald Polkinghorne, *Methodology for the Human Sciences: Systems of Inquiry*, (New York: State University of New York Press, 1983), 273.

32. J.P. Rothe, *Qualitative Research: A Practical Guide* (Ontario: RCI/PDE Publications, 1993), 21.

33. The term theoretical sampling was introduced by Barney G. Glaser and Anselm L. Strauss. They defined it as the process, whereby the "analyst jointly collects, codes, and analyses his data and decides what data to collect next and where to find them, in order to develop his theory as it emerges."(45) They further add, "the emerging theory points to the next steps—the sociologist does not know them until he is guided by emerging gaps in his theory and by research questions suggested by previous answers"(47). Barney G. Glaser and Anselm L. Strauss, *The Discovery of Grounded theory: Strategies for Qualitative Research* (Aldine Transaction, June 1, 1967).

34. Sharan Merriam B., *Qualitative Research and Case Study Applications in Education* (San Francisco: Jossey-Bass Publishers, 1998), 63.

35. Y.S. Lincoln and E.G. Guba, *Naturalistic Enquiry* (California: Sage Publishers. 1985). Also, see description of the term, "theoretical saturation," in Glaser and Strauss, "Strategies for Qualitative Research," 61.

36. Merriam B., "Case Study Applications," 64.

37. Ibid., 63.

38. M. Q. Patton, *Qualitative Evaluation Methods*, California: Sage Publishers, 1990. 182.

39. Jonathon A. Smith and Mike Osborn, Interpretative Phenomenological Analysis, in *Qualitative Psychology: A Practical Guide to Research Methods*, ed., Jonathon A. Smith (London: Sage Publishers, 2003), 55.

40. Ibid., 57.

41. Rothe, "Qualitative Research," 127.

42. Ibid.

43. Polkinghorne, "Systems of Inquiry," 272.

44. Limitations of the document analysis method include: bias of the author, reliability, missing or incorrect information. Limitations of the semi-structured interview are: respondent bias, the generation of a wide variety of data, a limited number of participants.

45. For example, the introduction of the Henry Hyde United States-India Peaceful Atomic Energy Cooperation Act of 2006; negotiations of terms of 123 Agreement; India's waiver from Nuclear Suppliers Group.

ONE

U.S.-India Civil Nuclear Agreement

Mapping the Debates

The 2005 U.S. nuclear rapprochement with India, a non-signatory of the Nuclear Nonproliferation Treaty (NPT) and a defacto nuclear weapon state, marked a significant policy shift initiating hitherto prohibited civilian nuclear technology trade. Not surprisingly, the U.S.-India agreement generated several controversies and debates as the Bush administration overturned its thirty-year-old domestic legislation as well as international rules for nuclear trade.[1] Some scholars viewed this as a radical shift in the approach of the United States, with the potential to derail the nonproliferation regime. As William Potter cautioned, "The stakes are very high and neither the United States nor the international community can afford to lose this nonproliferation match."[2] Other scholars applauded this as a significant step forward to engage India within the nuclear regime. As Harsh Pant emphasized, "The Indo-U.S. nuclear pact has virtually rewritten the rules of the global nuclear regime by underlining India's credentials as responsible nuclear state that should be integrated into the global nuclear order."[3]

The literature reflected a dominant tendency to examine the implications of the U.S.-India nuclear pact on the nuclear nonproliferation regime. Yet, ironically, there was dearth of an indepth analysis of the factors inducing this paradigmatic shift in the U.S. approach toward India, after three decades of nuclear estrangement. To establish the rationale for this book, this chapter examines the standard explanations offered in the literature and indicates their inadequacies in explaining the shift in the U.S. policy. Based upon a careful review of the literature, scholars can be characterized in three categories: "optimists" who believed that this agreement strengthens the nuclear nonproliferation regime (NPR); "pessimists" who opined that the nuclear deal has a definite negative impact; and cautious optimists who regarded it as a positive development, but suggested to establish criteria to ensure there is no domino effect. For the purpose of analysis, the debates related to the U.S.-India rapprochement have been categorized as the following: "responsible" nuclear behavior; proliferation begets reward; dealing with defacto nuclear states; nonproliferation compromised; power transition: dissatisfied (nuclear) state; democratic "bomb"; and counter-enlightenment: unravelling NPR. The categories are distinctly defined, yet, some interrelation can be expected.

"RESPONSIBLE" NUCLEAR BEHAVIOR

The persistent U.S.-India nuclear estrangement not only impinged on bilateral relations, it also kept the recalcitrant India outside the nuclear nonproliferation regime. On this account, some experts (Ashok Kapur,[4] Vinod Kumar,[5] T.V. Paul,[6] Mahesh Shankar[7]) exuded optimism that the nuclear rapprochement between the United States and India is a positive development. Paul called it a "radical initiative," otherwise, the nuclear estrangement between India and the West showed "no signs of ending."[8] The nuclear pact committed India to submit its civilian facilities to International Atomic Energy Agency (IAEA) safeguards and to sign the Fissile Material Control Treaty (FMCT), thereby bringing India into the nonproliferation net. Kapur argues, while NPT was "a bargain between two superpowers that was projected as the basis of international security," this agreement is a "bargain between an asymmetrical pair of powers that choose to come together in a challenging international [nuclear] environment." He also remarks that this agreement has "levelled the playing field in the sphere of nuclear negotiations between "nuclear haves" and "nuclear have-nots."[9] Kumar, extending the argument further, opines that hitherto India was not only absent in the nonproliferation regime, rather it was a target of the global nuclear export controls, thus, India remained a passive outsider. But the U.S.-India nuclear pact, with nonproliferation as an important component, has changed the equation. It has created vital space as well as a potential role for India to be proactive in "global antiproliferation efforts."[10]

The central premise of the NPT regime is nonproliferation of nuclear technology and weapons. Optimists argued that India, despite being an NPT outlier, has unilaterally followed the norm of nonproliferation. Therefore, India deserved recognition for its responsible behavior and thus, needs to be rewarded with nuclear assistance (Paul and Shankar,[11] Anupam Srivastava and Seema Gahlaut,[12] Lisa Curtis and Baker Spring[13]). In the nuclear nonproliferation sphere, "responsible" behavior has been defined as "strict controls on the diffusion of nuclear technology outside national boundaries."[14] Paul and Shankar argued that post-1974 peaceful nuclear test, India was punished for its "nuclear transgressions" and denied access to nuclear and related advanced technologies. Now, India has been rewarded due to "the exemplary voluntary restraint" it has displayed by exercising "strict controls over its nuclear knowhow and technology."[15] Thus, India represents a classic example of the carrot and stick approach inherent in the U.S. nuclear nonproliferation policy. This sets a precedent for other nations that maintain high nonproliferation standards to be rewarded similarly. Curtis and Spring agreed that India has been a "responsible steward of its nuclear assets." In fact, they argued that comparing India with other threshold countries like Iran or North Korea was "not only disingenuous, it is [was] bad foreign policy." India's responsible behavior, they argued, presents an objective criterion for civil nuclear cooperation with the defacto nuclear weapon states.[16]

Srivastava and Gahlaut, WMD export regulations specialists, compared India and China's nuclear nonproliferation behavior. They argued that, unlike China, India maintained "strong record of substantive compliance" with the nuclear regimes' norms of nonproliferation. That is, in the case of India there had been no authorized or inadvertent export of nuclear technology by the government or by private entities. Contrarily, China had been an active proliferator, supplied not only nuclear but also missile items to several countries, and, "repeatedly sanctioned" by the United States.[17] Thus, this deal emphasized the new criterion that stringent compliance with the norms of the NPT regime, not the mere formality of joining the treaty, signified the nonproliferation credentials of a state.[18]

Thus, the optimists highlight India's adherence to nonproliferation and lauds its stringent export controls as exemplary, responsible behavior. They exude confidence that bringing India within the nonproliferation regime, through the nuclear pact, will be beneficial. Understandably, the "responsible behavior" of any state that maintains strict control on nuclear technology, materials, and knowhow, deserves recognition. Nonetheless, in the context of the U.S.-India nuclear reconciliation several questions remained unanswered: First, these scholars did not discuss why India followed the norm of nonproliferation when signatories of the NPT, like China and North Korea, engaged in illicit proliferation activities. Second, for more than three decades India was typecast as a nuclear pariah and now it was being cast as a responsible nuclear state. Was it mere rhetoric to create support for the agreement or was it construction of a certain identity by India? Third, it is not clear whether recognition of "responsible" behavior of India meant that all the U.S.-India disagreements regarding the nonproliferation regime were resolved. Fourth, though the optimists recognized India's good record of curbing horizontal proliferation but appeared to overlook its vertical proliferation, that is, its indigenous weapons development. This corresponds to the narrow approach of the NPT-centric regime which attaches significance to controlling horizontal proliferation and considers vertical proliferation, by the NWS, as secondary.

PROLIFERATION BEGETS REWARD?

Pessimists emphasized that the U.S.-India nuclear pact had negative implications for the global nuclear order (Robert Einhorn,[19] Joseph Cirincione,[20] George Perkovich,[21] Gary Milhollin,[22] William Potter,[23] Jayantha Dhanapala,[24] Fred McGoldrick, Harold Bengelsdorf, and Lawrence Schienman[25]). They were apprehensive that this nuclear pact would be considered as a reward for nuclear crossover, and thus, might aggravate proliferation among nuclear threshold states and problem states, creating a "domino effect." Furthermore, the contention was that the United States despite being the norm leader, made nuclear technological cooperation conditional on recipients' implementation of selective IAEA safeguards. In the aftermath of U.S.-India nuclear cooperation it might be difficult "to dissuade some suppliers [nuclear powers] from providing nuclear assistance to countries of proliferation concern."[26] Instead, with the nuclear deal the United States has set a bad precedent by "giving nonproliferation goals a backseat" and accorded primacy to its commercial and foreign policy interests. This would send signals to other nuclear supplier states, including members of the Nuclear Suppliers Group (NSG), to seek commercial interests at the cost of the universal interest in nuclear nonproliferation.[27] Thus, weakening the export controls for India would enable other problem states, including Iran and Pakistan, as well as terrorist groups to take advantage of the enfeebled regulations. This would be an ominous development and eventually cause "nonproliferation amnesia," i.e., complete unravelling of the export controls regime.[28]

Furthermore, it was argued that the United States gave large concessions to India but made only minor gains (George Perkovich[29] Leonard Weiss,[30] Robert Einhorn[31]). Acceptance of the limited IAEA safeguards and the decision to separate India's civilian and military facilities were seen as only "symbolic" gains for the NPT regime. Perkovich opined that the "looseness" of the nuclear pact undermined nonproliferation objectives due to absence of corresponding strategic gains from India, including "containment of China."[32] That is, the United States neither extracted significant nonproliferation nor strategic concessions from India. In this context, Leonard Weiss emphasized that attempting to get India to abandon or rollback its nuclear arsenal in "the absence of any movement by the nuclear weapon states toward disarmament was politically quixotic." This U.S.-India pact was equivalent to giving India, an outlier, recognition as a "weapons state" without demanding the obligations expected of such states under the NPT; thus, undermining the basic principles of the treaty.[33]

The pessimists raised pertinent issues, including the point that the established nonproliferation norms cannot be overturned and if exceptions are made for a particular state then other states will also demand concessions albeit on different grounds. That is, this nuclear deal set a bad precedent and impinged on the credibility of the NPT regime. This was especially detrimental at a time when the United States was managing proliferation threats from Iran, North Korea, and post–9/11 terrorist groups.

Although the optimists and the pessimists differed in their perception of the consequences of the U.S.-India nuclear pact, yet, there was an interesting similarity in their approach. Both sides examined the nuclear pact from the angle "will it?" or "will it not?" abet the proliferation of nuclear weapons. That is, the main concern of the scholars was with the implications of the nuclear pact on the horizontal proliferation of the nuclear weapons. Such an approach that focused on the domino effect of the nuclear agreement, whether beneficial or detrimental, seemed embedded in Cold War thinking. It reflected the fear associated with the division of the world into blocs; that is, if one state falls into the Soviet camp, other states in the region will follow suit. This also reflected rigidity to accept the *sui generis* nature of nuclear proliferation challenges as well as adoption of innovative measures for dealing with them. This in turn reflected an absence of critical thinking in the nonproliferation discourse and demonstrated considerable lack of inclusion of the perspective of the other. India was constructed as a "nuclear pariah" but there was limited understanding of its peculiar nonproliferation behavior: Why, in the first place, did India refuse to accept the NPT? And why, being outside the nuclear regime, did India follow the norms of nonproliferation? In this context, Paul, author of *Power versus Prudence: Why Nations Forego Nuclear Weapons,* argued that states have "idiosyncratic reasons"—based on indigenous domestic and regional political security circumstances—for acquiring weapons and renouncing them. That is, they do not necessarily follow other states in decisions that require massive technological and economic investment.

DEALING WITH DEFACTO NUCLEAR STATES

Scholars also reflected cautious optimism as they attempted to bridge the divergent views of optimist and pessimist scholars (Dinshaw Mistry and Sumit Ganguly,[34] Dana R. Dillon and Baker Spring[35]). They argued that instead of specifying this change in nuclear policy as an India-specific change, the United States should formulate a criteria based policy that outlines a roadmap for engaging defacto nuclear states in civil nuclear cooperation. Allaying the pessimistic concerns, Mistry and Ganguly specified a multi-pronged criterion. That is, before the civil nuclear cooperation agreement, the defacto nuclear states: be subjected to nuclear embargo for twenty to thirty years; adhere to the nonproliferation regime; show an exemplary export control record; and pledge to renounce nuclear testing. Similarly, Dillon and Spring's criteria for civilian nuclear trade with potential defacto nuclear weapons states includes: a stable democracy with a rule of law; a record of nonproliferation and demonstrated respect for international nuclear nonproliferation regimes' obligations to nuclear weapon states; not being a sponsor of terrorism; firm separation between civilian and military nuclear programs; nonaggressive security policies; and willingness to consider limits on the number of nuclear weapons.

Though cautious optimists emphasized the need to establish rules for nuclear commerce with defacto nuclear countries, the criteria these scholars proposed were too broad and indeterminate. Nonetheless, they pointed to a loophole in the NPT regime, that was, the lack of post-proliferation management of defacto nuclear states. The NPT per se is exclusively focused on preventing the spread of nuclear weapons; there is no provision for dealing with states that cross the nuclear threshold. In this context, Avner Cohen and Thomas Graham Jr. emphasized the importance of integrating the nuclear states (India, Israel, Pakistan) through a "separate protocol" to the NPT. Such a protocol would require these states to adopt international export controls, prohibit nuclear testing, and eliminate fissile material production.[36]

REALIST OBJECTIVES V/S NONPROLIFERATION?

Some scholars argued that the United States, a leading promoter of the nuclear nonproliferation regime, had compromised the regime in pursuit of realist objectives. Consequently, other states too would enter into nuclear cooperation with defaulter states to achieve realist gains and nonproliferation goals would be sidelined in a growing trend. There was widespread consensus among scholars, whether optimists or pessimists, that the realpolitik interests of the United States encouraged its nuclear rapprochement with India—an emerging economy with immense strategic potential in Asia. A majority of scholars (Dinshaw Mistry,[37] Mario E. Carranza,[38] Ashley Tellis,[39] Sumit Ganguly,[40] George Perkovich,[41] Lisa Curtis,[42] Harsh Pant,[43] T.V. Paul and Mahesh Shankar[44]) identified the Bush administration's neorealist objective of forging a strategic partnership with India as the primary determinant of the U.S.-India nuclear rapprochement. Nonetheless, the absence of a clear-cut definition of the term "strategic partnership" created space for divergent interpretations. Embedded in the Cold War mindset, scholars suggested that the U.S.-India partnership primarily intended to maintain the balance of power in Asia, and specifically to contain China. Perkovich asserted, that Washington realized that to "dissuade or prevent China from competing harmfully . . . [the U.S.] must mobilize states on China's periphery to balance Chinese power." Therefore, the Bush administration realized:

> to win over India, the United States should change national and international laws and rules that bar technology cooperation with India due to India's nuclear-weapons and ballistic missile programs. Changing these rules is necessary to cement the partnership, and such changes also will help India bolster its strategic capabilities, including nuclear weapons and ballistic missiles, which will further balance China's strategic power.[45]

Similarly, Ashley Tellis remarked that the partnership aimed at preventing "Asia from being dominated by *any single power* . . . which may use aggressive assertion of national self-interest to threaten American presence, American alliances, and American ties with regional states" (emphasis added).[46] Tellis was also implicitly making a reference to China, as no other nation in Asia possesses the potential to dominate the region and threaten American interests. In this context, T.V. Paul opined, "The U.S. is driven by both strategic and economic considerations in its pursuit to eliminate nuclear friction with India."[47] That is, it is strategically important for the United States to develop India as a "potential counterweight" to China. Thus, the Indo-U.S. nuclear deal was seen as driven by American geopolitical interests.

Yet, other scholars (Curtis,[48] Tellis,[49] Michael A. Levy and Charles D. Ferguson[50]) considered the strategic partnership as an issue-based relationship entailing a convergence of post–Cold War interests, both global and regional in nature, such as: combating terrorism and religious extremism, curbing proliferation of Weapons of Mass Destruction, spreading democracy, diffusing economic development, protecting global commons such as sea lanes of communication, energy security,[51] and even HIV/AIDS.[52] In fact, Curtis termed the nuclear deal as the "centerpiece of the paradigm shift" in Washington's relationship with India. She stated, "If enacted, this [nuclear] agreement will mark a new era for U.S.-India ties. It will enable our two democracies to create a *freer, more stable, and more secure world*" (emphasis added).[53] Similarly, Pant remarked, "the road to a healthy strategic partnership between the two democracies had to include nuclear energy cooperation."[54] That is, a U.S.-India strategic partnership was contingent on the nuclear agreement.

The assumption that the U.S.-India nuclear agreement will promote a stable and comprehensive partnership akin to an alliance was flawed. Such a perception embedded in Cold War thinking presumed that India will function like an ally; this reflected a lack of understanding of India's foreign policy. Although India is a nascent democracy, nevertheless, issues related to foreign policy are debated vociferously in the public domain. Moreover, due to the nonalignment orientation in foreign policy—created by Pandit Nehru in the early years of its emergence—India was astute about retaining its autonomy in world affairs.[55] It would be a fallacy that India, like Cold War partners, would simply toe Washington's line, until there was appreciable convergence with the former's own interests.

The strategic partnership rationale defined the "containment of China" as the primary objective. This again reflected a false perception of the Indian foreign policy objectives. Definitely, India had certain bilateral issues with China, yet, the former believed in the principles of peaceful coexistence; and therefore, committed to avoid anything that would disturb its state of balance with China. Thus, the assumption that India would be willing to act as a balancer is a fallacy. In other words, a U.S.-India strategic partnership may be based on complementary interests but India will never be part of an alliance directed against any particular country, especially China. As Pant remarks, "If Americans are hoping to cultivate another Britain, or even another Australia, India, for sure, is not the right candidate to expend energies on."[56]

Undoubtedly, in the post–9/11 era, Washington's relations with India witnessed an unprecedented upward swing, especially, the Bush administration sought a strategic relationship with India. But to argue that the nuclear agreement is a mere extension of the positive swing in the relationship with India is problematic. It implies that the United States in order to further its realist objectives, made a quantum leap over the unresolved issues of nuclear estrangement with India. That is, the United States compromised the nonproliferation goals at the altar of foreign policy. The proposition that the purpose of the nuclear pact was mainly to establish the U.S.-India strategic partnership seems simplistic and linear. It deprives an in-depth understanding of the unprecedented change in U.S. nuclear nonproliferation policy after thirty years of estrangement with India. I contend that instead of the foreign policy context, the nuclear rapprochement needs to be explored in the backdrop of the nuclear nonproliferation regime. The current book attempts to overcome this gap in the literature and to provide an explanation for the U.S.-India pact within the context of the U.S. approach to the nuclear nonproliferation regime.

POWER TRANSITION: DISSATISFIED (NUCLEAR) STATE

Based on the power transition theory, T. V. Paul and Mahesh Shankar proposed that India—a state with nuclear weapons—be accommodated in the international nuclear order as it had the potential to become a dissatisfied state. They argued that the Nuclear Nonproliferation Treaty (NPT) "has no room for the orderly exit of a declining power or entry of a rising power."[57] The treaty is not dynamic enough to accommodate changes in the power distribution of the global nuclear order. Therefore, the nuclear rapprochement with India represented a pragmatic move by the Bush administration to enlist a rising power. Paul and Shankar regard it as similar to the accommodation of China, an "earlier dissatisfied power," which was integrated into the international order during the Nixon-Kissinger era.[58]

The power transition theory, developed by Organski,[59] in contrast to realism, posits that international order is hierarchical. There is constant competition among states for scarce resources and their objective is not simply, aggrandisement of power, rather maximization of net gains.[60] The dominant power establishes the international order with rules and regulations that "direct political, economic, diplomatic, and military interactions."[61] Thus, the international status quo designed by the current dominant power, the United States, can be described as a globalized, technology-driven, democratic, capitalist, nonproliferation oriented global order. The dominant power enforces the norms with the help of the great powers and one of the great powers is the "eventual challenger." A major conflict ensues when a dissatisfied great power, through internal growth, catches up with the dominant power. In this context, the traditional power transition scholars considered China as a potential challenger.[62] Paul and Shankar, on the other hand, view India to be a potential dissatisfied state. Ever since the NPT was signed in 1968, India had refused to accede to the NPT-centric nuclear nonproliferation regime and opposed its related treaties, such as the Comprehensive Nuclear Test Ban Treaty (CTBT) and the Fissile Material Control Treaty (FMCT). Furthermore, Paul and Shankar argue that the Indian nuclear tests, Pokhran I (1974) and II (1998), reflected India's desire for recognition as a nuclear weapons state as well as a global power. Therefore, they contended, if India is not recognized as a weapons state and accorded its due place in the nuclear nonproliferation regime, the consequences can be quite damaging. Dissatisfied states that perceive a discrepancy between their self-image and their position in the international order "are susceptible to ultranationalist and revisionist tendencies, growing increasingly defiant of a global order which refuses to recognize their claims."[63] Thus, Paul and Shankar asserted that the U.S.-India nuclear deal "upholds and strengthens" the nuclear nonproliferation regime and "suggest[s] to other rising powers that the system is flexible enough to allow for inevitable changes in the global distribution of power."[64]

There are several discrepancies in the explanation offered by Paul and Shankar. First, the construction of India as a "dissatisfied state" is not convincing enough. A dissatisfied state is akin to a revisionist state, but India, notwithstanding its attitude toward the nuclear nonproliferation regime, does not possess the underpinnings of a revisionist state. India's approach toward several international institutions, including its constant support of the United Nations system and pursuit of democratic norms, renders it a reformist state rather than a dissatisfied state. Amit Gupta defines a reformist state as "one that by and large accepts the structure and order of the international system but wishes to make incremental changes to it in order to improve its own power potential and status within the international system."[65] Although India refused to sign the NPT on the basis of inherent inequities, they were the first country to call for a comprehensive test ban, and were engaged in the Committee on Disarmament during NPT and CTBT deliberations. Also, India is a signatory of the Chemical and Biological Weapons Convention.[66] In this context, Paul and Shankar also recognized that, except for the nuclear nonproliferation regime, India has been constructively engaged in other spheres of international order. Thus, the questions arise: Is a dissatisfied state opposed to the entire international set up? Can a state be classified as dissatisfied only if it opposes a particular sphere of international order? That is, if India opposes the nuclear nonproliferation order, but is constructively engaged in other aspects of global order; would it still be considered a challenger?

Second, Douglas Lemke, a proponent of the power transition theory, has argued that conflict can be anticipated when the dissatisfied challenger acquires parity with the dominant power. That is, conflict between the challenger and the dominant power is dependent upon convergence of two conditions: achievement of parity and dissatisfaction. As Lemke puts it, "parity and the challenger's dissatisfaction are jointly necessary for a war, *a weak dissatisfied challenger is not to be feared*" (emphasis added).[67] But, through the nuclear technology transfers, the United States would speed up India's development and thereby help India transform into a great power. Viewed in this context, according to Paul and Shankar, India is a dissatisfied state, thus, its emergence as a great power would meet the conditions for conflict, as specified by Lemke. Then, it is in the best interests of the United States to ensure that India, a dissatisfied state, remains a weak state. That is, contrary to Paul and Shankar's argument, the United States should not offer assistance in nuclear technologies to India; because if India becomes a great power it could challenge the American preponderance. Third, Paul and Shankar's to incorporate India within the NPT regime would create a bad precedent; to appease the states that oppose the global nuclear order. This could prove detrimental to the nuclear nonproliferation regime.

DEMOCRATIC "BOMB" AND NONPROLIFERATION REGIME

The democratic peace thesis argues that democracies rarely go to war with each other.[68] The democratic peace thesis evoked a lot of interest, especially, in the post–Cold War era, as it is proposed that a world composed of democracies would enhance global security. President Clinton regarded democratization as the third pillar of his foreign policy. In his

State of the Union address, he stated, "Ultimately, the best strategy to insure our security and to build a durable peace is to support the advance of democracy elsewhere . . . they [democracies] also make better trading partners and partners in diplomacy."[69] Jack Levy even goes to the extent to assert that the democratic peace thesis is the "closest thing we have to an empirical law in the study of international relations."[70]

The democratic peace thesis was employed by several scholars, in varying degrees, to explain America's nuclear rapprochement with India (Jarrod Hayes,[71] George Perkovich,[72] Michael Levi and Charles Ferguson,[73] Dana R. Dillon and Baker Spring[74]). For the United States in its promotion of democracy, "the appeal of a deeper relationship with the world's largest democracy [India] was undeniable." This seemed to be the most plausible explanation for the positive engagement between the United States and India.[75] Hayes argued that the democratic peace thesis successfully explained the paradox in the U.S. nuclear nonproliferation policy. The Bush administration offered civil nuclear cooperation to India—which not only opposed the NPT but also crossed the nuclear threshold. At the same time, the pursuit of nuclear technology by Iran, a signatory of the NPT, was considered a threat. This is so because, "as a fellow democracy, the United States need have no fear of India's nuclear capabilities."[76] The Bush administration consistently emphasized the shared democratic identity with India, creating a "sense of partnership and trust. That trust endures despite Indian actions, like the 1998 test that betrayed U.S. wishes." This shared identity, Hayes argues, has enabled the desecuritization of India's nuclear arsenal while nondemocratic Iran was constructed as the "other" and, inevitably, this led to securitization of its nuclear program.[77]

Perkovich argued that, as an extension of the democratic peace thesis, Washington views the world as divided into "democratic friends" and authoritarian "foes." As a corollary to the democratic peace theory, Perkovich proposed the "democratic bomb" thesis. He argues that earlier the spread of nuclear weapons per se was viewed as the problem; now, it is non-democratic states with nuclear weapons that are regarded as the problem.[78] The "democratic-bombs-are-good" strategy has created space for pursuit of double standards in the U.S. nuclear nonproliferation policy. Perkovich remarked that, since the mid-1960s, the United States neither pressurised nor cajoled Israel to give up its nuclear arsenal. Similarly, pursuing the "democratic-bombs-are-good" strategy, the United States in its nuclear pact with India has abandoned its policy of prohibiting nuclear trade with any state that did not employ comprehensive safeguards.[79] In this context, Dillon and Spring averred that it will be challenging for Washington to strike a balance between its avowed commitment to nuclear nonproliferation objectives and the pursuit of nuclear cooperation with "friendly, democratic, *defacto* nuclear powers such as India."[80]

The democratic peace thesis is quite influential, yet, it does not provide a satisfactory explanation of Washington's nuclear rapprochement with India. In 1971, during the India-Pakistan war, the United States deployed a naval task force led by the *USS Enterprise*, a nuclear powered aircraft carrier, in the Bay of Bengal to threaten India with dire consequences. This episode defies the logic of the democratic peace thesis, as India was a democratic state and Washington had intervened on behalf of Pakistan which was under martial law. Wesley Widmaier has analyzed this 1971 "near-miss" between the United States and India from the constructivist perspective. He argues that it is a fallacy to "assume that all inferences regarding democracy must engender cooperation."[81] Nevertheless, India has been a democratic state for sixty-three years, and yet, for the last thirty years it was at the receiving end of the technological embargoes imposed by the United States. If, indeed, the United States considered democratic bombs as favorable, then why did Washington set up nuclear export controls in response to India's peaceful nuclear explosion in 1974? In 1998, when India overtly went nuclear, why did the Clinton administration impose sanctions instead of accepting the democratic nuclear arsenal? That is to say, why during the Bush era did this "shared democratic identity" lead to civilian nuclear cooperation, and why not earlier? Thus, the democratic bomb thesis raises more questions than it answers. Finally, democratic peace argument relates the nuclear reconciliation to U.S. foreign policy objectives and fails to provide an effective explanation.

COUNTER-ENLIGHTENMENT: UNRAVELING NONPROLIFERATION REGIME

The literature invariably linked U.S. nuclear rapprochement with India to the Bush administration. Several scholars (Sharon Squassoni,[82] Carranza,[83] William Walker,[84] Gary Milhollin,[85] and Joseph Cirincione[86]) hold the Bush administration responsible for the change in direction of U.S. nuclear policy toward India. Some attribute the transition in U.S. stance to the Bush administration's neorealist design to develop a strategic partnership with India; others believe it to be a by-product of the administration's disdain toward the nuclear nonproliferation regime. In this context, scholars invariably draw a comparison with President Bush's predecessor. President Clinton is regarded as an arms control enthusiast and an avid supporter of the nuclear nonproliferation regime. For instance, it was during the Clinton administration that the NPT was extended indefinitely at the 1995 Review Conference and its membership witnessed a substantial increase. Furthermore, due to Clinton's efforts, deliberations on the CTBT were successfully concluded and considerable progress was made toward the Fissile Material Control Treaty.

The general perception was that even though Clinton initiated a positive swing in U.S.-India bilateral relations, yet, he did not cross the nonproliferation redlines. That is, unlike Bush, he did not broaden relations with India at the expense of nuclear nonproliferation goals. Sharon Squassoni, a nonproliferation expert, contended that India "craved legitimization of its nuclear weapons" insisting that the United States lift the embargo on nuclear exports. Yet, "the U.S. policy, at least until the Bush administration, was that India had to freeze and roll back its nuclear weapons program."[87] Similarly, Carranza opines that "achieving a nuclear restraint regime in South Asia remained an important objective of American foreign policy until the end of the Clinton administration in January 2001." On the contrary, the Bush administration, in pursuit of neorealist goals, marked a distinct shift in U.S. foreign policy from "nonproliferation to post-proliferation toward South Asia." Carranza did not define what he meant by "post-proliferation," but it can be inferred that he meant the renunciation of the U.S. policy to push for a rollback of India's nuclear weapons and a tacit acceptance of India's defacto nuclear status.

This reversal of U.S. policy was linked to the broader nuclear doctrine of the Bush administration that included: indifference toward multilateral nuclear nonproliferation treaties such as the CTBT and the FMCT, unilateral withdrawal from the Anti-Ballistic Missile Treaty, cessation of the Strategic Arms Reduction Treaty (START), and lack of interest in pursuing nuclear disarmament.[88] Therefore, it was emphasized that the Bush administration, in a unilateral attempt, bent the rules of the nonproliferation regime and granted India access to nuclear technology without demanding equitable responsibilities.[89] Such an action, as Cirincione remarks, "seems to reward India's nuclear proliferation." It accords recognition to India as a nuclear weapon state "with all the rights and privileges reserved for those states [Nuclear Weapon States] that have joined the NPT, yet, without the same obligations."[90] In this context, Tellis opined that the apprehensions of an impending rivalry with China enabled "the realist as well as neoconservative factions" within the Bush administration to be more accommodative of "New Delhi's emerging nuclear capabilities."[91]

William Walker[92] particularly criticized the "counter-enlightenment" instincts of the Bush administration. He opined that the NPT represented a "grand enlightenment project" and reflected "a ubiquitous rationality and commitment to reason."[93] It was in the 1960s–1970s with the concerted efforts of the United States that an international nuclear order was constructed based on a "managed system of deterrence" and a "managed system of abstinence."[94] Under the Bush administration the pursuit of unilateral measures—such as abrogation of multilateral treaties, the Anti-ballistic missile (ABM) Treaty and the START—marked a distinct shift toward counter-enlightenment which would eventually unravel the NPT regime.[95] Contrary to the basic principle of the NPT that "nuclear weapons are intrinsically illegitimate," the Bush administration conferred "legitimacy on India's nuclear weapons program."[96] That is, President Bush "abandoned blanket condemnation" of all nuclear proliferation and created distinction between "bad" guys (Iraq and Iran) and "good" guys to pursue selective containment of nuclear weapons.[97] Moreover, as Cirincione argues, Bush's strategy "sought the elimination of regimes rather than weapons, believing the United States could determine which countries were responsible enough to have nuclear weapons and which countries were not. U.S. power, not multilateral treaties [like NPT], would enforce this judgment."[98]

Most of the issues raised by these scholars are compelling, yet, the counter-enlightenment argument does not provide a satisfactory explanation. First, Walker's thesis that the NPT is an enlightenment project orchestrated by the United States deserves some merit; beyond that, his assumption that the NPT was devised to achieve nuclear disarmament seems exaggerated. Walker overstates the extent to which western nations were committed to a grand enlightenment project; rather, the NPT was the result of a compromise reached between several states.[99] Second, the Bush administration's nuclear policy has been negatively compared to that of its predecessor. The question arises: If President Clinton was committed to strengthening the nuclear nonproliferation regime, then, why did he fail to prevent the twin nuclear crossovers in South Asia—India and Pakistan? In response to Walker's counter-enlightenment proposition, Ruhle remarks, "if the U.S. nonproliferation policy is different from that of 40 years ago, it is not because the U.S. has become more fundamentalistic, but because the [nuclear proliferation] problems it confronts have fundamentally changed."[100] That is, transition in the U.S. nuclear approach is not a consequence of the idiosyncrasies of the incumbent presidents; rather, it is a response to the changing global nuclear order. Third, the U.S. nuclear rapprochement with India is a relatively recent development and there is very little understanding of the circumstances under which the Bush administration granted India access to nuclear technology.

CONCLUDING REMARKS

The literature review highlights attempt of scholars to explore the rationale of the paradigmatic shift in the U.S. approach to attempt nuclear reconciliation with India, a defacto nuclear state and non-signatory of NPT. Nevertheless, scholars expressed unfavorable implications of the U.S.-India nuclear agreement for the global nuclear order and the abetment of horizontal proliferation. This reflects the dominant concerns of the nonproliferation discourse in which any development in the nuclear arena is assessed as a potential threat. Here, a parallel can be drawn with the Cold War period, when all international developments were analyzed vis-à-vis the Soviet threat and the domino theory pervaded the Western mind-set. In this context, Matthew Woods laments, "Forecasting the inevitable and dangerous spread of nuclear weapons is an enduring dimension of international relations."[101] He claims, "the international nuclear order results from the creation of inevitable and dangerous proliferation as an intersubjective reality that assumes an involuntary chain reaction and precludes the actual occurrence of such widespread, unstoppable proliferation."[102]

Interestingly, there was considerable lack of consensus among scholars over the question of whether U.S.-India nuclear cooperation is beneficial or detrimental to the nuclear nonproliferation regime. The optimists viewed it as a positive development for bringing India, a nuclear outlier, within the nuclear nonproliferation regime. Yet, unconvincing arguments were put forth: such as, (i) the consequences of leaving India, a dissatisfied nuclear state, outside the nuclear regime could be detrimental and (ii) an Indian democratic bomb is preferable to an Iranian or North Korean nondemocratic bomb within the nuclear nonproliferation regime. The pessimists, on the other hand, raised their concerns regarding nuclear cooperation with a non-signatory of the NPT. Pessimists argued that (i) the U.S.-India nuclear deal set a precedent that weaponization is rewarded and (ii) in pursuit of strategic gains, other nuclear weapons states might be encouraged to engage in nuclear cooperation with non-nuclear weapon states, in utter disregard for the global nuclear nonproliferation regime. As a corollary, the concern regarding the implications of the U.S.-India nuclear pact on the nonproliferation regime, gave rise to speculation that the Bush administration had lifted the technological embargoes against New Delhi in order to build a strategic partnership that would balance China's rising strength. It was argued that the nuclear issue was merely a "symbolic and technical" impediment[103] in the achievement of Washington's foreign policy objectives; therefore, the Bush administration made a quantum leap over the lingering nuclear issues and bent the rules of the nuclear nonproliferation regime. The perspective that Washington has compromised its nuclear nonproliferation objectives to achieve strategic interests affects credibility of the United States as a promoter of the nuclear nonproliferation regime. Such an argument is detrimental to the regime also, as other nuclear supplier states might be encouraged to pursue their strategic gains at the cost of nonproliferation objectives. However, in the absence of a detailed examination, including the rationale, of the U.S.-India nuclear pact, as well as lack of theoretical analysis to provide an objective understanding, precludes an assessment of its impact on the nuclear nonproliferation regime.

Thus, the review of literature suggests a significant empirical and theoretical deficit in our understanding of the transition in U.S. nuclear nonproliferation policy, which supposedly sidelined the nuclear nonproliferation regime to engage a challenger of the regime in nuclear cooperation. This demands a detailed investigation regarding the determinant/s of the paradigmatic shift in the U.S. nuclear nonproliferation policy: In other words, how the United States, a promoter of the nuclear nonproliferation regime, change its three decade old policy—from technological isolation to nuclear cooperation—toward India, a nonparticipant in the regime? Relatedly, the question arises: Does the U.S.-India nuclear agreement undermines the nuclear nonproliferation regime or brings India within global nuclear governance? This calls for a comprehensive analysis of the terms of the U.S.-India nuclear agreement and its implications for the nuclear nonproliferation regime.

To derive answers to these questions, this book examines the U.S.-India nuclear reconciliation in the backdrop of the nuclear nonproliferation regime rather than within a U.S. foreign policy context. To overcome the theoretical deficit, this book will employ regime theory to provide an objective analysis of the issues. The regime analysis would help to: (i) understand the global nuclear nonproliferation regime; (ii) assess India's position as a challenger to the nuclear regime; and (iii) examine the implications of the U.S.-India nuclear agreement on the nuclear nonproliferation regime—whether it is consistent with the fundamental elements of the regime or unravels them. Besides, it will examine the attempts by the Clinton and Bush administrations to deal with defacto nuclear states, that is, India. Thus, this book will attempt to conclude: whether the change in the U.S. nuclear nonproliferation policy toward India, culminating in the nuclear pact, represented a transformation of, or an adjustment within, the nuclear nonproliferation regime.

NOTES

1. The concerns raised in the debates in the U.S. and India, following the signing of the nuclear agreement, were quite divergent and focused on entirely different issues. This, in turn, reflected the disjuncture in their respective approach to the issue of nuclear weapons.

2. William C. Potter, "India and the New Look of US Nonproliferation Policy," *Nonproliferation Review* 12, no. 2 (July, 2005): 352.

3. Harsh V. Pant, "The U.S.-India Nuclear Pact and the Non-Proliferation Regime: Triumph of Politics over Institutions," paper presented at the 48th Annual ISA Convention, Illinois, 28 February–3 March 2007. pp. 2–3. (permission sought for citing, 6 March 2008).

4. Ashok Kapur, "Canada-India Nuclear Negotiations: Context and Process," in *Canadian Policy on Nuclear Cooperation with India: Confronting New Dilemmas*, ed., Karthika Sasikumar and Wade L. Huntley (Vancouver, B.C.: Simons Centre for Disarmament and Nuclear Proliferation Research, 2007).

5. Vinod A. Kumar, "Counterproliferation: India's New Imperatives and Options," *Strategic Analysis* (January–February, 2007).

6. T. V. Paul, "The US-India Nuclear Accord: Implications for the Non-Proliferation Regime," *International Journal* (Autumn 2007).

7. T.V. Paul and Mahesh Shankar, "Why the US-India Nuclear Accord is Good Deal," *Survival* 49, no. 4 (2007).

8. Paul, "US-India Nuclear Accord," 848.

9. Kapur, "Context and Process," 45.

10. Kumar, "New Imperatives and Options," 26 & 38.

11. Paul and Shankar, "Nuclear Accord is a Good Deal."

12. Anupam Srivastava and Seema Gahlaut, "India and the NPT: Separating Substantive Facts from Normative Fiction," *Strategic Analysis* 34, no. 2 (March, 2010).

13. Lisa Curtis and Baker Spring, *U.S. Nuclear Agreement with India: An Acceptable Deal for Major Strategic Gain,* Web Memo no. 1587 (Washington D.C.: The Heritage Foundation, August 14, 2007), 2.

14. Karthika Sasikumar, "India's Emergence as a 'Responsible' Nuclear Power," *International Journal* (Summer, 2007), 831.

15. Paul and Shankar, "Nuclear Accord is a Good Deal," 119.

16. Curtis and Spring, "U.S. Nuclear Agreement with India," 2.

17. Srivastava and Gahlaut, "India and the NPT," 286.

18. Ibid., 288.

19. Robert Einhorn, "Should the US Sell the Technology to India? Part I," *Yale Global* (8 November, 2005). Available at http://yaleglobal.yale.edu/display.article?id=6474 (accessed March 8, 2009).

20. Joseph Cirincione, "The US's Nuclear Cave-In," *Asia Times Online* (March 2006). Available at http://www.atimes.com/atimes/South_Asia/HC04Df03.html (accessed March 8, 2009); Cirincione, "Strategic Collapse," 2008.

21. George Perkovich, "Faulty Promises: The US-India Nuclear Deal," *Policy Outlook,* (Washington D.C.: Carnegie Endowment for International Peace, September 2005); George Perkovich, "Global Implications of the U.S.-India Deal," *Daedalus* (Winter 2010).

22. Gary Milhollin, "The U.S.-India Nuclear Pact: Bad for Security," *Current History* (November, 2006).

23. Potter, "US Nonproliferation Policy."

24. William Potter and Jayantha Dhanapala, "The Perils of Nonproliferation Amnesia," *The Hindu,* September 1, 2007.

25. Fred McGoldrick, Harold Bengelsdorf and Lawrence Scheinman, "The US-India Nuclear Deal: Taking Stock," *Arms Control Today* (October, 2005). Available at http://www.armscontrol.org/act/2005_10/OCT-Cover (accessed March 26, 2008).

26. Ibid.

27. Einhorn, "Technology to India"; Potter, "US Nonproliferation Policy"; Potter and Dhanapala, "Nonproliferation Amnesia."

28. Milhollin, "Bad for Security"; Potter and Dhanapala, "Nonproliferation Amnesia."

29. Perkovich, "Faulty Promises."

30. Leonard Weiss, "US-India Nuclear Cooperation: Better Later Than Sooner," *Nonproliferation Review* 14, no. 3 (November, 2007).

31. Einhorn, "Technology to India."

32. Perkovich, "Faulty Promises"; Einhorn, "Technology to India."

33. Weiss, "Better Late Than Sooner," 451.

34. Dinshaw Mistry and Sumit Ganguly, "The U.S.-India Pact: A Good Deal," *Current History* (November 2006).

35. Dana R. Dillon and Baker Spring, "Nuclear India and the Non-Proliferation Treaty," Backgrounder no. 1935 (Washington D.C.: The Heritage Foundation, May 18, 2006). Available at www.heritage.org/research/abm/missiledefense/bg1935.cfm (accessed February 12, 2009).

36. Avner Cohen and Thomas Graham Jr., "An NPT for Non-Members," *Bulletin of Atomic Scientists,* (May/June, 2004), 40.

37. Dinshaw Mistry, "Diplomacy, Domestic Politics, and the U.S.-India Nuclear Agreement," *Asian Survey* 46, no. 5 (September/October, 2006).

38. Mario E. Carranza, "From Nonproliferation to Post-Proliferation: Explaining the U.S.-India Nuclear Deal," *Contemporary Security Policy* 28, no. 3 (December, 2007).

39. Ashley J. Tellis, "What Should We Expect From India as a Strategic Partner," in *Gauging U.S.-Indian Strategic Cooperation*, ed., Henry Sokolski (Carlisle, PA: Strategic Studies Institute, 2007).

40. Mistry and Ganguly, "A Good Deal."

41. Perkovich, "Global Implications," 2010.

42. Lisa Curtis, "The Costs of a Failed U.S.-India Civil Nuclear Deal," Web Memo no. 1688, (Washington D.C.: The Heritage Foundation, November 2, 2007).

43. Pant, "Triumph of Politics over Institutions," 2–3.

44. Paul and Shankar, "Nuclear Accord is a Good Deal," 112.

45. George Perkovich, "Faulty Promises, 2.

46. Ashley Tellis, *The U.S.-India: Global Partnership: How Significant for American Interests?* Testimony before the House Committee on International Relations, 16 November, 2005, 3.

47. Paul, "The US-India Nuclear Accord," 848.

48. Curtis, "US-India Civil Nuclear Deal."

49. Tellis, "Global Partnership."

50. Michael A. Levi and Charles D. Ferguson, *US-India Nuclear Cooperation: A Strategy for Moving Forward*, Council Special Report, no. 16 (Washington D.C.: Council on Foreign Relations, June 2006).

51. Tellis, "India as a Strategic Partner." Also see, Robert D. Blackwill, "The India Imperative," *The National Interest*, 80 (Summer 2005); Levi and Ferguson, "US-India Nuclear Cooperation"; Scholars opine that given India's third largest Muslim population, the U.S. wants India to act as a "bulwark against the arc of Islamic stability running from the Middle East to Asia and to create a much greater balance in Asia." Alex Perry, "Why is Bush Counting on India?" *Time*, February 28, 2006. Also, Levi and Ferguson, 8.

52. Lisa Curtis, "New U.S. Alliance with India Forges Key Strategic Relationship," Commentary, (Washington D.C.: The Heritage Foundation, December 9, 2009).

53. Lisa Curtis, "Nuclear Crunch for U.S.-India," *The Washington Times*, September 23, 2008.

54. Harsh V. Pant, "A Fine Balance: India walks a Tightrope between Iran and the United States," *Orbis*, (Summer 2007): 500.

55. India was one of the founding leaders of the Non-Alignment Movement (NAM) along with Yugoslavia, Indonesia, Egypt, and Ghana. NAM was founded in 1961.

56. Pant "A Fine Balance," 508. Also, see, Amit Gupta, *The U.S.-India Relationship: Strategic Partnership or Complementary Interests?* (Carlisle, PA: Strategic Studies Institute, February 2005). He states, "India would be unwilling to be the type of military partner that the United Kingdom has been in U.S. global military efforts. The Indian unwillingness to commit to the first and second Gulf War coalitions is a case in point. Further, India does not have the type of historical and cultural-emotional ties that have forged a strong U.S.-Israel relationship" (15).

57. T.V. Paul, "The US-India Nuclear Accord," 856.

58. Paul and Shankar, "Nuclear Accord is Good Deal," 116.

59. A.F.K. Organski, *World Politics* (New York: Alfred A. Knopf, 1958), 315–16. "A powerful nation tends to set up a system of relations with lesser states which can be called an 'order' because the relations are stabilized. In time, everyone comes to know what kind of behavior to expect from others, habits and patterns are established and certain rules as to how these relations ought to be carried on grow to be accepted by all parties."

60. Jacek Kugler and A.F.K. Organski, "The Power Transition: A Retrospective and Prospective Evaluation," in *Handbook of War Studies*, ed., Manus I. Midlarsky (Boston: Unwin Hyman, 1988).

61. Douglas Lemke, "The Continuation of History: Power Transition Theory and the End of Cold War," *Journal of Peace Research* 34, no. 1 (February, 1997), 24.

62. Nonetheless, Douglas Lemke opines that although the People's Republic of China is regarded as a state dissatisfied with the international order because it is "neither democratic nor market-oriented," and due to "the fact that the Chinese growth process is inevitably based on huge foreign investment and trade, there exists 'real possibility' that the Chinese will be *satisfied* with the current international order before parity is reached." Lemke, "Continuation of History," 34.

63. Paul and Shankar, "Nuclear Accord is a Good Deal," 113–14.

64. Ibid.

65. Gupta, "The US-India Relationship," 11–12. Gupta writes, "Typically, the international system is viewed as being divided between status quo and revolutionary states. Status quo states are those that seek to maintain the structure of international system and the order that ensues from it. Revolutionary states seek to dismantle the structure and the order that goes with it, partially or completely. Revolutionary states have been described as rogue states, states of concern, and more recently, as the axis of evil."

66. Ibid.

67. Lemke, "Continuation of History," 24.

68. Kant's idea of peace between the liberal states was rediscovered and popularized by Michael Doyle. See Michael Doyle, "Kant, Liberal Legacies, and Foreign Affairs (I and II)," *Philosophy and Public Affairs* 12, no. 3 and 4 (Summer and Autumn 1983); also see Francis Fukuyama, "Liberal Democracy as a Global Phenomenon," *Political Science and Politics* 24, no. 4, (1991).

69. President Bill Clinton, *State of the Union Address*, January 25, 1994. Available at http://www.washingtonpost.com/wp-srv/politics/special/states/docs/sou94.htm (accessed 29 May, 2009).

70. Jack S. Levy, "Domestic Politics in War," in *The Origin and Prevention of Major Wars*, ed., Robert I. Rotberg and Theodore K. Rabb (New York: Cambridge University Press, 1989), 88.

71. Jarrod Hayes, "Identity and Securitization in the Democratic Peace: The U.S. and the Divergence of Responses to India and Iran's Nuclear Program," *International Studies Quarterly* 53 (2009).

72. George Perkovich, *Democratic Bomb*, Policy Brief no. 49 (Washington D.C.: Carnegie Endowment for International Peace, November 2006).

73. Levi and Ferguson, "Strategy for Moving Forward."

74. Dillon and Spring, "Nuclear India."

75. Levi and Ferguson, "Strategy for Moving Forward," 9.

76. Hayes, "Identity and Securitization," 988.

77. Ibid., 994.

78. Perkovich, "Democratic Bomb," 1.

79. Ibid., 2; Perkovich criticizes that such a "regime-centric strategy—trying to eliminate the bad regimes and reward the good ones—is risky; the combination of the two compounds the risk. . . . Pursuing nonproliferation through regime-change democratization can actually increase rather than reduce demand for nuclear weapons. Leaders in states such as Iran and North Korea and perhaps others have come to see nuclear weapons as the best bulwark against U.S. intervention. After all, the most accepted rationale for a state to seek nuclear weapons is to deter more powerful adversaries from threatening its sovereignty and territory" (3).

80. Dillon and Spring, "Nuclear India," 1.

81. Wesley W. Widmaier, "The Democratic Peace is What States Make of it: A Constructivist Analysis of the U.S.-Indian 'Near-Miss' in the 1971 South Asian Crisis," *European Journal of International Relations* 11, no. 3 (2005): 435.

82. Sharon Squassoni, "U.S.-Indian Deal and its Impact," *Arms Control Today* (July/August 2010). Available at http://www.armscontrol.org/act/2010_07-08/squassoni (accessed March 26, 2008).

83. Mario Carranza, "Can the NPT Survive? The Theory and Practice of U.S. Nuclear Nonproliferation Policy after September 11," *Contemporary Security Policy* 27, no. 3 (December, 2006).

84. William Walker, "Nuclear Enlightenment and Counter-enlightenment," *International Affairs* 83, no. 3 (2007).

85. Milhollin, "Bad for Security."

86. Joseph Cirincione, "Strategic Collapse: The Failure of the Bush Nuclear Doctrine," *Arms Control Today* (November, 2008).

87. Squassoni, "U.S.-Indian Deal."

88. Carranza, "Can the NPT Survive," 465.

89. Milhollin, "US-India Nuclear Pact," 371.

90. Cirincione, "Strategic Collapse."

91. Ashley Tellis, *India as a Global Power: An Action Agenda for the United States*, (Washington D.C.: Carnegie Endowment, July, 2005), 13.

92. Walker, "Nuclear Enlightenment."

93. Ibid., 431.

94. Ibid., 435–36.

95. Ibid.

96. Ibid., 448.

97. Carranza, "Can the NPT Survive," 501.

98. Cirincione, "Strategic Collapse."

99. For a critical discussion of Walker's enlightenment thesis, see, David S. Yost, "Analysing International Nuclear Order," *International Affairs* 83, no. 3 (2007); Joachim Krause, "Enlightenment and Nuclear Order," *International Affairs*, 83, no. 3 (2007); Pierre Hassner, "Who Killed Nuclear Enlightenment?" *International Affairs*, 83, no. 3 (2007); Michael Ruhle, "Enlightenment in the Second Nuclear Age," *International Affairs*, 83, no. 3 (2007).

100. Ruhle, "Enlightenment," 515.

101. Matthew Woods, "Inventing Proliferation: The Creation and Preservation of the Inevitable Spread of Weapons," *The Review of International Affairs* (Spring 2004), 416.

102. Ibid., 417.

103. Stephen Philip Cohen, *A Deal Too Far?* ORF-Brookings Paper, (New Delhi: Observer Research Foundation, ORF, February 28, 2006), 3; Also see, Harsh V. Pant, "The U.S.-India Nuclear Deal: The Beginning of a Beautiful Relationship," *Cambridge Review of International Affairs* 20, no. 3, (September 2007).

TWO

Nuclear Nonproliferation Treaty and India

An Anomaly

It is generally regarded that the United States led the establishment of the Nuclear Nonproliferation Treaty (NPT) centric nonproliferation regime in order to strengthen international security. Washington insisted that India join the regime as a nonnuclear weapon state (NNWS). India, on the other hand, not only refused to join the NPT, but also misused the western technological aid, intended for civilian purposes, to conduct a "peaceful" nuclear explosion (PNE) in 1974. Subsequently, in 1998, in stark opposition to the nonproliferation regime, India went overtly nuclear. Thus, the discourse portrays the United States as the leader and promoter of the regime while India is constructed as a nuclear pariah. I contend that this reflects a shallow understanding of the nuclear estrangement between the United States and India that lasted for more than three decades. Also, such a narrative is quite simplistic and embedded in the hegemonic proliferation discourse which is characteristically America-centric. As Itty Abraham avers, "The term 'proliferation' must give up any pretence to being an objective, analytic concept." Rather, the concept of proliferation is situated in the "political lexicon of IR and its use understood as political language: in this case a discourse which denotes the concern of some (states, intellectuals, media) with other's possession of nuclear weapons because of those other's alleged unwillingness to play by the 'rules of the game.'"[1]

Therefore, I contend that it is pertinent to gain an in-depth understanding of the nuclear disjuncture between the United States and India. In this regard, this chapter attempts to explore the following questions:

Why did India oppose the nuclear nonproliferation treaty? What caused the nuclear estrangement between the two countries? Why were the United States and India at extreme ends of the nonproliferation regime?

In the first section of this chapter, I attempt to clarify the fundamental disjuncture between American and Indian approaches to nuclear nonproliferation. The second section highlights India's role in negotiations for nuclear disarmament and critically analyses the framing of the nuclear nonproliferation treaty. The third section describes India's quest for advanced technology and the discord with Canada and the United States over technology transfer in the post-1970 era. The final section discusses a reorientation of the Indian approach that culminated in a peaceful nuclear explosion and deepened U.S.-India nuclear alienation. Basically, the United States and India envisioned disparate objectives and policies for the nuclear nonproliferation regime.

Even before the establishment of the nuclear regime, the United States and India had contending perspectives of nuclear nonproliferation. India, a member of the nonaligned nations (NAM), favored the negotiation of a treaty that focused on universal disarmament, that is, a treaty that included equitable vertical and horizontal nonproliferation. On the contrary, the United States favored the post–World War II nuclear weapons status quo and was concerned merely with the addition of new nuclear weapon states. Not surprisingly, the United States led the establishment of the nuclear nonproliferation regime, monopolized nuclear technology, and denied equitable access to dual-use technologies to the non-nuclear weapon states. India—an advocate of nuclear disarmament and arms control—was, ironically, marginalized in the establishment of the NPT-centric regime. Furthermore, India's pursuit of advanced technologies brought it into collision with the U.S.-led nuclear nonproliferation regime. The American objective of administering the spread of strategic technologies clashed with the Indian quest for advanced technologies for economic development and autonomy; this conflict resulted in the estrangement of the two countries. Thus, India became an anomaly for the nuclear nonproliferation regime, which in turn, created a schism in its relations with the United States.

NONPROLIFERATION: DIVERGENT PERSPECTIVES

The nuclear estrangement between the United States and India is narrowly attributed to the latter's defiance of the NPT. This perspective suffers from selective amnesia as it conveniently ignores that India was energetically engaged in nuclear disarmament negotiations throughout 1950s–1960s. Infact, India had pioneered a call for a comprehensive ban on nuclear testing as well as a freeze on nuclear fissile material. Subsequently, in 1988 in the United Nations General Assembly, the Indian prime minister, Rajiv Gandhi, laid out a bold initiative for the elimination of nuclear weapons by the year 2010. Francine Frankel, an India specialist, remarked that,

> The United States and India have long professed similar commitments to the eventual elimination of nuclear weapons. Yet, the United States' approach to nonproliferation, which asserts that universal membership of the 1970 Nonproliferation Treaty is the world's best hope for ultimate progress toward this goal, has been contested from the outset by India.[2]

That is, there was agreement on the goals but divergence in the means to attain them.[3] However, I contend that such an assertion is based on several erroneous assumptions, inter alia: first, the United States and India had similar objectives of nonproliferation; second, the NPT is an instrument with an ultimate goal of disarmament—eventual elimination of nuclear weapons, and finally, India was opposed to the nuclear nonproliferation per se. This reflects an acute lack of critical approaches in the proliferation discourse. The U.S.-India nuclear alienation was not a simple case of issue-based antagonism arising from India's refusal to sign the NPT. Rather, the United States and India had fundamental disagreements on the objectives and policies related to nuclear proliferation and this rendered them, in Philip Oldenburg's terms, "inevitable antagonists."[4]

The basic nuclear disjuncture between the United States and India brought them at odds during international negotiations on nuclear disarmament and arms control. Since 1945, international relations have been "overwhelmingly dominated" by U.S. concerns and dilemmas. This is reflected in the establishment of the nonproliferation regime. *A Report on the International Control of Atomic Energy*, also known as the Acheson-Lilienthal report, prepared by the U.S. State Department, emphasized the dual nature of nuclear technologies and the concomitant threat of proliferation. It stated, "The development of atomic energy for peaceful purposes and the development of atomic energy for bombs are in much of their course interchangeable and interdependent."[5] Moreover, the beginning of the Atomic Age coincided with the bipolar Cold War era, thus, it became imperative for the United States to thwart the threat of nuclear weapons, along with the threat of communism. An effective strategy to deal with both threats was "containment."[6] Washington was interested in controlling access to nuclear technology and thereby preventing acquisition of nuclear weapons by additional states. This warranted selective control of the nuclear materials and technologies, thus framed the concept of "proliferation." This approach is predominantly reflected in all the instruments of the nonproliferation regime, including the NPT, supplementary treaties, and multinational export controls.

Contrarily, India had a broader approach to the issue of nuclear weapons and sought to achieve nuclear disarmament at the global level. In fact, India was one of the few Third World nations that in 1950s and 1960s took the initiative to accomplish "nondissemination and nonacquisition"[7] of nuclear weapons at the global level. The dropping of the first atomic bomb over Hiroshima and Nagasaki on August 6, 1945 aroused a sharp reaction in India. Jawaharlal Nehru, the first prime minister of India, deplored the appearance of the atomic bomb as a *"weapon of war with its frightful and horrible powers of destruction."*[8] India's efforts to achieve disarmament were also motivated by a desire to give meaning to its political freedom as well as to achieve economic prosperity—investing in atomic energy, yet, reducing unproductive military expenditure. As the then India's Ambassador R. K. Nehru emphasized, "Disarmament and cuts in military expenditure would help [India] to release resources which should be utilized to the maximum extent for the purpose of development."[9]

DRAFTING OF THE NUCLEAR NONPROLIFERATION TREATY: A CRITICAL ANALYSIS

In 1954, an American series of nuclear tests code named *Operation Castle* created considerable concern about the nuclear fallout. Particularly, the test held on 1 March 1954, the *Bravo Shot* conducted on Namu Island, Bikini Atoll, produced a yield equivalent to about 15 megatons of TNT.[10] It was twice the expected yield and caused severe radiation beyond the restricted testing area. Radioactive contamination of 28 Americans and 236 residents of the nearby Marshall Islands was reported. The crews of a Japanese ship, *Fukuryu Maru* (Lucky Dragon), close to the restricted zone were unaware of the high radiation and suffered severe radiation sickness. After about two weeks the ship returned to Japan and, subsequently, one of the crew members succumbed to the radiation exposure. This incident drew significant international attention. Moreover, concerns regarding the contamination of tuna culminated in a boycott of the fish and heightened panic across Asian countries. Then, in a pioneering effort on April 2, 1954, the Indian Prime Minister, J. L. Nehru, called for a cessation of nuclear testing and an immediate standstill agreement on nuclear tests by the two superpowers until a comprehensive disarmament agreement was elaborated by the United Nations.[11] Again in December 1954, at the U.N. General Assembly (UNGA), India repeated its proposal for a total cessation of nuclear testing. In the light of Cold War tensions, the proposal did not have any immediate impact. Nevertheless, India's proposal to probe the effects of radiation was adopted unanimously, and in 1955 the United Nations Scientific Committee on the Effects of Atomic Radiation (UNSCEAR) was created.[12] Thus, India was instrumental in placing a comprehensive nuclear test ban on the international agenda. The superpowers did engage in intermittent talks and announced limited moratoriums on nuclear tests, yet, their mutual distrust prevented any substantial steps toward nuclear disarmament. In March 1962, under the aegis of the United Nations, the Eighteen Nation Disarmament Committee (ENDC) was established to engage the superpowers in nuclear arms control negotiations.[13] India was one of the eight nonaligned nations to participate actively in the deliberations of the ENDC.

The Cuban missile crisis of October 1962 and the narrow escape from nuclear war marked a turning point in superpower relations. In high-level ENDC discussions, the United States, the United Kingdom, and the erstwhile USSR negotiated the Partial Test Ban Treaty (PTBT) which was formally signed on August 5, 1963. The PTBT was significant in controlling nuclear fallout in the atmosphere, yet, by not including underground explosions it failed to realize the goal of a complete nuclear test ban. Nonetheless, in the context of the tense Cold War period, India hailed the conclusion of the PTBT as a significant step toward nuclear disarmament. Prime Minister Nehru, commented,

> It is highly important and significant because after years of discussions and arguments, this has happened and it breaks the ice as it were and gives an opportunity to go ahead with regard to disarmament and in putting an end, gradually, perhaps, to cold war attitudes of nations to each other.[14]

On August 8, 1963, the day the PTBT was opened for signatures, India became the first nonnuclear weapon state to sign the PTBT.[15]

Given the tense Cold War scenario, India, in a bid to overcome the looming threat of mutual annihilation, emphasized the adoption of several collateral measures enroute to global disarmament. In the ENDC, the leader of the Indian delegation stated, "There is no reason for us to wait for the conclusion of a disarmament treaty, or a draft of it, before we consider other things [collateral steps] or implement some of them."[16] That is, in the absence of progress toward a disarmament treaty, India emphasized adoption of certain subsidiary measures such as: nondissemination of nuclear weapons, a verified freeze on nuclear weapons, halting the manufacture of fissionable material, and a guarantee of the prevention of surprise nuclear attack.[17]

On September 15, 1965, India, along with other nonaligned nations, submitted a joint memorandum to the U.N. General Assembly (UNGA) outlining the basic approach for an appropriate treaty for thwarting the proliferation of nuclear weapons.[18] This led to the U.N. General Assembly Resolution 2028 for the initiation of deliberations in the ENDC on formulation of a nuclear nonproliferation treaty.[19] Subsequently, the Indian delegation in the ENDC participated vociferously in the deliberations to draft a treaty that would curtail both vertical and horizontal proliferation. Along the lines of U.N. Resolution 2028, the Indian representative, V.C. Trivedi, stipulated five conditions for a universal nonproliferation treaty; the treaty should: (i) lead to genuine nuclear disarmament; (ii) provide equitable obligations to nuclear weapon powers and nonnuclear weapon states; (iii) be linked to a comprehensive test ban; (iv) include a ban on production of weapons grade fissile material; and (v) should be fool-proof and contain no loopholes.[20]

Ironically, the United States declined to negotiate on the issue of nuclear disarmament. Rather, in the ENDC subcommittee, the United States carried out negotiations with the erstwhile Soviet Union along with some involvement of the U.K. The outcome was a draft Nuclear Nonproliferation Treaty which was submitted to the U. N. General Assembly on March 11, 1968. The draft treaty reflected the vested interests of the big powers in retaining and upgrading their nuclear arsenals while simultaneously controlling access to nuclear technology by the nuclear have-nots. Several states were critical of the inherent discrimination between nuclear haves and have-nots and refused to sign the NPT. Besides India, these included: China, France, South Africa, Argentina, Brazil, Pakistan, and Algeria.[21] India was greatly disappointed with the formulation of a partial and discriminatory treaty. The leader of the Indian delegation, V.C. Trivedi, called it a futile exercise of imposing *"nonarmament on unarmed countries"* (emphasis added).[22] On May 14, 1968, at the 57th Meeting of the First Committee of the U.N., the Indian ambassador M.A. Hussain, listed India's objections to the NPT as follows: the treaty (i) does not genuinely curb the proliferation of nuclear weapons; rather, it simply prohibits the dissemination of weapons to NNWS but does not constrain the continued manufacture, stockpiling, and sophistication of nuclear weapons by the existing NWS; (ii) accords a privileged status to the NWS; (iii) does not provide for balanced and equitable obligations between NWS and NNWS; (iv) does not constitute a significant step toward nuclear disarmament, and Article VI fails to place a judicial obligation for cessation of the nuclear arms race; and (v) is discriminatory with regard to IAEA safeguards and controls which are imposed only on NNWS.[23] Due to these objections India refused to sign the treaty.

Ironically, even though India was immersed in the nuclear negotiations, its concerns regarding vertical proliferation and disarmament were not accommodated. The formulation of the NPT is a classic example in international relations of how the dominant powers structure the global order in accordance with their interests. In this context, Robert Cox argues that the ontology of the powerful becomes universal, while the "perspectives of the less powerful are derided as irrational, ultimately forgotten, occulted, whether they are those of subordinated social groups or civilizations."[24] Not surprisingly, India being a nascent Third World nation its vision for an alternative nuclear order was easily sidelined. The Indian scholar S.D. Muni reflects, "The forces at work at the global level—the superpowers and the intensifying Cold War between them—were all too powerful and determined to shape the world in a way that suited their interests."[25]

It does not seem that nuclear disarmament was an immediate objective of the big powers. Rather, their exclusive focus was solely on preventing additional new nuclear powers from emerging which in the words of President Kennedy posed the "greatest possible danger." It was estimated that within a decade the number of nuclear weapon states could rise to 15–25.[26] An increase in the number of weapon states meant an increase in the potential for nuclear war. Not surprisingly, the main aim, as mentioned in the NPT was not nuclear disarmament, but prevention of a nuclear war arising from the dissemination of nuclear technology or weapons. The preamble of the NPT states, "*the* [horizontal] *proliferation of nuclear weapons would seriously enhance the danger of nuclear war.*"[27] Thus, contrary to the deliberations in the ENDC and India's emphasis, the NPT was framed with a narrow focus only on the horizontal spread of weapons, and not disarmament.

Furthermore, the commonly held misperception is that the NPT signifies an "underlying connection between nuclear disarmament and nuclear proliferation"[28] manifested in the legitimate "grand bargain" between nonnuclear weapon states (NNWS) and nuclear weapon states (NWS).[29] It meant, if the NNWS accede to the nuclear pact, they would receive peaceful nuclear technology from the NWS who, in turn, would commit themselves to achieving nuclear disarmament. That is, the NWS have the obligation to pursue global nuclear disarmament.[30] The Hans Blix Commission also notes that the original bargain of the NPT, is "the elimination of nuclear weapons through the commitment by non-nuclear weapon states not to acquire nuclear weapons and the commitment by the five nuclear weapon states to pursue nuclear disarmament."[31]

But a careful reading of Article VI of the NPT proves this to be a false assumption.

Article VI reads:

> *Each of the Parties to the Treaty undertakes to pursue negotiations in good faith on effective measures relating to cessation of the nuclear arms race at an early date and to nuclear disarmament, and on a treaty on general and complete disarmament under strict and effective international control.*[32]

Thus, this adroitly drafted Article makes it the prerogative of "*each of the parties to the Treaty*" that is, all signatories, not only the NWS, to take steps toward ending the nuclear arms race. Moreover, Article VI fails to provide for any detailed timeline or legally binding commitment on the signatories, and is therefore of mere symbolic value. In fact, it has been suggested that Article VI was included to make the treaty "attractive" and "saleable" to the nonnuclear weapon states, encouraging them to join the NPT system. It was intended to give the NNWS the impression that the nuclear haves would, at a future date, dismantle their nuclear weapons; so the nuclear inequality enshrined in the treaty is only for a limited time.[33] In fact, it is argued that overemphasis on Article VI and treating the NPT as a disarmament treaty can be counterproductive. The signatories to the treaty, especially the NNWS, might capitalize on the failure of the NWS' commitment to disarmament, using this as an escape route for themselves. Krause avers, it can be "dangerous, since it triggers off a logic which tends to undermine the whole treaty regime."[34]

The other part of the bargain through Article IV of the NPT recognizes the inalienable right of all signatories of the treaty to peaceful uses of nuclear energy.[35] Since the atomic energy is recognized as dual-potential, the sharing of nuclear technology and materials is not only heavily guarded, rather the NPT makes the nuclear have-nots dependent on the nuclear haves. Compared to the relatively absent restrictions on the NWS, the nuclear have-nots, intending to develop civilian nuclear programs, are subject to intense scrutiny. Thus, although the text of the NPT calls peaceful uses of nuclear energy "inalienable," in practice these rights are exercised under a system of compulsory safeguards and intensive monitoring.[36]

Contrary to William Walker's assertion that the NPT represented a "grand enlightenment project" pioneered by the United States,[37] the idea that it was the result of a political bargain between the two superpowers seems to be more convincing. Rebecca Johnson remarks that the NPT "was the product of tradeoffs in a distorted multilateral process ultimately shaped by the hegemonic power of the United States and the Soviet Union."[38] In a similar vein, Pierre Hassner laments that the NPT project, "relied on a great deal of hypocrisy on the part of most of its participants." It represented "an uneasy and fragile compromise based on the existing power relations" rather than "based on coherent long-term vision."[39]

The Nuclear Nonproliferation Treaty set up an arbitrary date and required all states that had not tested weapons by January 1, 1967 to renounce their capabilities and join the treaty as nonnuclear weapon states. On the other hand, states that had already crossed the nuclear threshold were not required to rollback and were admitted in the privileged position of nuclear weapon states. India could not join either of these categories. India had not yet conducted the nuclear tests and joining the treaty as a NNWS meant giving up its advanced civilian nuclear program as well as developmental aspirations. India had always maintained that it was willing to rollback technological capabilities based on a firm international commitment and significant progress toward disarmament. Nonetheless, India was excluded from participating in the nonproliferation regime except on the highly discriminatory terms and restrictions enforced by the powerful states. Infact, India's rival neighbor China was able to join the treaty as a nuclear weapon state, as prior to 1967, it had aggressively pursued a nuclear weapons program. At that stage, for India there was nothing to gain by renouncing its nuclear capabilities, neither the goals of nuclear disarmament nor curtailment of vertical proliferation. In this context, Jyotika Saksena asserts, in a sense, India "was penalized for not conducting a nuclear explosion before 1974."[40]

The next section discusses the significance India attached to the advanced technology to ensure self-reliance and economic development. In the post-1968 era, India's quest for technology created discord with Canada and the United States, and consequently, nonproliferation export controls were further strengthened.

INDIA'S QUEST FOR TECHNOLOGY

Post-independence, India, cognizant of its unpropitious circumstances, set out to confront economic vulnerabilities as well as the political and societal challenges of nation building. As a newly independent country in 1947, India's theater of insecurities was wider than the prevalent Western notion of security. Therefore, during the Cold War era when the great powers were "defining national security in terms of military power based on Morgenthau's realism,"[41] the Indian leadership envisioned achieving security through nonmilitary measures. Significantly, Nehru, the first premier of India, founded the survival strategy of the infant nation based on triple goals of self-reliance, national development, and technological advancement.[42] To this day, the triple goals permeate Indian policy-making. In 2001, a group of cabinet ministers drafted India's security document, *Reforming the National Security System,* it stated, "The more realistic and comprehensive approach to national security also includes economic strength, internal cohesion, and technological prowess."[43]

Reliance on advanced technology constituted an important cornerstone in Indian strategic thinking. India was aware that advanced technologies, both civilian nuclear energy and space, provided opportunities for societal transformation and development, and thereby, embarked on a quest for acquiring them.[44] Vikram Sarabhai, the father of the Indian space program, remarked:

> There are some who question the relevance of space [and nuclear] activities in a developing nation. To us, there is no ambiguity of purpose . . . we are convinced that if we are to play a meaningful role nationally and in the comity of nations, we must be second to none in the application of advanced technologies to the real problems of man and society which we find in our country.[45]

In this regard, it is important to mention that within four decades of investment, in terms of human and material resources, India's space program proved beneficial for societal development. With a modest investment of US$ 2.4billion, India developed a state of the art space program that is regarded as a "successful and cost-effective endeavour."[46]

It was Nehru's powerful, spirited leadership along with Homi Bhabha's genius and technical expertise that steered India's civilian nuclear energy policy toward the goals of achieving self-sufficiency and development through peaceful uses of nuclear energy. As early as 1944, Bhabha wrote to the Tata Trust urging them to establish a first-ever training and research institution for fundamental research in nuclear physics.[47] This was to ensure that India would be ready with both infrastructure and expertise at the dawn of the nuclear era. Thus, in June 1945 the Tata Fundamental Research Institute (TFRI) was established. Subsequently, scientific and industrial laboratories were established for the training of its scientists and to identify areas of importance to the progress and development of the country. Nonetheless, India's attitude toward the harnessing of nuclear energy was clear. In 1946 at a public meeting, Nehru said that the bomb was a "symbol of evil." He firmly believed that India, while developing nuclear energy for peaceful purposes, must never build nuclear weapons.[48]

India realized that self-reliance in research and development and continuous technological advancement were essential for retaining autonomy in international affairs. There were apprehensions that in the twentieth-century political colonialism between the North and the global South had been replaced by "technological colonialism." Technological aid involved the imposition of conditionalities and ensured significant "political and economic leverage for the donors."[49] In the Technological Policy Statement of 1983, India declared its objective as "attainment of technological competence and self-reliance to reduce vulnerability, particularly in strategic and critical areas, making the maximum use of indigenous resources."[50] Predictably, the quest for advanced technology put India at cross purposes with the Western world which in turn was intent on clamping down on dual-use technologies. In 1946, the United States, on the basis of the Acheson-Lilienthal report, submitted the Baruch Plan to the United Nations Atomic Energy Commission for international control of the atomic power programs. India opposed the Baruch Plan as it "sought to prohibit national research and development in atomic energy production."[51] This influenced the passing of the Indian Atomic Energy Act of 1948, "to provide for the development and control of atomic energy and purposes connected therewith"[52] and led to the establishment of the Atomic Energy Commission in 1948.[53] On August 4, 1956, India's first indigenously built experimental research reactor Apsara became critical, i.e., achieved its first chain reaction. It was also the first nuclear reactor in Asia to become critical.[54] It was a significant achievement for India, a developing country, as several industrialized countries were still importing similar units from the United States and Britain.[55] In fact, it is even suggested that "scaling up the [Apsara] reactor to prototype and production sizes was not an impossible task for Indian scientists."[56] Thus, by the late 1950s India was at an advanced stage in its civilian nuclear program.

CIRUS AGREEMENT: FALLOUT WITH CANADA AND THE UNITED STATES

In 1953, President Eisenhower, in his famous "Atoms for Peace" speech at the plenary meeting of the United Nations General Assembly, proposed to work with nonnuclear states for harnessing nuclear energy for peaceful purposes.[57] It led to nuclear cooperation with several countries including sales of research reactors and participation of foreign scientists in nuclear research projects. The Atoms for Peace project underlined the idea of international control of nuclear materials such as an international uranium bank. Rather than a humanitarian project aimed at directing peaceful uses of nuclear energy for development purposes, it was regarded as a significant step toward U.S. domination of the global nuclear energy market.[58] Frantz and Collins suggest that Washington "subsidized the spread of nuclear knowledge through the Atoms for Peace project to counter Soviet influence."[59] That is, to prevent the states interested in seeking nuclear technology from falling into the Soviet camp. Significantly, Homi Bhabha, father of the Indian nuclear program, was invited to preside over the first international conference on "Peaceful Uses of Atomic Energy" in Geneva in 1955.[60] At this stage, Indian and Western interests in harnessing peaceful nuclear energy appeared to converge, albeit temporarily.

In 1956, Canada signed a nuclear cooperation agreement with India and agreed to supply India with CANDU reactors. Subsequently, the United States also joined the nuclear pact and agreed to supply 10 tonnes of heavy water for the CANDU reactors. The so-called CIRUS (Canada India Reactor US)[61] reactor became critical on July 10, 1960, and fully operational in 1963. However, the Indian peaceful nuclear explosion (PNE) in 1974 proved to be the tipping point for cessation of the nuclear collaboration. It was alleged that India used the plutonium produced from the CANDU reactors to conduct the "peaceful" explosion in contravention of the CIRUS agreement. That is, India had diverted nuclear technologies imported from Western nations—intended for peaceful nuclear purposes—toward building nuclear warfare. Subsequently, it was reported that India also utilized the CANDU reactor as a "design prototype" to build Dhruva reactors for the production of plutonium.[62]

Internationally, there was mixed reaction to India's 1974 peaceful explosion. Yet, it was not an unexpected development, with the progress of China's nuclear weapons program, there seemed a possibility for India to rethink its approach towards development of nuclear weapons. Nonetheless, the Indian PNE created resentment within Canada. Initially, the belief was that India had broken the terms of the CIRUS agreement. As Robert Gillette puts it, India "had climbed into the nuclear clubhouse on the shoulders of Canadian technology and Canadian aid."[63] India was considered a defaulter on several counts: violation of the CIRUS agreement, betrayal of Canadian government's trust, misuse of Canadian aid, and challenge to the NPT system.

George Bindon and Sitoo Mukherjee, who conducted detailed research on the India-Canada nuclear collaboration, regard the Canadian reaction as "exaggerated." The Indian detonation was to some extent "predictable." Since 1955 India had at several international fora emphasized the necessity of conducting peaceful nuclear explosions for developmental purposes.[64] Moreover, scholars also challenge the patronizing picture of the North-South technological aid. They refute that Canada's technological assistance enabled a "technologically backward India to enter the nuclear club." Instead, it was more a case of two equal partners sharing in the establishment of a high technology industry. It was a symbiotic relationship, with Canada also gaining from the counter-transfer of Indian nuclear knowhow.[65] Furthermore, several scholars have suggested that the deal with India was significant for the subsequent commercialization of the Canadian nuclear reactor. "Without India's participation the eventual success and acceptance of the CANDU system as a viable commercial product would have been less likely."[66] In fact, Sullivan has commented that before the CIRUS agreement Ottawa was eager to ensure that India selects Canada as the preferred supplier for its second research reactor instead of the United States or the United Kingdom. Therefore, Canada was willing to provide technical assistance "with minimal restrictions and *no* controls over the fuel rods."[67] The agreement simply stated peaceful uses and the Indian government, as Sullivan points out, merely "undertook" that the by-products of the CIRUS reactor would be used for peaceful purposes alone.[68] Thus, there were hardly any safeguards attached to the sale of the reactors.[69]

Though, in May 1974, Canada suspended the nuclear agreement, yet Mitchell Sharpe, then secretary of state for external affairs, clarified that India did not break any legal agreement.[70] The reaction and the sense of betrayal felt in Canada, although legally unfounded, was not entirely unreasonable. The CIRUS agreement was signed in 1956, more than a decade prior to the signing of the NPT. At that time there was considerable ambiguity regarding the definition of peaceful nuclear explosions and safeguards. With the coming into force of the NPT in 1968 there was an increased emphasis on safeguards and controls on technology sharing with nonnuclear weapon states. Articles II and III of the NPT eliminated the distinction between "peaceful" nuclear explosion and nuclear weapon test. Moreover, the NPT prohibited the conduct of nuclear tests, be it for peaceful or military purposes by the non-nuclear weapon states, i.e., the states which had not tested a device by January 1, 1967. Accordingly, in 1971, Canada, signatory to the NPT, insisted that India retrospectively redefine the peaceful clauses in the 1956 agreement. The Canadian request was turned down by the then Indian prime minister, Indira Gandhi.[71] Canada was eager to establish itself in the emerging nuclear energy sector and was thus in competition with other supplier states. Thus, as a supplier, it was natural for Canada to feel concerned about the potential repercussions of India's PNE, and the use of plutonium from the CIRUS reactor, on the commercialization of the CANDU technology.

Nonetheless, the Indian peaceful nuclear explosion (PNE) of 1974 made Western nations conscious of existing loopholes in the nonproliferation accord and heightened their dilemmas regarding the potential use and misuse of nuclear technologies and the concomitant chain-reactions. Henry Kissinger remarked, "The Indian nuclear explosion . . . raises anew the spectre of an era of plentiful nuclear weapons in which any local conflict risks exploding into a nuclear holocaust."[72] Suddenly, post-1974 India became a "nuclear pariah."[73] In response to the Indian nuclear test, the U.S. Congress passed the Nuclear Nonproliferation Act of 1978 (NNPA). This act barred nuclear exports including any "source material, special nuclear material, production or utilization facilities, and sensitive nuclear technologies" unless the recipients—nonnuclear weapon states—accepted IAEA safeguards on all its nuclear facilities, including those deemed for peaceful purposes. It is important to note that the new criteria for U.S. nuclear trade did not require signing of the NPT, only acceptance of the full-scope safeguards.[74] India's position on nuclear safeguards was quite clear; it would not accept discriminatory safeguards. Thus, the NNPA rendered India ineligible for nuclear trade with the United States.[75] It has been argued that the nonproliferation controls have largely emerged in "defensive" response to India's nuclear and missile advancements. While India's 1974 nuclear detonation impelled the secret formation of the London Club, later called the Nuclear Suppliers Group (NSG), Indian development of space technology inspired the formation of the Missile Technology Control Regime (MTCR).[76] Brahma Chellaney remarks that the nuclear friction between India and the United States is actually an "intense struggle between one country's determination to control the global diffusion of sensitive technologies and another country's resolve rooted in security considerations to build technological independence."[77]

India was the recipient of nuclear technology and thus obliged to follow the conditions and rules of technology transfer as established by the supplier nations since in 1974 India had defaulted in the Western perception it deserved reprimand and sanctions. Thus, Canada called off the nuclear deal and the United States, which was less vocal, introduced the NNPA and excluded India from technology sharing arrangements. Viewed from the western perspective, the Indian PNE had the potential to create a domino effect, with other developing countries following suit and diverting peaceful nuclear technologies to military purposes. Quite logically, then, India had to be restricted and this explains the imposition of technological embargoes against India. India came to be regarded as a pariah but, significantly, was not considered a rogue state.

INDIA'S CHALLENGE TO THE NPT: AN ANOMALY

The PNE of 1974 reflected a change in India's stance from a nation at the forefront of nuclear disarmament negotiations to a nation with demonstrated nuclear capability. This change resulted from an underlying reorientation of India's approach to international arms control and disarmament—from an outward oriented global disarmament policy to an inward focused self-reliant approach to national security. Initially, India was largely guided by a "sense of urgency to reduce international political tensions in a world containing a growing stockpile of nuclear weapons."[78] Also, based on its historical struggle for freedom, India felt a moral obligation to employ the Gandhian principles of nonviolence and equality in the international arena to achieve peace and security for all nations. This was reflected in its active participation in the international negotiations for elimination of nuclear weapons. It is estimated that in the ENDC (1962–1965), India presented seventy-four major statements and during the NPT negotiations (1965–1968) Indian representatives delivered thirty-seven major speeches.[79] But, post-1968 era, India gradually withdrew from center stage in disarmament negotiations. India not only refused to sign the NPT that resulted from these negotiations, with the PNE it posed a considerable challenge to the nonproliferation regime. That is, India went from being a supporter to a challenger of international arms control.

Michael Sullivan identifies four reasons for this change: the 1962 border war with China, the death of Prime Minister Nehru in May 1964, China's testing of its first nuclear explosion, and the military conflict with Pakistan in 1965.[80] Rather, I contend that these may be contributing factors, but were not the main reasons for the change in India's attitude to arms control. Primarily, it was India's disillusionment with the discriminatory regime and the lack of substantial steps to curtail vertical proliferation and elimination of nuclear weapons that caused a shift in Indian stance toward arms control.

Post-1962 Sino-India war, which led to a humiliating defeat of India, any advancement in the Chinese nuclear program created considerable insecurity in the Indian political circles and increased the demand for nuclear weaponization. Yet, Prime Minister Nehru, the main protagonist of peaceful uses of nuclear energy, resisted any plans for militarization of the existing nuclear technology. Moreover, in 1954 India had initiated the call for a comprehensive test ban and since 1962 was engaged in nuclear disarmament deliberations in the ENDC. Thus, Nehru did not consider it ethical for India to conduct nuclear tests. On March 25, 1963, during discussions of grants for the Department of Atomic Energy, a suggestion was made that the government's no bomb policy should be reviewed and the issue should at least be kept open. Nehru commented, "On the one hand, we are asking the nuclear powers to give up their tests. How can we, without showing utter insincerity of what we have always said, go in for doing the very thing [conduct nuclear test] which we have repeatedly asked the other powers not to do?"[81]

Since the mid-1950s China had been aggressively pursuing its nuclear weapons program and conducted its first nuclear test in October 1964. Within a period of thirty-two months China test fired a nuclear capable missile and conducted several nuclear tests, including a thermonuclear explosion, i.e., a hydrogen bomb, in June 1967. Meanwhile, in India there was scathing criticism from the opposition and some ruling Congress party members insisted on a change in the Indian position on nuclear weapons. On May 10, 1966, the day after the third Chinese nuclear test, the external affairs minister, in response to the debate in the Lok Sabha, stated:

> *We had made a careful assessment of the situation in consultation with our service chiefs and atomic energy experts even when the first nuclear device was exploded by China. The mere fact that China has exploded its third explosion does not vitiate the earlier conclusion, [not to conduct nuclear test] though at the same time, the policy is kept under constant review. In any serious review, account has to be made not only of Chinese tests but of relevant factors, especially progress made in the discussions relating to nuclear disarmament in which many countries are participating.*[82] (emphasis added)

Intervening in the discussion, the then prime minister Indira Gandhi said, "I do not think our policy is at all a negative one; I think it is a very positive policy. We are building our atomic power. Of course, we are using it for peaceful purposes; but in the meantime, we are increasing our know-how and other competence."[83] This shows that India was not eager to immediately respond to the Chinese nuclear weapons program with its own nuclear test explosions. Thus, it also refutes the erroneous perception in the West that "India's nuclear policy is essentially a response to the security threat from China."[84] Even after a decade of weaponization in China, India did not proceed to build nuclear weapons. Though, undeniably, there was a subtle change in India's stance. India was neither aggressive in building nuclear weapons, nor was it vehemently opposed to the option of weaponization—as witnessed earlier during the Nehru era (1947–1964). Rather, India, which had submitted a joint memorandum in September 1965 to the UNGA for formulation of a nonproliferation treaty, was pursuing a wait and watch policy. It was energetically pursuing a demand for nuclear disarmament and was attempting to establish certain collateral measures, such as a ban on nuclear testing and a freeze on nuclear armaments, in the interregnum. Undoubtedly, the call for disarmament was not only moralistic, it was also guided by India's security considerations. Since any success in curtailment of vertical proliferation, such as a freeze on nuclear build-up, would have taken care of the nuclear weaponization in India's immediate neighbourhood, vis-a-vis China, besides providing a global reduction in nuclear threat.

India was quite disillusioned with the outcome of the nuclear negotiations and institution of a discriminatory and illusory NPT regime. Contrary to its earlier urgency to initiate peace between the superpowers, India in the late 1960s became apprehensive of the superpower tactics to manipulate the international nuclear order in accordance with their vested interests. During the drafting of the NPT, India charged the superpowers with "atomic collusion." This position is aptly captured by Sullivan, "Since the drafting of the NPT, India has become more fearful of an agreement made by the two superpowers over the heads of the nonnuclear weapon states than of the absence of agreement due to lack of communication on the part of the Big Two."[85] That is, it was the framing of the NPT in the narrow horizontal proliferation terms and lack of consideration for India's concerns for both disarmament and development that influenced the change in India's stance. This explains the withdrawal of India from its previous active role at the international level. There are suggestions that even in the mid-1960s India was technologically prepared to conduct a peaceful nuclear explosion.[86]

Nonetheless, it was in the post-1968 scenario that disillusionment with "superpower imperialism in international security,"[87] combined with other geopolitical factors, influenced the then prime minister Indira Gandhi to give the green light for a peaceful nuclear explosion in 1974. One significant factor which probably proved to be a catalyst in India's calculations for PNE was the overt anti-India support offered by the United States to Pakistan in the 1971 Indo-Pak war. In the early 1970s, Pakistan gained significance for Washington in the nascent U.S.-China rapprochement. Therefore, during 1971 war, the United States sent its state of the art nuclear armed aircraft carrier *Enterprise* in the Bay of Bengal to threaten India. This not only underlined the political utility of the nuclear weapons to the Indian establishment, but also reinforced the inherent discrimination in the global nuclear order, that privileged states possessing nuclear weapons could target unarmed states.

The Indian PNE challenged the NPT regime in several ways. First, the nuclear test proclaimed as "peaceful" violated Articles II and III of the NPT that assumed there is no difference between peaceful and military explosions. Technically, there is no difference in peaceful and military explosions. Yet, by calling it a peaceful explosion India displayed its intent to use nuclear energy exclusively for development purposes. Second, the Indian PNE challenged the distinction between nuclear weapon states and nonnuclear weapon states. The NPT distinction between NWS and NNWS was based on a date: January 1, 1967. All states that had conducted nuclear explosions before this date were considered NWS and therefore were eligible to conduct future nuclear tests for both peaceful and military purposes. States that had not conducted nuclear tests by January 1, 1967 were barred from crossing the nuclear threshold, including peaceful explosions. The Indian PNE conducted after the NPT came into force in 1970 "circumvents that date and makes that distinction useless—legally and politically."[88] Finally, the PNE placed India in an ambiguous category—India demonstrated its nuclear weapons capability but refrained from building nuclear arsenal. In this context, K. Subrahmanyam remarks that, the Indian policy of nonalignment was alien to the Western and Communist notions of foreign policy and was therefore regarded as a facade, similarly, "the sponsors of the NPT argue that a country can be only a nuclear weapon power or a nonnuclear power." They fail to recognize that there can be a third category. The Indian PNE and the subsequent declaration that India does not propose to manufacture nuclear weapons made India an ambiguous nuclear state.[89] In response to a deteriorating security environment, the PNE demonstrated that India had the capacity to build nuclear weapons. The PNE also reflected India's policy to abstain from the development of nuclear weapons while retaining the option to go nuclear if the security environment so demanded.

Paradoxically, India, which was energetically involved in negotiations for nuclear nonproliferation, became an anomaly for the NPT-centric regime. From being a supporter of global nuclear disarmament and arms control, India became a challenger of the NPT regime. This anomalous relation with the NPT regime estranged India's relations with the United States.

NOTES

1. Itty Abraham, *The Making of the Indian Atomic Bomb: Science, Secrecy and the Postcolonial State* (London, Zed Books, 1998), 15.
2. Francine R. Frankel, ed., "Preface," in *Bridging the Nonproliferation Divide: The United States and India* (Centre for the Advanced Study of India, University of Pennsylvania, Lanham, MD: University Press of America, 1995), xi.
3. Ibid., xii.
4. Philip Oldenburg, "India and the United States: Accidental or Inevitable Antagonists?" *Asian Survey* 15, no. 4 (Winter 1988/89): 220.
5. A Report on the International Control of Atomic Energy, Prepared for the Secretary of State's Committee on Atomic Energy, Publication 2498, (Washington D.C.: Department of State, March 16, 1946), 4. Available at http://www.foia.cia.gov/cgi/1946/03%20-%20March%201946/Report_on_the_International_Control_of_Atomic_Energy_16_Mar_1946.PDF (accessed January 12, 2009). The report suggested establishment of an International Atomic Development Authority. On the basis of this report, the United States submitted Baruch Plan to the United Nations.

6. Containment, the strategy employed by the United States, was a conglomeration of the political, military and economic strategies to stall the influence of the Soviet communism. The containment strategy was formulated by George Kennan. He stated: "the main element of any United States policy toward the Soviet Union must be that of long-term, patient but firm and vigilant containment of Russian expansive tendencies." George Kennan, "The Sources of Soviet Conduct," *Foreign Affairs* 25, no. 4 (July 1947): 575.

7. K.D. Kapur, *Nuclear Non-Proliferation Diplomacy: Nuclear Power Programmes in the Third World* (New Delhi: Lancers Books, 1993), 294.

8. Jawahar Lal Nehru, *India's Foreign Policy: Selected Speeches, September 1946–61* (New Delhi: Ministry of Information and Broadcasting, 1961), 187.

9. As quoted in A.K. Chopra, *India's Policy on Disarmament* (New Delhi: ABC Publishers, 1984), 8.

10. TNT, trinitrotoluene, is a unit for measuring energy output of nuclear explosions. It also reflects the destructive potential of the nuclear weapons. Hiroshima bomb had a yield of 12–15 TNT while the bomb dropped on Nagasaki had a yield of 21 TNT.

11. Robert Divine, *Blowing on the Wind: The Nuclear Test Ban Debate 1954–60* (New York: Oxford University Press, 1978), 3; Stephen J. Ledogar, "Concluding the Negotiations," *Disarmament* 18, no. 1 (1995): 135; Savita Datt, "A Comprehensive Test Ban: Prospects," *Indian Defense Review* (January 1995): 22.

12. United Nations Scientific Committee on the Effects of Atomic Radiation possesses the mandate to assess and report on the levels and effects of exposure to ionizing radiation on the world population. It is still in existence and its 58th session is expected to be held in March 2011. For more information, see, http://www.unscear.org/unscear/en/about_us.html (accessed January 21, 2011).

13. Although these talks failed to accomplish a comprehensive nuclear test ban or complete nuclear disarmament, yet, the deliberations did lead to some limitations on nuclear tests. These included: Partial Test Ban Treaty (PTBT) in 1963, Nuclear Nonproliferation Treaty (NPT) in 1970, Threshold Test Ban Treaty (TTBT) in 1974, and Peaceful Nuclear Explosions Treaty (PNET) in 1974. The PTBT prohibited nuclear weapon test explosions under the jurisdiction or control of a party in the following environments: the atmosphere, including outer space or underwater, including territorial waters or high seas. The treaty did not prohibit underground explosions. Threshold Test Ban Treaty as the name suggests, prohibited underground nuclear weapons tests with a yield of more than 150 kilotons. The United States was concerned about the verification measures of the yield of nuclear tests and this aspect delayed the ratification of the TTBT for 16 years. It was only in 1987 that the United States and erstwhile USSR began negotiations for new procedures and methods of verification. After a long wait the treaty entered into force in December 1990 with a new verification protocol. Ironically, by 1990 the value of the threshold of 150 Kilotons was no more relevant and thus, this treaty ended up being a politically expedient measure. Moreover, the provisions of the TTBT did not extend to the underground nuclear explosions for peaceful purposes. Therefore, the United States and the S.U. signed Peaceful Nuclear Explosions Treaty on May 28, 1976. Through this treaty, the threshold limit of the TTBT was extended to the underground nuclear tests also. But again, due to the verification issues it was also not ratified by the U.S. and came into force only in 1990. For a critical analysis of these nuclear test limitation measures, see, Vandana Bhatia, "Toward a Comprehensive Test Ban," (paper presented at the Graduate Students Conference, University of Delhi, South Campus, 1996).

14. Nehru, "India's Foreign Policy," 187.

15. K. Subrahmanyam, "India First Country to Accede to Partial N-Test Ban Treaty," *The Times of India*, February 13, 1995; Also see, Chopra, 91.

16. Krishna Menon, *Remarks at the Eighteen Nations Committee on Disarmament*, Final Verbatim Record of the Conference of the Eighteen Nation Committee on Disarma-

ment, 5th Meeting (ENDC/PV5, United Nations General Assembly, March 20, 1962), 35.

17. R. K. Nehru, *Remarks at the Eighteen Nations Committee on Disarmament*, Final Verbatim Record of the Conference of the Eighteen Nation Committee on Disarmament, 162nd Meeting (ENDC/PV162, United Nations General Assembly, January 31, 1964), 14.

18. *Disarmament Commission, Official Records: Supplement for January-December 1965*, Document DC/227, (New York: United Nations, 1966), 40, 44. The group of eight non-aligned nations, in the Eighteen Nation Committee on Disarmament (ENDC), besides India, included: Brazil, Burma, Ethiopia, India, Mexico, Nigeria, Sweden, and United Arab Republic.

19. United Nations General Assembly Resolution 2028, Non-Proliferation of Nuclear Weapons, Twentieth Session, November 19, 1965, 7. The resolution emphasized, inter alia, "The Treaty should be void of any loopholes which might permit nuclear or non-nuclear powers to proliferate directly or indirectly, nuclear weapons in any form." And, the treaty should also "embody an acceptable balance of mutual responsibility and obligations of the nuclear and non-nuclear powers."

20. As cited, K. Subrahmanyam, "India's 'NO' to observer at NPT Extension Conference," *Times of India*, January 25, 1995.

21. Joseph Nye, "New Approaches to Nuclear Proliferation Policy," *Science* 256 (May 29, 1992): 1294. However, several of these states reversed their original positions and signed the treaty in early 1990s. France and China joined NPT in 1992 after 22 years of the treaty coming into force.

22. V.C. Trivedi, *Remarks at the Eighteen Nations Committee on Disarmament*, Final Verbatim Record of the Conference of the Eighteen Nation Committee on Disarmament, 298th Meeting (ENDC/PV298, United Nations General Assembly, May 23, 1967), 16.

23. As cited in, K. Subrahmanyam, "Indian Attitudes Towards NPT," in Nuclear Proliferation Problems, Bhupendra Jasani, ed., (Almquist and Wiksell: Stockholm International Peace Research Institute, SIPRI, Stockholm:, 1974), 259–60.

24. Robert W. Cox (ed) "Introduction," in *The New Realism: Perspectives on Multilateralism and World Order* (New York: United Nations University Press, 1997), xxii.

25. S.D. Muni, "India and the Post-Cold War World," *Asian Survey* 31, no. 9 (September 1991): 863.

26. As quoted, Graham Allison, "Nuclear Disorder: Surveying Atomic Threats," *Foreign Affairs* 89, no. 1 (January/February 2010): 74; Also quoted in, Glenn Theodore Seaborg, *Kennedy, Krushchev and the Test Ban* (Berkeley: University of California Press, 1981), 199.

27. Text of the Nonproliferation Treaty. Available at http://www.un.org/en/conf/npt/2005/npttreaty.html (accessed March 16, 2009). Michael Ruhle, "Enlightenment in the Second Nuclear Age," *International Affairs* 83, no. 3 (May 2007): 514.

28. David Holloway, "The United States and the NPT 'Double Bargain,'" in *Nuclear Proliferation and International Order: Challenges to the NPT*, ed., Olav Njolstad (New York: Routledge Global Security Series, 2011), 151.

29. It is also called as the double bargain. In 2009, the U.S. president, Barack Obama remarked that the double bargain, underlying the NPT, means that " the countries with nuclear weapons will move towards disarmament, countries without nuclear weapons will not acquire them, and all countries can access peaceful nuclear energy." Obama's Speech in Prague, April 5, 2009. Available at www.cfr.org/proliferation/Obamas-speech-prague-april-2009/p20960 (accessed March 26, 2010).

30. Avner Cohen and Thomas Graham Jr., "An NPT for Non-Members," *Bulletin of Atomic Scientists* (May/June 2004), 40; Holloway, 154.

31. *The Weapons of Mass Destruction Commission, Weapons of Terror: Freeing the World of Nuclear, Biological and Chemical Arms*. Stockholm: Weapons of Mass Destruction Commission, 2006, 62.

32. Text of the Treaty on Nonproliferation of the Nuclear Weapons.

33. Ruhle, 514; Also see, Rebecca Johnson, "Rethinking the NPT's Role in Security: 2010 and Beyond," *International Affairs* 86, no. 2 (March 2010). Johnson mentions, "The United States and Soviet Union accepted Disarmament obligations as an objective or even a common good, but because they had to, in order to get some key governments on board. Countries such as Sweden, Italy and Germany made it clear that they would not forego nuclear weapons in the long term, if the possession of such nuclear armaments by others would confer lasting high value in terms of status, security, or power projection. This was the original reason for the Article VI disarmament obligations and for the NPT given an initial duration of 25 years" (438).

34. Joachim Krause, "Enlightenment and Nuclear Order," *International Affairs* 83, no. 3 (2007), 485–86.

35. Article IV mentions: "Nothing in this Treaty shall be interpreted as affecting the inalienable right of all the Parties to the Treaty to develop research, production and use of nuclear energy for peaceful purposes without discrimination and in conformity with Articles I and II of this Treaty.2. All the Parties to the Treaty undertake to facilitate, and have the right to participate in, the fullest possible exchange of equipment, materials and scientific and technological information for the peaceful uses of nuclear energy. Parties to the Treaty in a position to do so shall also co-operate in contributing alone or together with other States or international organizations to the further development of the applications of nuclear energy for peaceful purposes, especially in the territories of non-nuclear-weapon States Party to the Treaty, with due consideration for the needs of the developing areas of the world." Text of the Treaty on Nonproliferation of the Nuclear Weapons.

36. See, Nobuyasu Abe, "The Current Problems of the NPT: How to Strengthen the Non-proliferation Regime," *Strategic Analysis* 34, no. 2 (March 2010): 219; Arvind Gupta, "NPT Review Conference 2010: Issues and Prospects," *Strategic Analysis* 34, no. 2 (March 2010): 226.

37. William Walker, "Nuclear Enlightenment and Counter-Enlightenment," *International Affairs* 83, no. 3 (May 2007).

38. Rebecca Johnson, "Rethinking the NPT's Role in Security: 2010 and Beyond," *International Affairs* 86, no. 2 (May 2010): 431.

39. Pierre Hassner, "Who Killed Nuclear Enlightenment?" *International Affairs* 83, no. 3 (May 2007): 455–56.

40. Jyotika Saxena, "Regime Design Matters: The CTBT and India's Nuclear Dilemma," *Comparative Strategy* 25 (2006): 220.

41. Rajpal Budania, *India's National Security Dilemma: The Pakistan Factor and India's Policy Response* (New Delhi: Indus Publishing Company, 2001), 16.

42. This approach toward development of science and technology for self-reliance was pursued by several visionaries of India: Homi Bhabha, Rajiv Gandhi, Vikram Sarabhai, M. S. Swaminathan, and the former president of India, APJ Abdul Kalam.

43. Reforming the National Security System, Recommendations of the Group of Ministers, (New Delhi: Cabinet Secretariat, Government of India, February 2001), 6.

44. The leading space agency, Indian Space Research Organization, ISRO was formed in 1969 and the space program was institutionalized in 1972.

45. Dr. Vikram Sarabhai, at the First Unispace meet at Vienna in 1968. As quoted, in V.A. Thomas and P.S. Goel, "Indian Space Program and National Development," *Advances in Astronautical Sciences* 117 (2004): 16.

46. Frank Morring Jr. and Neelam Matthews, "Third World Rising," *Aviation Week and Space Technology* 161, no. 20 (November 22, 2004), 46.

47. R. L. M. Patil, *India-Nuclear Weapons and International Politics* (Delhi: National Publishing House, 1969), 20. Also, see, Leonard Weiss, "India and the NPT," *Strategic Analysis* (March 2010): 256. Dr. Homi Bhabha received his PhD in nuclear physics from University of Cambridge in 1934.

48. G.G. Mirchandani, *India's Nuclear Dilemma* (New Delhi: Popular Book Service, 1968), 3.

49. C. Subramaniam, "Science as an Instrument of Economic Progress," in *Science and Technology in India*, ed., Vadilal Dagli, (New Delhi: S. Chand and Company, 1982), 52.

50. Technology Policy Statement 1983, Department of Science and Technology, Ministry of Science and Technology, Government of India, 1983. Available at http://www.dst.gov.in/stsysindia/sps1983.htm (accessed March 26, 2010).

51. V.C. Trivedi, *Remarks at the Eighteen Nation Disarmament Committee*, Final Verbatim Record of the Conference of the Eighteen Nation Committee on Disarmament, 334th Meeting (ENDC/PV334, United Nations General Assembly, September 28, 1967), 5.

52. Lok Sabha Debates, Parliament of India, Third Series, no. 2, August 20, 1962, Column 2885.

53. See, Mirchandani, 5; Emeka Ohajunwa, *Disarmament and Nuclear Proliferation in India-U.S. Security Relations 1947–1990* (New Delhi: Chanakya Publications, 1992), 124. The 1948 Atomic Energy Act of India also brought Atomic Energy under the control of the Central government. The Department of Scientific Research and an Institution for Research and development of Atomic Energy at Trombay were created. Later, in 1954, Nehru in his capacity as the prime minister assumed the charge of the newly created Department of Atomic Energy. This is regarded as the first phase of the Indian nuclear program when India established nuclear and fuel processing plants. Also, the Geological Survey of India was established for the purpose of exploring and locating the minerals for advancing the nuclear program; *Global Fissile Material Report 2010: Balancing the Books; Production and Stocks, Fifth Annual Report of the International Panel on Fissile Materials* (Princeton: IPFM, Princeton University, New Jersey, 2011), 117. It notes, "From the very beginning, India's Department of Atomic Energy was generously funded and it embarked on an ambitious program aimed at having indigenous capability for covering the entire fuel cycle."

54. R. R. Rao, "India's Nuclear Progress: A Balance Sheet," *India Quarterly* 30 (October-December 1974): 248.

55. Michael J. Sullivan III, "Indian Attitudes on International Atomic Energy Controls," *Pacific Affairs* 43, no. 3 (Fall 1970): 357. "Only the enriched uranium fuel element came from abroad that was provided in 1955 by Great Britain which also supplied the second enriched uranium charge for Apsara in 1965. Under the terms of a bilateral agreement, Great Britain has policed the safeguards arrangement to ensure no fissile by products were diverted to weapons use."

56. Rao, 248.

57. See, Eisenhower's famous "Atoms for Peace" speech at the plenary meeting of the United Nations General Assembly, December 1953. Available at http://www.atomicarchive.com/Docs/Deterrence/Atomsforpeace.shtml (accessed March 22, 2009).

58. Leonard Weiss, "Atoms for Peace," *Bulletin of Atomic Scientists* 59, no. 6 (November 2003): 257.

59. Douglas Frantz and Catherine Collins, *The Nuclear Jihadist: The True Story of the Man Who Sold the World's Most Dangerous Secrets and How We Could Have Stopped Him* (New York: Twelve, 2007), 361.

60. Dev Kant Borooah, "Introduction," in *Atoms for Peace: An Exposition of India's Nuclear Policy*, ed., Balwant A. Desai, (Bombay: All India Congress Committee, 1975), 5; Regarding the conference, Weiss remarks, "It was the largest scientific meeting ever held until then with an estimated 2,500 participants. The atmosphere was euphoric and much information previously held secret, was shared in public sessions. French scientists revealed the process of plutonium extraction and the United States declassified significant amounts of data and technology. . . . Many nuclear scientists in countries that later became of proliferation concern received training in the United States or with U.S. funding."; Turkey was the first country to sign the nuclear cooperation agreement, followed by Israel (n.10).

61. *Global Fissile Material Report 2010*, 117–18. It is a heavy water moderated, light water cooled, natural uranium fueled reactor based on the Canadian NRX reactor. It

was refurbished in 2003 and resumed operation in 2007; Also, as per the US-India civil nuclear agreement it was proposed to be shut down in December 2010.

62. Dana R. Dillon and Baker Spring, "Nuclear India and the Nonproliferation Treaty," *Backgrounder*, no. 1935, (Washington D.C.: The Heritage Foundation, May 18, 2006), 4; Mario Carranza, "From Non-Proliferation to Post-Proliferation: Explaining the U.S.-India Nuclear Deal," *Contemporary Security Policy* 28, no. 3 (2007): 466.

63. Robert Gillette, "India: Into the Nuclear Club on Canada's Shoulders," *Science* 184, no. 4141 (7 June 1974): 1053.

64. Therefore, Bindon and Mukherjee question why Canada waited until the actual detonation, in 1974, to call off the nuclear agreement. Bindon and Mukherjee, 222.

65. Kapur, "Some Hypotheses and Lessons," 314.

66. Bindon and Mukherjee, 220 and 224. Also see, Gillette, 1053; Kapur, "Some Hypotheses and Lessons," 314.

67. Sullivan, "Indian Attitudes," 358.

68. Ibid.

69. Weiss, "India and the NPT," 258.

70. See, Kapur, "Some Hypotheses and Lessons," 313; In May 1974, Mitchell Sharpe stated, "the Indian government [had] not broken any agreement that it [had] entered into." As quoted in, George Bindon and Sitoo Mukherjee, "Canada-India Cooperation," *Research Policy* 7 (1978): 230; Also see, Gillette, 1055.

71. Kapur, "Some Hypotheses and Lessons," 313; Bindon and Mukherjee, 231–32; Also, see, Ashok Kapur, "India and the Atom," *The Bulletin of Atomic Scientists* 30, no. 7 (September 1974), 29.

72. The US Department of State, Bulletin no. 1875 (2 June 1975), 707.

73. Michael A. Levy and Charles Ferguson, "U.S.-India Nuclear Cooperation: A Strategy for Moving Forward," *Council Special Report* (Washington D.C.: Council for Foreign Relations, February 2007), 3.

74. See, P.R. Chari, "An Indian Reaction to U.S. Nonproliferation Policy," *International Security* 3, no. 2 (Autumn 1978): 58–59; Carranza, "From Non-Proliferation to Post-Proliferation," 466; Leonard S. Spector, *Status of U.S. Sanctions Imposed on India and Pakistan* (Monterrey: James Martin Center for Nonproliferation Studies, August 2001), 3.

75. Weiss, "India and the NPT," 26. Weiss informs, "The law contained a narrow 18–24 month window to allow President Carter, unless blocked by a vote of Congress, to grandfather two shipments of nuclear fuel for the Tarapur reactors while attempting to persuade India to satisfy the new export criteria. . . . The 18–24 month window in the NNPA closed without India's acquiescence to full scope safeguards, making India ineligible for nuclear trade with the United States" (26).

76. Manoj Joshi, "Curbs on Missile Technology," *The Hindu*, November 1989; Brahma Chellaney, "Non-proliferation: An Indian Critique of U.S. Export Controls," *Orbis* (Summer 1994), 44. Two major developments in India's space program created the urgency for the developed nations to evolve missile technology controls—first, the successful tests (July 1980 and May 1981) of satellite launch vehicle, SLV-3 and its potential military applications; and second, the inception of Integrated Missile Development Program (IGMDP) in 1983. Initially, in November 1982, through the National Security Decision Directive no. 70, the American president expressed determination to stop missile proliferation. Later, in 1984, MTCR was set up clandestinely and was announced formally on April 16, 1987—after India conducted its first IGDMP missile Trishul.

77. Chellaney, "An Indian Critique," 44.

78. Michael J. Sullivan III, "Reorientation of Indian Arms Control Policy, 1969–1972," *Asian Survey* 13, no. 7 (July 1973), 691.

79. Sullivan, "Reorientation of Indian Arms Control," 696.

80. Ibid.

81. G.G. Mirchandani, *India's Nuclear Dilemma* (New Delhi: Popular Book Service, 1968), 23.

82. Lok Sabha Debates, Parliament of India, May 10, 1966, Column 15712.
83. Ibid.
84. Kapur, "India and the Atom," 29.
85. Sullivan, "Reorientation of Indian Arms Control Policy," 697.
86. See, Shyam Bhatia, *India's Nuclear Bomb* (Sahibabad: Vikas Publishing, 1979), 130; K. Subrahmanyam, "Nuclear Policy Perspective," *World Focus* (January 1988): 45; Rao, "India's Nuclear Progress."
87. Kapur, "India and the Atom," 29.
88. Ibid.
89. K. Subrahmanyam, *Self-Reliance and National Resilience: The Indian Nuclear Policy* (New Delhi: Abhinav Publishing, 1975), 128.

THREE

Pokhran II

Defiance of the Nuclear Nonproliferation Regime

Divergent approaches to nonproliferation created a persistent nuclear stalemate between the United States and India, especially in the post-1968 period.[1] The United States engaged in a nuclear arms race with the erstwhile Soviet Union found it convenient to intermittently harp on the Nuclear Nonproliferation Treaty (NPT) in talks with India. On the other hand, post-1974 Pokhran nuclear tests, India had pragmatically located itself in an ambiguous position with regard to nuclear weapons. In the post–Cold War era, change in the global nuclear order and the advent of the Clinton administration created some stirrings in the U.S.-India nuclear equation; subsequently both states were shaken from their slumberous deadlock. In the mid-1990s, the Clinton administration was actively engaged in global efforts to strengthen the nuclear nonproliferation regime; it supported an indefinite extension of the NPT (1995) and the formulation of the Comprehensive Test Ban treaty (1996). India not only opposed the indefinite extension of the NPT but also refused to sign the CTBT. Yet, nothing was as outrageous as India's five nuclear test explosions, in 1998, at Pokhran (hereafter Pokhran II). Brajesh Mishra, the former National Security Advisor of India (1998–2004) remarked years later that "one either changes the policy to suit the environment or changes the environment to suit the policy. The nuclear tests [Pokhran II] helped us change the environment."[2]

This chapter focuses on the determined pursuit of nuclear nonproliferation by the Clinton administration and India's continued defiance of the nonproliferation regime. The first section briefly discusses the antagonistic relationship between the United States and India. The second section analyzes the Clinton administration's "cap, rollback, and eliminate" approach to nuclearization in South Asia. The third section highlights the expansion of multilateral ties between the United States and India. The fourth section critically analyzes India's opposition to the indefinite extension of the NPT and the framing of the CTBT. The fifth section discusses the imposition of sanctions on India by Washington in the aftermath of India's Pokhran II nuclear tests. The final section analyzes the flawed U.S. nuclear diplomacy toward India. Pokhran II posed an unprecedented challenge to the NPT as India established itself as a defacto nuclear weapon state. These tests forced a serious review of the hitherto policy of "denial and isolation" pursued by the United States toward India. These tests dismantled the existing U.S.-India nuclear stalemate and catalyzed the need to redesign U.S. nuclear nonproliferation policy toward India.

INEVITABLE ANTAGONISTS

The trajectory of the U.S.-India relations post–1968, i.e., NPT-era, presents an interesting case. Relations between the two countries became estranged due to the disjuncture in their approach to the NPT in specific, and objectives of the nuclear nonproliferation regime in general. Regimes are complex social institutions bound to "reflect the prevailing structure of power in [international] society." Oran Young remarks, "Regimes are never neutral with respect to their impact on the interests of participating actors."[3] In the aftermath of India's 1974 peaceful nuclear explosion, the United States undertook the task of strengthening nuclear and missile export controls. This led to the establishment of export cartels like the Nuclear Suppliers Group (NSG),[4] the Zangger Committee,[5] and the Missile Technology Control Regime (MTCR).[6] These cartels prevented dual-use technology cooperation with India, a non-signatory of the NPT. Interestingly, thereafter, the United States neither felt the necessity nor the urgency to bargain with India on nuclear issues, yet, sporadically insisted that India join the NPT as a nonnuclear weapon state. India was not ready to accede to the discriminatory nuclear nonproliferation regime and continued to develop nuclear and space programs, so, the stalemate persisted. Donald Puchala and Raymond F. Hopkins argue that "the tenets of the international regime come to match with the values, objectives, and decision-making procedures of the pre-eminent participant or participants. A regime need not serve the common or separate interests of every participant very well or even at all."[7]

Otherwise too, U.S.-India relations, except for intermittent periods of warmth and cooperation, were largely estranged in the Cold War period. During the Reagan administration (1981–1989) some attempts were made to initiate U.S.-India cooperation on defense and advanced technology.[8] As the Cold War waned the threat of advanced U.S.-origin military technology from India passing into Soviet hands had considerably reduced. Former Department of Defense official Joseph McMillan suggests that the Reagan administration believed in promoting "India's indigenous military and defense capability."[9] President Reagan recognized the rising power of India and wanted to wean India away from the Soviet camp. In the 1980s, India, too, was attempting to outgrow the Soviet influence. India wanted to play a proactive role in international affairs, and once again assert its identity in the global order. Specifically, it was interested in diversifying its defense trade and diminishing its dependence on defense equipment and spare parts supplies from the Soviets.[10]

During the first Gulf War (1991–1992) American combat aircraft were flying from bases in South East Asia to Gulf destinations. India, in an unprecedented move, allowed the American aircrafts to refuel in Bombay.[11] This was an important decision by India considering the fact that the U.S. action was directed against a fellow nonaligned state, Iraq.[12] Yet, in 1992, India was taken aback when the United States took a punitive measure to thwart the progress in India's civilian space program. In accordance with the Missile Technology Control Regime (MTCR), the United States imposed sanctions on both the Indian Space Research Organization (ISRO) and the Russian space agency (Glavkosmos), and prevented the sale of cryogenic engines to India.[13] The U.S. defined the Russian cryogenic engine as an "MTCR Category I" item and claimed that the ISRO-Glavkosmos deal violated MTCR guidelines. According to the U.S. Defense Authorization Act of 1991, the president is obliged to impose sanctions against any company or country selling MTCR listed items to non-MTCR signatories.[14]

The disintegration of the Soviet Union marked a significant systemic change and "fundamentally altered" the interests of America and India.[15] The Soviet Union was not only a source of "diplomatic and political support" for India, the former was also its "long-time weapons supplier."[16] As Ambassador Thomas Pickering emphasizes, "the subtraction of the Soviet Union," represented the loss of a "potential strategic alternative" for India. He opined that India's geopolitical scenario had been radically changed as the Soviet Union "was no longer there and no longer a dependable alternative."[17] On the American side, the collapse of the Soviet Union created an opportunity to develop closer relations with India. Especially, the Clinton administration "recognized that India was a free agent and they might as well try to make sure it was part of the American consensus."[18]

Additionally, the end of the Cold War marked the decline of the Soviet-style economy. In India, signs were visible that the state-led economy was performing dismally. Nonetheless, the then Indian Prime Minister Rao and his finance minister, Manmohan Singh, acted swiftly to initiate a transition toward policies of economic liberalization. Ambassador Pickering, who was posted in India during 1992–1993, recollects, "heroic people in India were quick to call attention" to the economic stagnation. Thus, "historically, we saw the beginnings of the change in India."[19] The liberalization of the Indian economy can be called India's second "tryst with destiny, as it unleashed unprecedented opportunities for economic growth."[20] Significantly, the overhauling of the Indian economy—from state-led socialist economy to market-based—created space for a symbiotic relationship with the global economy.[21] The American corporate sector was quick to view India's potential as a huge market for U.S. capital, technology, and goods. Robin Walker, an expert on South Asia, opines that the liberalization of the economy concomitantly unleashed a technological revolution and led to "astounding technology trade." In fact, he argues that the U.S.-India trade was a classic case of a government following its corporate sector in opening up a relationship with another country (India).[22]

Thus, with the end of the Cold War there were high expectations that the United States would find a natural partner in India. Dennis Kux, the author of *Estranged Democracies*, proposed that the "most logical policy" for Washington would be "to treat India as a significant Asian power." He advocated that the United States "should seek friendly relations, including expanded security relations . . . India is large enough and economically and militarily of sufficient importance that the Indo-U.S. relationship could have strategic importance in its own right."[23]

In view of the post–Cold War potential for growth of U.S.-India bilateral relations, Clinton adopted a dual-track policy with India. On the one hand, the Clinton administration made an earnest attempt to improve the apathetic relationship with India; on the other hand, vigorous efforts were made to make India follow Washington's dictates and accede to the nonproliferation regime. Nevertheless, India refused to follow U.S. directives in the nuclear nonproliferation sphere and, thus, the nuclear divergence persisted.

CLINTON'S APPROACH: "CAP, ROLLBACK, AND ELIMINATE"

With the disintegration of the Soviet Union, proliferation of the weapons of mass destruction (WMD) emerged as a significant threat. In the post–Cold War era there were significant concerns about the emergence of new nuclear states coupled with the "spread of nuclear weapons and knowledge"[24] among rogue states and terrorist groups. Thus, the Clinton administration was faced with a challenging global nuclear order and nonproliferation was high on Clinton's foreign policy agenda.

In the South Asian region, the presence of two nuclear states, India and Pakistan, drew significant attention.[25] Despite the technological embargoes imposed by Washington, India persistently refused to sign the treaty and Pakistan linked its signatures to India's. Moreover, since the 1980s, some concerns arose regarding India's advancements in the indigenous missile program, especially the buildup of nuclear capable missiles. In February 1993, Congressional Research Service (CRS) report pointed out that India had enough fissionable material to produce seventy-five or more nuclear weapons while Pakistan could make ten to fifteen weapons. Both countries had missiles and aircraft capable of carrying nuclear weapons with variable limitations in efficiency and accuracy. The CRS report also specified that while India's nuclear program was largely self-sufficient, Pakistan had obtained the nuclear technology from abroad.[26] Subsequently, the director of Central Intelligence, James Woolsey, in his Congressional testimony stated, "The arms race between India and Pakistan poses perhaps the most probable prospect for future use of weapons of mass destruction, including nuclear weapons." He also warned that both countries were capable of assembling nuclear weapons on short notice.[27]

The increasing nuclearization in South Asia stoked fear of the looming threat of nuclear war in the region. U.S. intelligence reports revealed that in the year 1990 India and Pakistan had narrowly escaped a nuclear war.[28] It was reported that the intelligence satellites had noticed an "intense increase in Pakistan radar activity." There were strong indications that Pakistan was ready for war. It was reported that Pakistan had prepositioned and armed its F-16 aircraft.[29] Richard Kerr, the then deputy director of intelligence for the Central Intelligence Agency, regarded the India-Pakistan conflict as the "most dangerous situation," even "more frightening than the Cuban missile crisis."[30] The Indian government disputed the validity of the intelligence claims that in 1990 it was on the verge of a nuclear exchange with Pakistan.[31] It was also suggested that the intelligence reports were a ploy of the United States to project "an exaggerated over-nuclearized scenario" in South Asia in order to allow the Americans to dictate nonproliferation measures to the region.[32]

Nonetheless, a prominent scholar, Devin T. Hagerty, argues that the 1990 no-war was a possibility that did not occur because of "existential deterrence." That is, the knowledge of each side's nuclear capability and the fear that any military hostility could escalate into nuclear war deterred both India and Pakistan.[33] This phenomenon of the absence of nuclear war due to the opaque nuclear situation between the subcontinental twins is also described as "nonweaponized deterrence"[34] and "recessed deterrence."[35] Even though a "direct, interstate conflict" was avoided due to incipient nuclearization, it was suggested that the next war could result from "domestic turmoil and spillover."[36] This realization focused attention on the Kashmir dispute between India and Pakistan, and its potential to transform into an unwanted nuclear situation in the subcontinent. Thus, on several occasions the Clinton administration raised the Kashmir issue which infuriated the Indian establishment. On October 28, 1993, Assistant Secretary of State Robin Raphael claimed Kashmir to be a disputed territory and thereby questioned India's legitimacy of rule.[37] Earlier, President Clinton, in his September address to the United Nations General Assembly, had also remarked that India had violated human rights in Kashmir. India considered this anti-India stance on Kashmir to be an attempt to pressure it to give up its nuclear option.[38]

The threat of nuclearization and associated dangers in South Asia encouraged the Clinton administration to pursue its nonproliferation goals vigorously. In May 1993, the White House report to the Congress, *Progress Toward Regional Nonproliferation in South Asia,* emphasized, "Nonproliferation is a high priority" and declared the intention to "*pursue a comprehensive, incremental and long term approach that seeks to cap, then reduce over time, and finally, eliminate weapons of mass destruction and their means of delivery from the region*" (emphasis added).[39] Thereafter, Washington renewed its pressure on India to sign the NPT and insisted on other measures to curb the danger of nuclear proliferation in the region such as halting the production of fissile material and accepting international safeguards on nuclear facilities.

The Clinton administration at several occasions suggested that nonproliferation arrangements in South Asia could be enacted through multilateral conferences. In a bilateral dialogue with India, the Clinton administration proposed a five nation conference (including the United States, Russia, China, Pakistan, and India) to reach a denuclearization arrangement for the subcontinent. Subsequently, a nine-nation conference was also mooted. In April 1994, Strobe Talbott, the deputy secretary of state, visited India specifically to emphasize the "cap, rollback, and eliminate" objectives of the administration. He also proposed a nine-nation multilateral conference based on the formula 5+2+2. That is, the five permanent members of the U.N Security Council (the United States, Russia, China, France, the U.K.), Japan and Germany, besides India and Pakistan.[40] India declined these regional initiatives as they were flawed on several counts. First, in gross disregard of the China factor in Indian strategic calculations, these proposals put forward by the Clinton administration included China as a prominent member. It had long been recognized that, "India could not accept the status quo of China's legitimate and exclusive regional possession of nuclear weapons."[41] India regarded any regional denuclearization arrangement to be unacceptable without the curtailment of Chinese nuclear capabilities. China was also responsible for abetting Pakistan's nuclear and missile programs. Thus, these proposals reflected Washington's lack of perception of the regional geopolitical dynamics and India's security concerns.[42] Second, these proposals meant increased international surveillance and interference in the South Asian region; a possibility that India had acutely avoided during the Cold War. Third, the inclusion of Japan and Germany was seen as a strategic move as these were also India's major trade partners. Finally, New Delhi was not in favor region-specific solutions including a regional/sub-regional nuclear weapon-free zone; India considered these as only partial and discriminatory measures. The nuclear weapons and the delivery vehicles have global reach, therefore, even if the Indian subcontinent was denuclearized, India could still be a target of a nuclear attack. Thus, pragmatically speaking, India was opposed to any regional-level capping measures until and unless these were linked to global disarmament.[43] Indian Atomic Energy Commission Chairman R. Chidambaram denounced the U.S. nonproliferation initiatives in the region, stating,

> India has observed the longest moratorium on nuclear bomb explosions. So we don't have to take lessons on morality from the U.S. or anyone else . . . we are not in favor of any regional capping effort or having countries broker a deal between India and Pakistan on the nuclear question.[44]

The Clinton administration had little success in implementing the "cap, rollback, and eliminate" objectives in the hitherto neglected South Asian region. In a desperate bid, the United States offered thirty-eight F-16 combat aircrafts to Pakistan, granting it a one-time exception in the Pressler Amendment[45] *in lieu* of international safeguards and inspections on its nuclear installations. Pakistan rejected this offer,[46] yet, it created a furor in India. It reflected the Clinton administration's dearth of understanding of the political dynamics in the region.[47] Furthermore, F-16 combat planes are capable of carrying nuclear weapons, therefore, this offer highlighted contradictions in the U.S. nuclear nonproliferation policy. Washington was attempting to denuclearize the region, yet, on the other hand, was willing to offer nuclear capable aircrafts to Pakistan—a nation which was under the U.S. scanner for illicit proliferation practices.

President Clinton adopted a coercive policy to make India follow U.S. dictates on nuclear nonproliferation. The administration displayed little interest in pursuing dialogue to bridge the nuclear divide, and made no attempt to understand the security concerns behind India's desire to retain its nuclear capabilities. India and the United States continued to be "stuck in the nuclear narrative."[48] In this context, George Perkovich remarks, "The United States continued to pursue proposals to cap India's nuclear and missile programs. The Indians neither accepted nor rejected these proposals, indicating a *decorous stalemate*" (emphasis added).[49]

BROADENING OF BILATERAL TIES

The Clinton administration, cognizant of the emerging market potential of India, sought an "enlargement of the template of the Indo-U.S. relationship."[50] Interestingly, there was keen interest on both sides to forge new multidimensional connections. In April 1994, during a six-day historic visit to Washington of then Indian Prime Minister Narasimha Rao, mutual interests in trade and development were explored. Contentious issues such as Kashmir, human rights, missiles, and nuclear proliferation were relegated to the background and discussed privately among the leaders.[51] Soon after the summit meeting, there was an increase in the pace and scope of high-level exchanges that endeavored to engage India in several spheres. U.S. Energy Secretary Hazel O'Leary visited India in mid-1994 and again in February 1995. In January 1995, William Perry became the first American secretary of defense to visit India after a gap of seven years. During this trip, he signed the *Agreed Minute on Defense Relations*, with his Indian counterpart, Minister of Defense Mallikarjun. This agreement called for building a new strategic relationship and a "Defense Policy Group" (DPG) was established. The DPG mandate was to: review strategies in the post–Cold War era, promote exchange of senior officials and military officers, and launch training and joint exercises among the armed forces.[52] This was considered a significant breakthrough in U.S.-India relations.

Following Perry's visit, U.S. Commerce Secretary Ron Brown led "the largest American business group ever to visit India."[53] He signed an agreement with his Indian counterpart to establish a "Commerce Forum," a joint venture between government officials and business executives to promote bilateral economic relations. The delegation returned home with $4 billion dollars' worth of trade and investment, and this was "just the beginning for American companies ready to exploit India's free market economic changes."[54] Secretary Brown's visit marked a "'capstone' toward forging a new relationship between India and the U.S."[55] Thus, the economic significance of India was realized by the business community as well as the Clinton administration. According to Warren Christopher, the then U.S. secretary of state, India's economic reform plan created favorable conditions for "unprecedented trade and investment." Christopher averred, "Our investment in India has increased more in the last year [1993] than it had in the preceding four decades of Indian independence."[56] By the end of 1995, the United States had emerged as India's "biggest trading partner and a source of 40 percent of foreign investment in the country."[57]

DEEPENING OF NUCLEAR GULF

Despite the expansion of bilateral ties evident in the high-level visits and significant economic and defense pacts, nuclear divergence between the United States and India persisted. Because India was considered a proliferation threat, domestic legislation and international export controls restricted the scope of defense and security cooperation with India. Robin

Raphael, in a statement before the Subcommittee on Near Eastern and South Asian Affairs, reiterated that "nonproliferation is a high priority" for the Clinton administration. She allayed the concerns that the development of economic relations with India would weaken the U.S. nonproliferation objectives. She remarked, "Some commentators have incorrectly argued that expanding U.S. economic objectives in South Asia should or will undercut our efforts to advance other key interests, such as nonproliferation or human rights."[58] Raphael emphasized that the growth of bilateral relations were conditional to finding "common ground on this vital issue of nonproliferation."[59]

During the years 1993–1996, the United States made energetic efforts to strengthen the nonproliferation regime with the indefinite extension of the NPT and the signing of the CTBT. This accentuated the nuclear divergence between the United States and India. The NPT review conference was scheduled for April 1995.[60] The United States stepped up pressure on India to sign the treaty. India reiterated that it would not sign any discriminatory nonproliferation agreement that is not linked to a phased elimination of nuclear weapons. Initially, India's Foreign Secretary, K. Srinivasan, had claimed that India may attend the NPT review conference as an observer, but this led to widespread domestic criticism. In the words of K. Subrahmanyam, a prominent Indian security analyst, "Let us not spoil our unique record of unrelenting opposition to nuclear weapons by even giving an iota of our recognition to the NPT by sending an official observer."[61] Thus, India abstained from the NPT extension conference. On May 11, 1995, after prolonged negotiations, the treaty was extended for an indefinite period based on the proposal put forward by Canada.[62]

The NPT, undeniably, has played a role in slowing down nuclear proliferation. Thus, it is preferable to the anarchy that could have ensued in its absence.[63] Yet, in the post–Cold War era, the 1995 NPT Review Conference provided an opportunity to remove the inequalities and discrepancies in obligations between nuclear weapon states (NWS) and nuclear nonweapon states (NNWS) enshrined in the treaty. The disarmament clause, Article IV, of the NPT could have been strengthened and linked to a phased program of elimination of nuclear weapons. As Michael J. Mazarr remarks, the Clinton administration had "a historic chance to reverse the nuclear arms race of the last 40 years."[64] However, President Clinton showed tremendous lack of innovative thinking and strategic vision. The NPT, which perpetuated inequality and focused parsimoniously on horizontal proliferation alone, was given a new lease of life without any significant reforms.

The Clinton administration also actively engaged in negotiations for framing the CTBT in the Conference on Disarmament (CD) in Geneva.[65] This reflected a significant change in the U.S. position on a comprehensive test ban. India had called for a nuclear test ban in 1954 when the

United States had conducted only about fifty nuclear tests.[66] Throughout the Cold War, the United States did not consider nuclear test ban to be in its national interest, therefore, opposed it. At that time, the United States raised concerns about the inadequacy of the verification measures to assess nuclear tests conducted by the Soviet Union. To overcome this issue of verification, in 1984, India, along with other nations, established a group called the Six Nation Initiative to provide seismic monitoring services.[67] This again proved to be a vain attempt to bridge the gap between the superpowers for the resumption of dialogue on a nuclear test ban.

The rationale behind the U.S. opposition to comprehensive nuclear test ban was mainly to maintain nuclear superiority vis-à-vis the Soviets. This superiority required periodical nuclear tests to ensure the reliability and safety of the existing nuclear stockpile as well as for miniaturizing and upgrading the weapons. Seaborg and Loeb emphasize that the main reason was "the determination to 'modernize' the U.S. stockpile by adding new weapons considered more suitable to future needs."[68] According to statistics, in the period 1945–1992 the United States conducted 1,030 nuclear tests individually. This number rises to 1,054 if the 24 tests held jointly with the U.K. are included.[69] Since 1961, the United States conducted nuclear tests every year, with a record high of 56 nuclear tests in 1962. Ironically, during the period 1965–1968 when negotiations for a nuclear nonproliferation treaty were being held, the United States held 184 nuclear test explosions. By 1970, when the NPT came into force, this number had increased to 269.[70] At the end of 1992, after conducting six nuclear tests, President George H. W. Bush announced a unilateral moratorium. The United States altered its position due partly to the disintegration of the Soviet Union, America's arch rival and partly to the approaching NPT extension expected in 1995. A successful extension of the NPT was contingent upon U.S. progress toward a comprehensive test ban. Moreover, by the 1990s the United States had perfected simulation testing and had accumulated enough data to use computer assisted nuclear testing.

Although the nuclear test explosions by a nuclear weapon state are legally not in contravention of the Nuclear Nonproliferation Treaty, nonetheless, oppose the spirit of nuclear nonproliferation per se. Initially, in the 1950s–1960s when India had advocated a comprehensive test ban the immediate objective was to curtail nuclear fallout and its implications for the health of humans and the environment; subsequently, the CTBT was seen as a step toward genuine global disarmament. It was intended that with the cessation of nuclear tests, no new nuclear states would emerge and existing nuclear weapon powers would be unable to maintain or upgrade their nuclear arsenals. That is, the CTBT was initially aimed at preventing "qualitative and quantitative development of weapons."[71]

Nonetheless, in 1996, the CTBT, like the NPT, was not linked to a well-defined disarmament program nor did it restrict nuclear weapon powers from enhancing their nuclear arsenals. Rather, the CTBT was formulated at a time when the nuclear weapon powers, including the United States, had conducted hundreds of tests and had gathered enough data to conduct simulation tests. Once again, the United States seemed apathetic to incorporating measures to curb vertical proliferation. Moreover, the treaty banned only nuclear test explosions, not virtual nuclear tests. Thus, the CTBT, like the NPT, became an instrument to merely curb horizontal proliferation.[72] As John D. Holum avers, the United States had conducted over 1,000 nuclear tests, the highest number of nuclear tests by any country. Allaying concerns regarding the implications of the CTBT for the U.S. security interests, Holum stated, "It is possible under current circumstances to maintain our stockpile safely and reliably without explosive testing . . . the test ban is not an agreement that we will, through attrition and lack of confidence, get rid of our nuclear arsenal. On the contrary, the plan includes stockpile stewardship."[73] He further remarked, instead, *"we gain security to the extent we lock all nations in place on the nuclear weapons learning curve"* (emphasis added).[74] Similar sentiments were echoed in the Shalikashvilli report, which affirms, the CTBT "is compatible with keeping a safe, reliable U.S. nuclear deterrent and is an important part of global [read, horizontal] non-proliferation efforts."[75]

For these reasons discussed above, India had little faith in the credibility of the CTBT negotiations in the Conference of Disarmament (CD), January 1994–August 1996. Arundhati Ghose, the Indian ambassador to the CD, vociferously opposed the draft of the treaty. She aptly averred that the scope of the treaty was quite narrow, saying, it *"does not fulfill the requirement of a comprehensive ban [but rather it is] a nuclear weapon test explosion ban treaty."* This was not the CTBT that India had envisaged in 1954 as a step toward nuclear disarmament.[76] It was simply "a (horizontal) nonproliferation treaty."[77] India's main objections were that it was not linked to a global disarmament framework and allowed selective proliferation. It was not comprehensive in the true sense of the term as it banned only nuclear weapons explosions but allowed subcritical tests and computer simulations by advanced nuclear states.[78] In this context, the Indian prime minister remarked,

> As the PTBT (Partial Test Ban Treaty) drove testing underground, we do not wish the CTBT to drive testing into laboratories by those who have the resources to do so. We must ensure that the CTBT leaves no loophole for activity either explosive based or nonexplosive based, aimed at the continued development and refinement of nuclear weapons.[79]

Finally, the then Indian foreign secretary, Salman Haider, specified India's position that it would not sign the CTBT but would continue to press for the total elimination of nuclear weapons in a time-bound framework.[80]

Another dispute between the United States and India arose over the entry into force (EIF) clause of the CTBT. On the suggestion of the British delegation, led by Sir Michael Weston, the EIF clause was linked to the mandatory signatures of the forty-four nations that had agreed to host the seismic stations as part of the international monitoring system. This was viewed by New Delhi as an attempt to coerce India to sign and ratify the treaty. Therefore, India offered to withdraw its initial proposal to host a seismic station. The Indian delegation maintained that forcibly putting India's name on the forty-four-nation list contravened the Vienna Convention on treaties that forbids compelling a sovereign state to sign a treaty not in its national interest.[81] Despite several attempts by the Clinton administration to make India not to reject the CTBT's EIF clause and to sign the treaty, India rejected the proposed draft of the CTBT at the Conference on Disarmament in Geneva.[82]

Thus, on both occasions—the NPT Review Conference and the CTBT negotiations—the divergence between India and the United States seemed unbridgeable and represented a dialogue of the deaf with total lack of understanding on both the sides. The CTBT was signed and in a repeat of history, India's demands for nuclear disarmament and global nonproliferation, were neglected. During the negotiations of the 1996 CTBT, the objective of the United States was to engage Russia and China in some control and verification measures, particularly on-site inspections and satellite surveillance.[83]

While the U.S.-India stalemate on nuclear issues persisted, the Clinton administration undertook another initiative to improve relations with New Delhi and launched the "Strategic Dialogue" in October 1997. It entailed a series of high level visits to India with a focus on building specific areas of cooperation. President Clinton was planning to visit India in the fall of 1998 as part of this new initiative, but the plan was shelved after India conducted Pokhran II nuclear test explosions.[84]

POKHRAN II: IMPOSITION OF SANCTIONS

Within two years of the conclusion of the CTBT, India exercised its nuclear option. On May 11 and 13, 1998, India conducted a series of nuclear tests code named "Shakti," meaning "Power." These tests were conducted at Pokhran, in the Indian state of Rajasthan, where India had conducted its sole peaceful nuclear explosion in 1974.[85] The Pokhran II nuclear tests conducted by India created a strong global ripple effect and elicited immediate worldwide condemnation.[86] Especially, for the Clinton administration the Indian nuclear tests were a rude shock, as the nonproliferation objective was high on its foreign policy agenda. Besides several diplomatic efforts at the regional level, to "cap, rollback, and eliminate" Indian nuclear capabilities, the administration was engaged at the global level in strengthening the nonproliferation regime—as evident in the NPT review and the conclusion of the CTBT.[87] Thus, the Pokhran II nuclear tests openly challenged U.S. efforts to curb proliferation of nuclear weapons as well as its attempts to expand relations with India. President Clinton condemned the nuclear tests in the strongest words and referred to South Asia as the "most dangerous place on the earth." On May 12, 1998, President Clinton categorically stated his intention to take stringent actions if India carried out any further nuclear tests. He said:

> I want to make it very, very clear that I am deeply disturbed by the nuclear tests which India has conducted, and I do not believe it contributes to building a safer 21st century. The United States strongly opposes any new nuclear testing. This action by India not only threatens the stability of the region, it directly challenges the firm international consensus to stop the proliferation of weapons of mass destruction. . . . As most of you know, our laws have very stringent provisions, signed into law by me in 1994, in response to nuclear tests by nonnuclear weapon states. And I intend to implement them fully.[88]

Subsequently, the U.S. ambassador to India, Richard Celeste, was recalled to Washington for consultation. White House Press Secretary Mike McCurry remarked that India's decision to conduct nuclear tests "runs counter to the effort the international community is making to promulgate a comprehensive ban on such testing."[89] National Security Advisor Samuel Berger expressed that the United States was "deeply disappointed" by the Indian decision to "test nuclear weapons." Later, at a conference he said that the nuclear tests conducted by India "blew the lid off South Asia's long simmering rivalry" and "threaten to trigger a full-fledged nuclear and missile race in the region."[90] It has been reported that immediately after the first day's tests, President Clinton assured the Indian government that sanctions could be avoided if India would halt future tests and deployment of nuclear weapons.[91] But after a gap of one day India conducted further nuclear tests. On May 13, 1998, in response to India's second round of nuclear test explosions and in accordance with his legal obligations, President Clinton imposed sanctions[92] on India under the Arms Control Export Act, also known as the Glenn Amendment.[93]

The next immediate objective of the Clinton administration was to prevent a snowball effect in the subcontinent, especially the nuclear crossover by India's rival neighbor i.e., Pakistan.[94] President Clinton made a strong appeal to the government of Pakistan to refrain from conducting nuclear tests. He stated, "I also urge India's neighbors not to follow suit—not to follow down the path of a dangerous arms race."[95] Later, a high level team led by the deputy state secretary was dispatched to Islamabad to deter the Pakistanis from crossing the nuclear threshold. Pakistan was to be suitably rewarded with incentives ranging from the delivery of F-16 aircraft to a revival of economic and military funding.[96] In spite of the U.S. efforts, Pakistan also conducted nuclear tests, and on May 30, 1998 came under the Glenn Amendment sanctions net. Since 1990, Pakistan had already been facing sanctions under the Pressler Amendment[97] and the Symington Amendment.[98]

Sanctions under the Glenn Amendment imposed on India and Pakistan, included: (i) termination of U.S. foreign assistance except humanitarian or food and agricultural assistance; (ii) termination of U.S. government sales of defense articles, designs, and services, as well as revocation of licenses for sale of items on the U.S. Munitions List; (iii) termination of all foreign military financing; (iv) denial of government backed credit or financial assistance; (v) prohibition of financial or even technical assistance from any international financial institution; (vi) prohibition of loans or credits from U.S. banks, except for purchase of food or agricultural commodities; (vii) prohibition of licensing exports by the commerce department; and (viii) denial of credit or other export-import bank support for exports.[99] By law, the sanctions were to remain in place until Congress passed legislation to remove them.[100] The Clinton administration also ordered the Nuclear Regulatory Commission to cease ongoing nuclear safety dialogue with India.[101] Subsequently, U.S. professionals working in areas of sensitive technologies were restricted from visiting India and vice-versa. For instance, permission was not granted for eight senior U.S. physicists from the Fermi National Accelerator Lab and the Argon National Lab to participate in an international symposium on particle physics at the Tata Institute of Fundamental Research (TIFR) in Mumbai—as the TIFR was included in the sanctioned entities list issued in November 1998.[102] Charles Ferguson, a nonproliferation expert, recalls that Indian nuclear energy scientists were also denied visas to visit the United States.[103]

U.S. officials emphasized that the sanctions had a "rehabilitative purpose"[104] to encourage India and Pakistan to respect international nonproliferation norms. Karl Inderfurth, the assistant secretary for south Asian affairs, in his testimony on July 13, 1998, stated, "It is not the intention of the United States or any of our international partners to isolate India or Pakistan. We are not trying to engage in punishment for its own sake."[105] Clinton administration officials emphasized that the sanctions were not targeted against the people of these countries; rather, they were intended to "influence the affected governments."[106] As Inderfurth stated, "we do not wish for unnecessary harm to fall upon the civilian populations of either country—particularly the poor and the less fortunate."

POKHRAN II: DEFIANCE OF NUCLEAR REGIME

Varied explanations have been offered for the Pokhran II nuclear weapons explosions and crossing of the nuclear threshold by India. These include: domestic politics; ideological factors; national security threats from China and Pakistan; status and power motivations; technological advancement; and the scientific-technological complex.[107] There has been little discussion of the role of the nonproliferation regime, and the resultant inequitable nuclear order, in instigating India's nuclear weaponization. I contend that the Pokhran II nuclear tests reflected India's defiance of the strengthening of the nuclear regime in the 1995–1996 period. In the post-1970 era, India, having been excluded from the nonproliferation regime, conducted a peaceful nuclear explosion and thus carved a third way for itself in the global order of nuclear haves and nuclear have-nots. As a nuclear capable nonnuclear weapon state, India retained a position of considerable strategic ambiguity. It proved to be a pragmatic policy, enabling India to achieve diverse objectives simultaneously.[108] By choosing not to weaponize, India could credibly emphasize global disarmament, yet, retained the option to advance technologically and develop nuclear weapons.

But in 1995–1996, the NPT was extended without significant revisions to overcome its inherent discrepancies, and the signing of the CTBT reinforced selective and discriminatory nonproliferation approach. The NPT extension led to the perpetuation of the inherent inequality between NWS and NNWS, without any substantial progress toward nuclear disarmament.[109] Similarly, the CTBT, framed as an instrument of horizontal nonproliferation, endorsed the inequality and limited the learning curve of only the nuclear have-nots.[110] India had opposed these measures as contradictory to its objectives and refused to sign either of the treaties. The lack of accommodation of Indian concerns increased its "sense of isolation and vulnerability."[111] There was no scope for India to join the global nonproliferation regime except by compromising its nuclear policy objectives.

Furthermore, India realized that after the CTBT came into force in 1999, it would be impossible to exercise its option to conduct nuclear tests. Christine Fair remarks, for India "the opportunity costs of not testing were precipitously increasing." Especially after the conclusion of the CTBT, India perceived "the noose to be tightening."[112] Therefore, India felt encouraged to exercise its nuclear option and thus broke the nuclear impasse with the Pokhran explosions. In fact, even China and France, the de jure nuclear weapon states, prior to signing the CTBT also completed series of tests to collect enough data for future upgrading through computer simulations.[113] As Jyotika Saksena remarks, contrary to the stated purpose to curtail nuclear test explosions, the 1996 CTBT's flawed design "provided reasons for states to conduct tests before the treaty foreclosed such an option altogether."[114]

FLAWED U.S. NUCLEAR DIPLOMACY: CALL FOR CHANGE

The Pokhran II tests proved to be a major challenge for the Clinton administration. Despite its efforts to prevent nuclearization in South Asia it was faced with the emergence in quick succession of not one but two defacto nuclear states. The Pokhran II tests generated a "nationwide churning process" within the United States.[115] This led to an intensive assessment of the flawed nuclear nonproliferation policy toward India, and of the broader policy toward the South Asian region. An independent task force, convened by two Washington based prestigious think-tanks—the Brookings Institution and the Council on Foreign Relations—argued that it was "a critical juncture for re-examining U.S. [nonproliferation] policy toward South Asia."[116]

First, U.S. intelligence agencies failed to detect preparations for the 1998 nuclear test.[117] U.S. intelligence had monitored the Pokhran test site for several years and yet failed to detect the imminent test.[118] Richard Shelby, chairman of the Senate Intelligence Committee, called it "a colossal failure of our intelligence-gathering."[119] Raj Chengappa, in his book *Weapons of Peace,* considers India's success in evading the CIA a triumph in itself.[120] Nonetheless, it was difficult to decide whether it was "an intelligence failure, or simply a failure to be intelligent."[121] The U.S. State Department was held responsible for its inability to judge India's motivations as well as its determination to go overtly nuclear. Stephen Cohen, a prominent south Asian scholar, lamented that the detonation of nuclear devices in May 1998 marked "one of the great failures of the recent American policy—all the more so because it was foreseeable and preventable."[122]

Second, ever since India's peaceful nuclear explosion in 1974, the United States was aware of the impending possibility of nuclear tests and overt weaponization in India.[123] Therefore, for twenty-four intervening years, the main aim of the U.S. nonproliferation policy, including the technological isolation, was to thwart India's nuclear crossover. Thus, the 1998 tests proved to be a debacle of the hitherto punitive nuclear approach toward India, exclusively "based on sticks and stones."[124] Stephen Cohen, in his testimony to the Senate Foreign Relations Committee, remarked, "Our diplomacy constrained by restrictive and highly specific legislation, had nothing to offer but threats, and these failed to work." Instead, he argued, this led to the strengthening of "the anti-American groups in both countries [India and Pakistan] as well as those who sought to build and deploy nuclear weapons."[125] In a similar tone, Marshall Bouton argued that the Indian nuclear tests were the result of the

U.S. policy of "denial and isolation" pursued since 1974 and that this policy could have further damaging effects.[126] In the post-1998 scenario, it was believed that sanctions would make India more defiant, instead, the United States should engage India in nuclear bargaining and offer certain incentives—such as transfer of civilian nuclear technology.[127] Thus, the need for an innovative approach was increasingly emphasized, for the United States to function positively as an "honest broker and not as a punitive voice."[128]

Interestingly, Selig Harrison laid out an elaborate incentives-based approach and suggested seeking Congressional approval to resume technology transfers to India hitherto prohibited by the Nuclear Nonproliferation Act of 1978. This, he argued, would create a positive atmosphere in which the U.S. could elicit several concessions from India—first, application of international safeguards on all its reactors, besides the Tarapur reactor already under IAEA safeguards; second, a "binding *dejure* commitment" from India, in addition to its voluntary restraint, not to export nuclear technology to other states; finally, a compromise to sign the CTBT or other credible measure for cessation of future nuclear testing. Contrary to the punitive approach, Harrison argued that nuclear bargaining would be both politically and economically beneficial to the United States. The nuclear energy industry of the United States would benefit economically[129] and Washington would gain political leverage into the hitherto isolated nuclear program of India. Such a strategy could enlist India's support and help prevent the proliferation of nuclear weapons on the subcontinent. For instance, in case of North Korea, the Clinton administration, through the 1994 Agreed Framework, had agreed to facilitate the construction of two light water reactors in return for the cessation of plutonium production at the *Yongbyon* research reactor.[130] Consequently, the United States was able to curtail North Korea's ability to obtain enough fissile material to build sizeable nuclear bombs.[131] Richard Haass also advocated engaging nuclear India. He argued, "not all proliferation is bad" and therefore, the United States should treat adversarial and friendly states differently. He reasoned that "discrimination is at the heart of the entire nonproliferation regime. . . . Double standards, and triple standards if need be, are what realistic and successful foreign policy is all about."[132] Thus, there was considerable support for enlisting India's association with international nuclear and missile control regimes to contain the proliferation of weapons of mass destruction.[133]

Third, the issue of nuclearization in South Asia raised concerns about the Chinese involvement in the proliferation of weapons of mass destruction (WMD) in the subcontinent. This, in turn, reflected a failure of the U.S. Commerce Department to curtail missile technology proliferation in the garb of satellite exports to China. Gary Milhollin, director of the Wisconsin Project on Nuclear Arms Control, stated, "We asked the Indians to show restraint in nuclear testing, but we were unwilling to put restraints on our own satellite companies by sanctioning China for missile proliferation."[134] Evidently, the discriminatory policy of the U.S. administration gives China access to sensitive missile technology and, on the other hand, "slaps India for trying to protect itself from the consequences of this improved technology."[135] The transfer of American missile technology to China was quite detrimental. It aided China, the so-called "world's worst proliferator"[136] in promoting Pakistan's development of WMD. China was also employing American technology to make deadlier missiles with multiple warheads.[137]

Finally, it was realized that, compared to China, India was a "benign" proliferator; India had crossed the nuclear threshold and built its own nuclear program but it had never proliferated technologies to others. Stanley A. Weiss pointed out that India was not only the first country to call for global nuclear disarmament, but also it had never proliferated nuclear or missile technologies. He stated:

> From 1974, when it [India] first exploded an atomic device to last [1998] May, when it came out of the closet with five underground explosions, it watched China conduct more than 40 nuclear tests. [Moreover] India has not broken any international treaties. It never signed the 1970 nonproliferation treaty or the 1996 test ban treaty.[138]

Newt Gingrich, then speaker of the U.S. House of Representatives, lambasted the Clinton administration's policy of accommodation toward China. He argued the United States silently accepted the conduct of forty-five nuclear tests by China, yet, "roared with outrage when a democratic Indian government chose to test its capability."[139] Despite the repeated violation of its nonproliferation obligations, China still received "virtually unrestricted" dual-use American high-technology exports, and India, a benign proliferator, was being denied technological access.[140] Thus, there was growing support for adoption of a nuclear bargaining approach to engage India in the broader nonproliferation regime.

This chapter reviewed the considerable efforts of the Clinton administration (1993–1998) to "cap, rollback, and eliminate" the nuclear weapon capability of India; yet it failed to prevent India from crossing the nuclear threshold. On the contrary, the strengthening of the nuclear nonproliferation regime—through the indefinite extension of the NPT and, particularly, through formulation of the CTBT, also an instrument of selective nonproliferation—motivated India to weaponize its nuclear capability. In 1998, India conducted five nuclear test explosions in Pokhran, thereby breaking the nuclear impasse between the United States and India. Consequently, Pokhran II was perceived as a failure of U.S. nuclear diplomacy singularly based on its punitive measures toward India. The Pokhran II nuclear explosions disrupted the U.S.-India nuclear stalemate and catalyzed a frantic search in Washington for options to deal with the challenge posed by India to the nuclear nonproliferation regime.

NOTES

1. This chapter draws upon material reprinted by permission of Taylor & Francis LLC (http://www.tandfonline.com) from Bhatia, Vandana, "Non-proliferation Policy of the Clinton Administration toward India: Shifting of Nuclear Goalposts?" *Comparative Strategy* 32(3): 261–82.

2. Brajesh Mishra as quoted in, "Nuclear Tests helped Change the Environment," *The Hindu*, May 14, 2003.

3. Oran R. Young, "Regime Dynamics: The Rise and Fall of International Regimes," in Andrew Linklater, ed., *Critical Concepts in Political Science*, Volume 2, (New York: Routledge, 2000), 744.

4. Nuclear Suppliers Group, formerly known as 'the London Club,' held its first meeting in London, November 1975.

5. Zangger Committee, also called the NPT Exporters Committee, took shape during the 1971–1974 period.

6. Missile Technology Control Regime was formed in 1987 by the Western advanced nations to prevent the proliferation of advanced technologies related to the unmanned delivery vehicles, including nuclear capable.

7. Donald J. Puchala and Raymond F. Hopkins, "International Regimes: Lessons from Inductive Analysis," *International Organization* 36, no. 2 (Spring 1982): 247.

8. Waheguru Pal Singh Sidhu, *Enhancing Indo-U.S. Strategic Cooperation*, Adelphi Paper no. 313, (London: The International Institute for Strategic Studies, 1997), 38–39. In 1982 President Reagan and Indira Gandhi signed the *U.S.-India Science and Technology Initiative*. In 1984, A *Memorandum of Understanding on Sensitive Technologies, Commodities, and Information* was also signed by the two countries.

9. An Interview with Joseph McMillan, Senior Research Fellow, National Defense University, Washington D.C., February 2009. Previously, McMillan had served as the Principal Director of Near Eastern and South Asian Affairs, Department of Defense. In his official capacity, during the Reagan administration, McMillan met the Indian delegation including, Dr.K. Santhanam and Dr. V.S. Arunachalam, for negotiating the sale of Light Combat Aircrafts (LCA) to India.

10. See, Jyotika Saksena and Suzzane Grillot, "The Emergence of Indo-U.S. Defense Cooperation: From Specific to Diffuse Reciprocity," in *Engaging India: U.S. Strategic Relations with the World's Largest Democracy*, ed. Gary Bertsch, Seema Gahlaut and Anupam Srivastava, (New York: Routledge, 1999).

11. Mohan J. Malik, "India's Response to the Gulf Crisis: Implications for Indian Foreign Policy," *Asian Survey* 31, no. 9 (September 1991): 853. However, subsequently, yielding to domestic pressure, Prime Minister Chandrashekhar, withdrew the use of transit and refuelling facilities for the U.S. aircrafts (856); Also see, Major Jerome M. Conley, *Indo-Russian Military and Nuclear Cooperation: Implications for U.S. Security Interests*, INSS Occasional Paper 31, Proliferation Series (Colorado: USAF Institute for National Security Studies, USAF Academy, February 2000), 13.

12. After initial hesitation, India supported *UN Resolution 678* which authorized use of force if Iraq failed to withdraw from Kuwait by January 15, 1991, the specified date.

13. In January 1991, India signed an agreement with *Glavkosmos*, the Russian space agency, for purchasing the Cryogenic engines and technology for use in the geosynchronous satellites. Due to time constraints in achieving its space program objectives, India decided to purchase the Cryogenic technology from abroad rather than develop it indigenously. Interestingly, in 1990, besides *Glavkosmos*, India had received offers for similar engines from the General Dynamics, USA and *Arianespace*, France. But these did not materialize as the American offer did not include the transfer of technology and the French Space Agency offer was not economically viable; "U.S. Continues to Embargo High Tech Defense Exports to India," *Defense and Foreign Affairs Weekly*, August 13–19, 1990, 1; *The Hindu*, May 23, 1992; "Cryogenic Deal With Russia," *Strategic Digest*, November 1993, 1843.

14. The sanctions imposed ban on the commercial transactions of the two space agencies—ISRO and Glavkosmos. It also affected the U.S. government contracts with the two firms which covered items like super-computers and telescopes. However, both Russia and India claimed that Washington's allegations about violations of the MTCR were motivated, to discourage competitors in commercial space launch business. Nonetheless, in July 1993 Russia succumbed to the western pressure and cancelled the sale of cryogenic engines to India. Manoj Joshi, "Dousing the Fire: Indian Missile Program and the United States Nonproliferation Policy," *Strategic Analysis* 17, no. 5 (August 1994); Brahma Chellaney, "Nonproliferation: An Indian Critique of U.S. Export Controls," *Orbis* (Summer 1994): 44.

15. Interview with Daniel Markey, Senior Fellow for India, Pakistan and South Asia, Council of Foreign Relations, Washington D.C., February 2009.

16. Christine Fair, "Learning to Think the Unthinkable: Lessons from India's Nuclear Tests," *India Review* 4, no. 1 (January 2005): 33.

17. Interview with Ambassador Thomas Pickering, March 2009.

18. Markey, interview.

19. Amb. Pickering, interview.

20. On the eve of India's independence, midnight of August 14, 1947, the Prime Minister Nehru claimed the historic moment as "*India's Tryst with Destiny*." Although, the liberalization of the Indian economy unleashed unprecedented opportunities for economic growth and development, yet, it does not mean that the *Nehru-Mahanoblis* model based on the socialist economy was entirely unsuccessful. During the initial years of independence, when the foundations of India's democratic structures and government institutions were being laid, the state controlled economy played a significant role.

21. With the liberalization of the economy, India's economic interests changed and led to a change in the trading partners. Post-1991, Russia lost its position as India's major trading partner. Actually, with the collapse of the Soviet economy, its successor state, Russia could neither sustain the pre-1990 established level of rupee-based trade, nor, could be a source for inflow of investments and capital in India.

22. Interview with Robin Walker, National security scholar, Truman Security Project, Washington D.C. He states, "As the American companies went in the late 1990s, in 2000 Clinton visited and made the first visit [of the American President] to India in several decades."

23. Dennis Kux, *India and the United States: Estranged Democracies, 1941–1991* (California: Sage Publications, 1994), 451.

24. Joseph Nye, "New Approaches to Nuclear Proliferation Policy," *Science* 256 (May 29, 1992): 1293.

25. Since 1980s there were several reports that Pakistan was aggressively pursuing nuclear weapons and missile development with external support, mainly China and North Korea. Yet, prior to 1998, unlike India, it never conducted a nuclear test.

26. Richard P. Cronin and Barbara Leitch LePoer, *South Asia: U.S. Interests and Policy Issues*, CRS Report for Congress, no. 93–243 (Washington D.C.: Congressional Research Service, February 12, 1993), 4–5.

27. *Testimony of the Director of Central Intelligence Agency*, James Woolsey, Senate Governmental Affairs Committee, 103rd Congress, 1st Session, Washington DC, February 24, 1993, 12.

28. Seymour Hersh, "On the Nuclear Edge," *New Yorker* (March 29, 1993): 56–57; In early 1990, India exasperated with the continued clandestine Pakistan's support to the insurgents in Indian Kashmir, started preparations to carry out strikes at the terrorist training camps based in Pakistan. Based on the intelligence reports, the Pakistani establishment gave orders to arm F-16s with nuclear weapons—to overcome the conventional inferiority vis-a-vis India. These developments were picked up the American intelligence. Earlier, too in 1987 there had been a Brasstacks Crisis, in which India's military was carrying out significant peacetime exercises which was misread by Pakistani side as India's preparations for war. For details on these two crises see,

Sumit Ganguly, "Indo-Pakistani Nuclear Issues and the Stability/Instability Paradox," *Studies in Conflict and Terrorism* 18, (1995): 325–334; Also see, Stephen P. Cohen, "1990: South Asia's Useful Crisis," (paper presented to the Annual Meeting of the American Association for the Advancement of Science, Chicago, February 6–7 1992); Devin T. Hagerty, "The Power of Suggestion: Opaque Proliferation, Existential Deterrence, and the South Asian Nuclear Arms Competition," *Security Studies* 2, no. 3–4 (Spring-Summer 1993).

29. Hersh, "Nuclear Edge."

30. As quoted, Ibid., 57.

31. "Singh Denies Reports on Indo-Pak Nuclear War," *The Hindustan Times* (New Delhi), March 25, 1993.

32. Vinay Kumar Malhotra, ed., "U.S. Latest Initiatives on Nonproliferation in South Asia and Indo-U.S. Relations," in *Indo-U.S. Relations in the Nineties* (Delhi: Anmol Publications Pvt. Ltd, 1995), 32.

33. Devin T. Hagerty, "Nuclear Deterrence in South Asia: The 1990 Indo-Pakistani Crisis," *International Security* 20, no. 3 (Winter 1995/96): 80.

34. George Perkovich, "A Nuclear Third Way in South Asia," *Foreign Policy* 91 (Summer 1993). See, Perkovich's article for details of "non-weaponizsed deterrence" regime; Also see, *Preventing Nuclear Proliferation in South Asia,* Report of the Study Group, chaired by Arthur A. Hartman, (New York: Asia Society, 1995). The study group in its report supported establishment of a non-weaponized deterrence regime in South Asia.

35. Air Commodore Jasjit Singh, "Prospects for Nuclear Proliferation," in *Nuclear Deterrence: Problems and Perspectives in the 1990s*, ed. Serge Sur, (New York: UNIDIR, 1993), 66.

36. Sumit Ganguly, "Indo-Pakistani Nuclear Issues and the Stability/Instability Paradox," *Studies in Conflict and Terrorism* 18 (1995): 329.

37. *The Hindustan Times*, October 29, 1993.

38. Malhotra, "Initiatives on Nonproliferation," 20.

39. U.S. Department of State, *Report to Congress on the Progress Toward Regional Nuclear Nonproliferation* (Washington D.C.: U.S. Department of State, May 5, 1993), 3.

40. Raj Chengappa, "Nuclear Dilemma," *India Today*, April 30, 1994, 46.

41. William Schneider, "*Policy Issues and Implications of Nuclear Testing by India and Pakistan*," Statement before the Subcommittee on Near Eastern and South Asian Affairs, on The Crisis in South Asia, Part II, Senate Foreign Relations Committee, U.S. Congress, June 3, 1998. Available at http://www.fas.org/spp/starwars/congress/1998_h/s980603-schn.htm (accessed April 29, 2009).

42. Marshall M. Bouton, "Heed South Asia's Concerns," *Far Eastern Economic Review* 161, no. 26 (June 25, 1998).

43. Mitchell Reiss, *Bridled Ambition: Why Countries Constrain their Nuclear Capabilities*, (Washington DC: Woodrow Wilson Centre Press, 1995), 201; Thomas W. Lippman, "U.S. Effort to Curb Nuclear Weapons in Peril as India Insists on Limits for China," *Washington Post*, July 7, 1994.

44. Dr. Rajagopalan Chidambaram, Chairman of India's Atomic Energy Commission, Interview by Raj Chengappa, "Say 'No' to Regional Capping," *India Today* (April 30, 1994), 50.

45. The Pressler Amendment was introduced in 1985 by the U.S. Congress as a new section *620E(e) in the Foreign Assistance Act (FAA).* It mandated annual certifications by the U.S. president to the Congress that Pakistan was not building a nuclear explosive device, and that the American aid was not being misused towards funding Pakistan's nuclear program. Since 1985 till 1989, the U.S. administration continued to certify that Pakistan did not possess a nuclear explosive device. It was in 1990 for the first time that the George H.W. Bush administration was unable to issue the required certification, this triggered the Pressler Amendment sanctions. It coincided with the end of the Cold War which considerable lessened Pakistan's significance as a front-line state against the Soviet troops in Afghanistan region. Pakistan had already made full pay-

ment for the F-16s. Yet, in accordance with Pressler Amendment, neither did the United States deliver the F-16s nor did Washington return Pakistan's payment; thus, this issue lingered on.

46. Interestingly, Pakistan refused this proposal of the supply of 38 F-16s in lieu of accepting IAEA safeguards—even though Pakistan had already made the full payment for these aircrafts.

47. John F. Burns, "India Rejects U.S. Bid for Nuclear Pact with Pakistan," *New York Times*, March 26, 1994.

48. Satu P. Limaye, "U.S.-India Relations: Stuck in Nuclear Narrative," *Comparative Connections* 3, no. 1, April 2001.

49. George Perkovich, *India's Nuclear Bomb: The Impact on Global Proliferation*, updated edition, (Los Angeles: University of California Press, 2001), 347.

50. Bhabani Mishra, "India-U.S. Relations: A Paradigm Shift," *Strategic Analysis* 29, no. 1 (Jan-March 2005): 79.

51. Perkovich, *"India's Nuclear Bomb,"* 347.

52. *The Hindustan Times*, January 13, 1995.

53. John F. Burns, "U.S. Ends A $4 Billion Visit to India," *The New York Times*, January 18, 1995. Burns mentions that Clinton administration had stepped up efforts to promote American exports and accordingly, the Commerce department identified 10 emerging markets to be targeted, including India.

54. Ibid. The deals included areas likely to make fastest strides in the emerging economy of India.

55. Ibid. As early as 1993, the U.S. had emerged as India's largest trading partner with trade valued at 7.4 billion; also with $800 million in direct investment American companies were the largest investors in India.

56. Warren Christopher, "Strengthening U.S. Relations with South Asia," Speech by the U.S. Secretary of State to the South Asian Association for Regional Cooperation, New York City, September, 29, 1994, Bureau of Public Affairs, *U.S. Department of State Dispatch* 5, no. 40 (3 Oct, 1994): 656.

57. Ranbir Vohra, *The Making of India: A Historical Survey*, 2nd edition, (New York: M.E. Sharpe, 2000), 288.

58. Robin Raphel, *Nonproliferation Policy in South Asia*, Statement before the Subcommittee on Near Eastern and South Asian Affairs, Senate Foreign Relations Committee, 9 March 1995, *U.S. Department of State Dispatch* 6, no. 12 (Washington D.C., March 20, 1995).

59. Ibid.

60. This review conference was held in accordance with the Article X.2 of the NPT which states that after twenty-five years of entry into force, a conference of NPT members would decide whether to keep the treaty in force indefinitely or extend it for an additional fixed period or periods. Significantly, by the time the Fifth Review Conference was held in 1995, 38 states had acceded to the NPT thus, raising its membership to 178. In 1995, France and China joined as Nuclear Weapon States, because they had manufactured and exploded nuclear explosive device prior to January 1, 1967. Whereas, rest of the thirty-six states joined as Non-Nuclear Weapon States (NNWS). In 1991, South Africa dismantled its six nuclear weapons and joined the NPT. In 1992, Belarus, Kazakhstan, and Ukraine agreed to give up the nuclear weapons deployed by the erstwhile Soviet Union on their territories and joined the NPT. Argentina and Brazil halted their advanced nuclear programs and joined the NPT in 1995 and 1998, respectively.

61. K. Subrahmanyam, "India's 'No' to Observer at the NPT Extension Conference," *Times of India*, January 25, 1995; For the debate in India on the NPT extension, see, Savita Pande, "Future of NPT and India–Any Options?" *Strategic Analysis* (July 1994): 452; "India and NPT Extension: a Case for Total Disarmament," *The Times of India*, February 15, 1995.

62. The options were limited: Either an indefinite unconditional extension, as advocated by the United States and its allies or a limited extension for a period of fifteen to

twenty-five years. Stephen W. Young and Daniel T. Plesch, *A Permanent Nonproliferation Treaty,* Newsletter on International Security Policy, 45, 1 June 1995. Available at http://www.basicint.org/pubs/BReports/BR45.htm#AP (accessed April 29, 2009).

63. Rebecca Johnson, "Rethinking the NPT's Role in Security: 2010 and Beyond," *International Affairs* 86, no. 2 (2010): 438; Stephen I. Schwartz, "Reconciling Indian Nuclear Cooperation and the International Proliferation Regime," in *Canadian Policy on Nuclear Cooperation with India: Confronting New Dilemmas,* ed., Karthika Sasikumar and Wade L. Huntley (Vancouver: Simons Centre for Disarmament and Non-Proliferation Research, Canada, 2007), 133.

64. Michael J. Mazarr, "Clinton Foreign Policy R.I.P.," *The Washington Quarterly* 21, no. 2 (Spring 1998): 13.

65. The ENDC was subsequently reorganized and renamed Conference of the Committee on Disarmament. In 1978, the First Special Session of the UN General Assembly recommended the establishment of the "Committee on Disarmament." Finally, in 1984, the forum was renamed "Conference on Disarmament."

66. U.S. Department of Energy, *United States Nuclear Tests: July 1945-September 1992,* DOE/NV-209-REV15 (Las Vegas, Nevada: Nevada Operations Office, December 2000), xi.

67. K.Subrahmanyam, "India 'First' Country to Accede to Partial N-Test Ban Treaty," *The Times of India,* February 13, 1995. The countries in the six-nation initiative, included Mexico, Sweden, Argentina, Greece and Tanzania.

68. Glenn T. Seaborg and Benjamin S. Loeb, "Make the Partial Test Ban Comprehensive," Bulletin *of the Atomic Scientists* 4, no. 7 (May 1987): 3.

69. U.S. Dept. of Energy, *"United States Nuclear Tests,"* xi; Also see, Stephen I. Schwartz, ed., *Atomic Audit: The Costs and Consequences of U.S. Nuclear Weapons since 1948,* (Washington D.C.: Brookings Institution Press, 1998).

70. U.S. Dept. of Energy, *"United States Nuclear Tests,"* xi; Also see, Robert Standish Norris and Thomas B. Cochran, *U.S. Nuclear Tests July 1945 to December 1992* (Natural Resources Defense Council, Washington D.C., February 1994), 1. "The U.S. practice for more than 3 decades was not to announce all nuclear tests." On December 7, 1993, 204 previously unannounced tests were declared.

71. Arundhati Ghose, "Negotiating the CTBT: India's Security Concerns and Nuclear Disarmament," *Journal of International Affairs* 51, no. 1 (Summer 1957): 245.

72. Mutimer, "Testing Times," 17.

73. John D. Holum, Director of the U.S. Arms Control and Disarmament Agency (USACDA), Remarks at a Press Conference, U.S. Arms Control and Disarmament Agency. Washington D.C., December 10, 1996.

74. John D. Holum, Director, USACDA, Statement before the Subcommittee on International Operations and Human Rights of the Committee on International Relations, U.S. House of Representatives, March 5, 1997.

75. "Clinton Urges U.S. Congress to Ratify CTBT," *Times of India,* January 7, 2001; The Shalikashvilli report is available at http://www.carnegieendowment.org/2001/01/04/findings-and-recommendations-concerning-ctbt-shalikashvili-report/d4j (accessed June 10, 2010).

76. Arundhati Ghose, *Statement at the Plenary Meeting of the Conference on Disarmament,* Geneva, June 20, 1996. Available at http://www.fas.org/news/india/1996/ctbt_cd_june_20_96.htm (accessed October 21, 2010).

77. Arundhati Ghose, "Maintaining the Moratorium: A Defacto CTBT," *Disarmament Forum* 2, United Nations Institute for Disarmament Research, UNIDIR, Geneva (2006): 24.

78. For India's objections to the CTBT, also see, Savita Pande, *CTBT: India and the Nuclear Test Ban Treaty* (New Delhi: Siddhi Books, 1996); Christopher Bellamy, "India Pose Threat to Nuclear Test Ban Treaty," *Independent* (London), 21 June 1996.

79. A.B. Vajpayee, Prime Minister of India, Statement to the UN First Committee on Disarmament, October 1995.

80. Sunil Narula, Ludwin Joseph, Ramananda Sengupta, "CTBT: In Isolation Ward Again," *Outlook India*, July 17, 1996.

81. Bharat Karnad, *Nuclear Weapons and Indian Security: The Realist Foundations of Strategy*, (New Delhi: Macmillan, 2002), 391; Narula *et al*, "In Isolation Ward."

82. It is reported that President Clinton wrote to the Indian Foreign Minister Gujral asking him not to reject the treaty. Also, U.S. Secretary of State Warren Christopher, during his meeting with Naresh Chandra, the Indian ambassador to the United States, urged India not to block the CTBT at the CD. See, Karnad, "Nuclear Weapons and Indian Security," 392; Perkovich, "India's Nuclear Bomb," 383.

83. Arundhati Ghose, "Negotiating the CTBT: India's Security Concerns and Nuclear Disarmament," *Journal of International Affairs* 51, no. 1 (Summer 1997): 254. She was the head of the India's delegation that participated in the CTBT negotiations at Geneva in 1996.

84. Amb. Pickering, interview. In his capacity as the undersecretary for political affairs, State Department, Pickering helped launch this strategic dialogue with India; Also see, Malhotra, "Latest Initiatives," 34.

85. "India Explodes Three Nuclear Devices at Pokhran," *The Hindu*, May 11, 1998; *Official Press Release*, External Publicity Division, Ministry of External Affairs, Government of India, New Delhi, May 11, 1998. Available at http://www.meadev.gov.in/news/official/19980511/official.htm. (accessed February 15, 2009). On May 11, the Indian prime minister, Atal Bihari Vajpayee, declared that India conducted three nuclear tests at the nuclear test site in Pokhran, in the state of Rajasthan. According to the Prime Minister, a fission device, a low-yield device, and a thermonuclear device were tested. The tests did not result in the release of any radioactive material in the atmosphere. Later, in an official press release the Indian government stated that these tests have proven India's capability for a weaponized nuclear program and "are expected to carry Indian scientists towards a sound computer simulation capability which may be supported by sub-critical experiments if considered necessary."; On May 13 India conducted two more sub-kiloton nuclear tests and declared that the planned test series "Operation Shakti" was complete. These tests were conducted "to generate additional data for improved computer simulation of designs and for attaining the capability to carry out sub-critical experiments, if considered necessary." The official statement stated that no radioactivity was released in the atmosphere. *Planned Series of Nuclear Tests Completed*, Official Press Release, External Publicity Division, Ministry of External Affairs, Government of India, May 13, 1998. Available at http:www.meadev.gov.in/news/official/19980513 (accessed February 15, 2009).

86. Canada deplored the nuclear tests conducted by India and recalled its high commissioner. Peter Walker. "Canada Recalls High Commissioner," *The Asian Age* (New Delhi), May 14, 1998; Lloyd Axworthy, the foreign affairs minister, urged India to renounce nuclear weapons program and sign the NPT and CTBT. *The Hindustan Times*, May 12, 1998; Australia also withdrew its high commissioner to India, Rob Laurie. Subsequently, after the conduct of the second round of tests by India, Canberra suspended bilateral defense relations with India, including withdrawal of Australia's defense advisor stationed in New Delhi. *The Australian*, May 14, 1998; The Australian government called the tests as "outrageous acts" and ill-judged "which could have most damaging consequences for security in South Asia and globally." *The Times*, May 13, 1998; The Chinese government expressed its shock and condemned the tests. It appealed for a "unified stand" by the international community and demanded immediate cessation of nuclear weapons development by India. *The Hindustan Times*, May 14, 1998; France criticized Indian nuclear tests, yet, it the imposition of sanctions by the United States *The International Herald Tribune*, May 14, 1998.

87. Internationally, during the Clinton era, there were several successes in the nonproliferation sphere, including: abandoning of nuclear weapons by several countries, such as Ukraine, Kazakhstan, and Belarus; U.S.-Russian cutbacks; renunciation of South Africa's covert nuclear capability; and increase in the membership of NPT as France, China, Brazil and Argentina acceded to the treaty. Dennis Kux, "U.S.-Pakistan

Relations as the Twentieth Century Ends," in *Pakistan 2000*, ed., Charles H. Kennedy and Craig Baxter (American Institute of Pakistan Studies, Lanham, MD: Lexington Books, 2000), 68–69.

88. Bill Clinton, Statement of the President on India's nuclear tests, Office of the Press Secretary, White House, May 12, 1998; Stephen Lee Myers, "Nuclear Anxiety: The Policy; Clinton To Impose Penalties on India Over Nuclear Tests," *New York Times*, May 13, 1998; James Bennet, "Nuclear Anxiety: The President; Clinton Calls Tests a 'Terrible' Mistake and Announces Sanctions against India," *New York Times*, May 14, 1998.

89. "U.S. Disappointed, Sanctions Likely," *The Hindu*, May 12, 1998.

90. Samuel R. Berger, Assistant to the President for National Security Affairs, Remarks at the Carnegie International Non-Proliferation Conference, Carnegie Endowment for International Peace and Security, Washington D.C., January 12, 1999.

91. Richard Cronin, Barbara Leitch LePoer, Jonathan Medalia and Dianne Rennack, *India-Pakistan Nuclear Tests and U.S. Response*, CRS Report for Congress (Washington D.C.: Congressional Research Service, updated November 24, 1998), CRS-28.

92. As per the *section 102 (b)4 Arms Export Control Act*, President has thirty days time frame to decide about implementing the sanctions. Yet, in case of both India and Pakistan, President Clinton applied sanctions within a couple of days of conduct of the nuclear tests.

93. Glenn Amendment, adopted 1977, *Sec 102(b) of the Arms Export Control Act*, formerly *Sec.670 of the Foreign Assistance Act of 1961* as amended. This amendment prohibits U.S. foreign assistance to any non-nuclear weapons state (as defined by the nuclear non-proliferation treaty) that carries out a nuclear test explosion; For extensive discussion of the sanctions imposed on India and Pakistan, see, Jeanne Grimmett, *Nuclear Sanctions: Section 102(b)of the Arms Control Export Act and Its Application to India and Pakistan*, CRS Report no. 98–486 (Washington D.C.: Congressional Research Service, updated September 19, 2001). For details on the Glenn Amendment, see Randy J. Rydell, "Giving Nonproliferation Norms Teeth: Sanctions and the NNPA," *The Nonproliferation Review* 6, no. 2 (Winter 1999).

94. Although, this study focuses on the U.S. nuclear nonproliferation policy toward India, yet, the repeated reference to Pakistan in the discussion becomes inevitable. This is so because, the issue of India's nuclearization evoking U.S. response was linked to the fears of nuclear arms race in South Asia. Also, Pakistan justified its nuclear program by projecting the threat from India, due to latter's conventional military superiority.

95. Myers, "Nuclear Anxiety: The Policy."

96. Kux, "U.S.-Pakistan Relations," 69. It is reported that before Pakistan conducted the nuclear tests, President Clinton in an attempt to prevent a nuclear breakout spoke four times with the Pakistani government.

97. For further information on Pressler Amendment and the issue of F-16s, see footnote 42.

98. The Symington Amendment, adopted in 1976, *Sec 101 of the Arms Export Control Act*, formerly *Sec. 669 of the Foreign Assistance Act of 1961* as amended. This amendment prohibits U.S. assistance to any country involved in trafficking in nuclear enrichment equipment or technology outside of international safeguards.

99. Testimony of the Undersecretary of Commerce for International Trade, Ambassador David L. Aaron, Hearing on India-Pakistan Nuclear Proliferation, Subcommittee on Asia and the Pacific, House Committee on International Relations, 105th Congress, 2nd Session, Washington D.C., June 18, 1998. Available at http://www.fas.org/spp/starwars/congress/1998_h/98061806_npo.html (accessed May 2, 2009).

100. Aaron, testimony, June 18, 1998.

101. Interview with a senior official at the Nuclear Regulatory Commission (NRC) Washington D.C. (anonymity requested).

102. Pallava Bagla, "Washington Blocks 8 U.S. Scientists from TIFR Physics Seminar," *Indian Express* (Mumbai), January 15, 1999. Nonetheless, twenty-five U.S. scientists from non-government institutions attended the symposium.

103. Interview with Charles Ferguson, February 2009.

104. Mistry, "Diplomacy," 755.

105. Karl Inderfurth, Testimony before the Subcommittee for Asia and the Pacific, Senate International Relations Committee, U.S. Senate, Washington DC. July 13, 1998.

106. Amb. Aaron, testimony, June 18, 1998.

107. See, Perkovich, "India's Nuclear Bomb"; Sumit Ganguly, "India's Pathways to Pokhran II: The Prospects and Sources of New Delhi's Nuclear Weapons Program," *International Security* 23, no. 4 (Spring 1999); Ashley J. Tellis, *Behind the India's Bomb: The Politics and Strategy of Nuclear Deterrence* (Santa Monica: RAND Corporation, 2001); Stephen Cohen, *India: Emerging Power* (Brookings Institution Press: Washington D.C., 2002). Itty Abraham, *Making of the Atomic Bomb* (London: Zed Books, November 1998).

108. Deepa M. Ollapally, "Mixed Motives in India's Search for Nuclear Status," *Asian Survey*, 41, no. 60, (November/December 2001).

109. Mutimer, "Testing Times," 13.

110. Ghose, "Maintaining the Moratorium," 25.

111. Schneider, "Policy Issues and Implications."

112. Christine Fair, "Learning to Think," 52.

113. Ghose, "Maintaining the Moratorium," 25; Jyotika Saksena, "Regime Design Matters: The CTBT and India's Nuclear Dilemma," *Comparative Strategy* 25 (2006): 209.

114. Saksena, "Regime Design," 209.

115. Mishra, "A Paradigm Shift," 80.

116. Morton H. Halperin and Richard N. Haass, "Our Misguided South Asia Nuclear Policy," *The Washington Post*, September 13, 1998.

117. Several opinions have emerged regarding Indian deception of the U.S. spy satellites and intelligence agencies. The vast pool of data provided by the Indian Space Research Organization (ISRO) regarding the orbits and timings of the spy satellites helped the Indian team of scientists and engineers to work in a calculative manner, when the satellites were not overhead, to evade detection. Moreover, the preparations for the 37th test of the Trishul short-range surface-to-surface missile at Chandipur, Orissa, were also used to divert attention from the Pokhran nuclear test site; Chairman of the Indian Atomic Energy Commission, R. Chidambaram also points out that the failure to detect India's sub-kiloton explosions was due to "software and analytical inadequacies" of the foreign seismologists in the face of "separated, simultaneous explosions." This failure exposed the weaknesses of the Comprehensive Test Ban Treaty (CTBT) monitoring system. According to Chidambaram, the seismic method was not the best way to assess India's nuclear tests since the seismic results could be manipulated. The DAE released accelerometer results after the tests. See, T.S. Gopi Rethinaraj, "Indian Blasts Surprise the World, but Leave Fresh Doubts," *Jane's Intelligence Review*, July 1998, 19–22 ;"Nuclear Power, India's Important Need," *The Hindu* (Chennai), October 31, 1998; R. Jeffrey Smith, "CIA Missed Signs of India's Tests, U.S. Officials Say," *The Washington Post*, May 13, 1998; Bill Gertz, "India Blasts take U.S. Intelligence by Surprise," *Washington Times*, May 12, 1998.

118. David Albright, "The Shots Heard 'Round the World," *The Bulletin of Atomic Scientists* 54, no. 4 (July–August 1998): 21. Albright provides a good discussion of several debates on the Pokhran II nuclear tests—the yield estimate, thermonuclear explosion, and the detection failure.

119. As quoted, "Don't Blame the CIA," *The Economist*, 23 May 1998.

120. Raj Chengappa, *Weapons of Peace: Secret Story of India's Quest to be a Nuclear Power* (New Delhi: Harper Collins, 2000), 17. Chengappa examines India's quest since 1974 laden with political calculations, manipulations, missed opportunities and hurdles for the right opportunity to conduct the nuclear tests.

121. "Don't Blame the CIA," op cit.

122. Stephen, P. Cohen, Testimony on Political and Military Developments in India, Near East and South Asia Subcommittee, Senate Committee on Foreign Relations, Near East and South Asia Subcommittee, May 25, 1999. Available at http://www.brookings.edu/testimony/1999/0525india-cohen.aspx?p=1 (accessed March 24, 1999).

123. Perkovich, "India's Nuclear Bomb," 185.

124. Cohen, testimony, May 25, 1999.

125. Ibid.

126. Bouton, "South Asia's Concerns."

127. Ibid.

128. Bernard E. Trainor, "U.S. Should not Deplore New Nuclear States: It Should Help Them Curb Risks," *The Boston Globe*, June 4, 1998.

129. Selig S. Harrison, "India's Muscle Flexing is Over. Let the Bargaining Begin," *The Washington Post*, May 17, 1998. Interestingly, the U.S.-India nuclear agreement of 2005 includes some of the suggestions made by Harrison.

130. Stephen M. Walt, "Two Cheers for Clinton's Foreign Policy," *Foreign Affairs* 79, no. 2 (March-April 2000): 72. Japan and South Korea also were involved in the Agreed Framework.

131. Ibid.

132. Richard Haass, "The U.S. Role in India's Nuclear Tests," *The Washington Times*, May 14, 1998.

133. Stephen P. Cohen, *A New Beginning for South Asia*, Policy Brief no. 55, (The Brookings Institution, Washington D.C., January 2000): 3–4.

134. Director, Wisconsin Project on Nuclear Arms Control, Gary Milhollin, Testimony before the Committee on Armed Services, U.S. Senate, July 9, 1998. Available at http://www.fas.org/spp/starwars/congress/1998_h/980709gm.htm (accessed January 10, 2009). Milhollin argued that American government's export policy on satellites enabled Chinese companies to sell missile components to Pakistan without fear of retribution. In fall of 1992, China exported complete missiles to Pakistan, but now, China is exporting missiles "piecemeal." He criticized Clinton administration for transferring the subject of sale of satellites and related technologies to the Commerce Department. This he argued insulated sale of satellites from missile related sanctions. Under the regulations of the Commerce Department a missile-related item loses its identity as a missile item if it is incorporated into a commercial satellite. The export of satellites would not be blocked by the Commerce Department even though the satellites contained items that can be used in the missiles. Thus, the missile related sanctions are easily evaded; Also see, Shirley A. Kan, *China: Possible Missile Technology Transfers From U.S. Satellite Export Policy: Background and Chronology*, CRS Report for Congress no. 98–485F, Washington D.C.: Congressional Research Service, updated August 13, 1998.

135. Newt Gingrich, "Letter on the Indian Nuclear Tests," Office of the Speaker, The House of Representatives, Washington D.C., 14 May, 1998. Available at http://www.indianembassy.org/pic/Congress/newt_gingrich.htm (accessed January 10, 2009).

136. Stanley A. Weiss, "India should be at the Top of Washington's Contact List," *The International Herald Tribune*, November 16, 1998.

137. Gingrich, "Letter"; Regarding Washington's concerns on China's role in proliferation of nuclear and missile related technologies, also see, *Proliferation: Chinese Case Studies*, U.S. Congressional Hearings, Special Weapons, Subcommittee on International Security, Proliferation and Federal Services, Committee on Governmental Affairs, U.S. Senate, April 10, 1997; Shirley A. Kan, *China's Proliferation of Weapons of Mass Destruction: Current Policy Issues*, CRS Issue Brief for Congress, Congressional Research Service, May 16, 2001; For details on China-Iran nuclear and missile technology related transfers, see, John W. Garver, *China and Iran: Ancient Partners in a Post-Imperial World* (Seattle: University of Washington Press, 2006).

138. Weiss, "Top of Washington's Contact List."; Moreover, the U.S. had significant concerns regarding Chinese transferring nuclear and missile technologies to Iran. In October 1991, Richard Solomon, assistant secretary of state for East Asia and the

Pacific, stated that China had sold nuclear related technologies to Iran despite assurances to address U.S. concerns. "Report Says Iran Seeks Atomic Arms," *New York Times*, October 31, 1991.

139. Gingrich, "Letter on the Indian Nuclear Tests"; Also see, Harrison, "India's Muscle Flexing."

140. Weiss, "Top of Washington's Contact List," op cit.

FOUR

Post-Pokhran II (1998–2000)

Shifting Nuclear Goalposts?

The qualitative transformation of the U.S.-India relationship is usually traced to the Clinton era.[1] It is commonly perceived that the Clinton administration contributed immensely to change in the "structure and substance" of the bilateral relationship; yet, Clinton's predisposition toward strengthening global nuclear nonproliferation precluded any concessions in its nonproliferation objectives.[2] On the other hand, Clinton's successor, President George W. Bush, is held accountable for changing the U.S. nuclear approach toward India and, thereby, of compromising Washington's nonproliferation interests. This I argue is problematic and necessitates revisiting the developments during the Clinton administration in the post-Pokhran II era. As discussed in the previous chapter, the Clinton administration maintained significant pressure on India to follow the global nonproliferation norms and vociferously opposed the nuclear tests. Consistent with his highly acclaimed commitment to nonproliferation, President Clinton slapped sanctions on India after the Pokhran II nuclear tests. Yet, the following questions need to be explored: Was the United States consistent in its approach toward India? Were the sanctions maintained with the same intensity as they were imposed? Did the administration stick to its oft proclaimed goals of "cap, rollback, and eliminate"? What were the nonproliferation benchmarks that the Clinton administration established in its dialogue with India? And, most significantly, did the administration achieve them? The answers to these questions will help us analyse whether President Clinton also contributed to changing the nuclear stance toward India.

The first section of this chapter examines the effectiveness of the sanctions strategy employed by the Clinton administration in the aftermath of the Pokhran II tests. The second section focuses on the Strobe Talbott-Jaswant Singh (hereafter, Talbott-Singh) dialogue initiated between the U.S. and India. It also analyzes the four nuclear benchmarks that were established by the Clinton administration for the nuclear bargaining process with India. The third section critically analyzes the Clinton administration's post-proliferation strategy toward nuclear India. The final section examines the (in)significance of the U.S.-India dialogue and the perceptible change in bilateral relations. I contend that President Clinton changed the "structure and substance" of the relationship with India, but in the process he also shifted the nuclear goalposts with respect to India. First, the administration demonstrated an acute lack of substantial post-proliferation strategy to deal with nuclear India. The measures initially taken by the United States, imposing sanctions and the nuclear bargaining, proved to be ad hoc and reactionary. Furthermore, it also revealed a considerable vacuum in the nonproliferation regime to deal with nuclear India. Second, following the May 1998 Pokhran II tests, U.S. nonproliferation objectives in the Indian subcontinent underwent a distinct shift from the earlier "cap, rollback, and eliminate" stance to simply maintenance of "nuclear restraint." This, in turn, implied a tacit acceptance of India's (and Pakistan's) nuclear weapons. Third, in the post-Pokhran II environment, the U.S. approach toward nuclear India changed from coercive to conciliatory. The unprecedented dialogue that ensued between the United States and India led to harmonization of the bilateral relationship, yet failed to extract any substantial commitment from nuclear India. Fourth, during the Clinton era, the removal of the persistent irritant—Washington's demand for India to sign the NPT as a nonnuclear weapon state (NNWS)—from the U.S.-India nuclear narrative, considerably narrowed their nuclear nonproliferation divide. The above aspects, to a great extent, cleared the languishing nuclear debris between Washington and New Delhi and created space for the succeeding administration to bridge the nuclear divide with India.

THE FIASCO OF SANCTIONS

After the peaceful nuclear explosion in 1974, India retained its nuclear capable status and maintained ambiguity about its nuclear weapons. In response, the United States imposed technological embargoes and instituted export controls to prevent India from gaining access to sensitive technologies. Yet, surprisingly, except for intermittently demanding that India sign the Nuclear Nonproliferation Treaty (NPT), the United States never undertook a major initiative to bring India within the nonproliferation fold. India existing outside the nonproliferation regime, as an anomaly, continued to advance technologically, relying on its indigenous resources and expertise. The United States was seemingly caught unawares when India tested its nuclear weapons within two years of the conclusion of the Comprehensive Test Ban Treaty (CTBT). The Indian nuclear crossover exposed yet another flaw in the NPT-centric regime, i.e., lack of a post-proliferation mechanism. I contend that the nonproliferation regime, obsessively focused on prevention of proliferation, has no effective measures to deal with a post-proliferation situation. The United States was quick to impose sanctions under the Glenn Amendment—originally devised to prevent states from going nuclear—but these failed to be effective in post-proliferation scenario. The imposition of sanctions proved to be ad hoc and reactionary measure by the Clinton administration and failed to make nuclear India accede to the nonproliferation regime.

Sanctions, or penalties, are imposed with the intention of altering the behavior of other states or entities.[3] Aside from punitive action for crossing the nuclear threshold, the sanctions imposed on India (and Pakistan) were meant to achieve two additional objectives. First, the sanctions reflected the administration's avowed commitment to nuclear nonproliferation. As Talbott put it, the sanctions were "a part of our effort to keep faith with the much larger number of nations that have renounced nuclear weapons despite their capacity to develop them."[4] Second, the sanctions exemplified high economic and political costs for states that crossed the nuclear threshold and thereby were meant to serve as a disincentive. In imposing the sanctions the State Department claimed to send "a strong message to would-be testers."[5] Thomas Graham Jr. proposed retaining the sanctions until both countries agreed not to "weaponize" or "deploy the weapons."[6] The Clinton administration set specific objectives that would need to be reached by India and Pakistan before the sanctions could be removed: first, nuclear testing must be halted; second, the CTBT must be signed immediately and without conditions; third, missiles must not be tested or deployed; fourth, cooperation in ongoing negotiations of the Fissile Material Cut-off Treaty (FMCT) in Geneva; fifth, restraints must be maintained and formalized with respect to sharing sensitive goods and technologies with other countries; and finally, bilateral tensions must be reduced, including the friction concerning Kashmir.[7]

Ironically, sanctions imposed on other states can also have implications for the country employing them, necessitating a careful assessment of the possible ramifications before their invocation. As Richard Haass, aptly advises, "Economic sanctions are a serious instrument of foreign policy and should be employed only after consideration no less rigorous than what would precede military intervention."[8] In his testimony to the Senate Task Force on Economic Sanctions, Haass cautioned that economic intervention, like military intervention, has costs, but these are usually invisible and rarely figure in the state budget. Nonetheless, sanctions do impinge on the economy, not only in terms of loss of sales but also in "forfeited opportunities."[9] He argued that several countries attach high value to commercial transactions and are hesitant to impose sanctions, but the United States simply forges ahead, even unilaterally.[10]

This was the first time ever that the Glenn Amendment was invoked to impose sanctions, without any inference of its efficacy. Alongside, concerns arose that the Glenn sanctions imposed on India and Pakistan might impinge on the commercial and political interests of Washington. The Clinton administration was eager to minimize "to the extent possible the impact [of the sanctions] on U.S. business and labour."[11] Since early 1990s, India's economic liberalization policies led to an upsurge in the U.S.-India economic relations—the United States emerging as India's largest trading and investment partner. By 1996, the total U.S. investment in India had peaked to $1.1 billion. In 1997, U.S. exports to India reached $3.6 billion, while U.S. imports from India totalled $7.3 billion.[12] This meant that U.S. businesses had a stake in the stable functioning of the Indian economy. David L. Aaron, the undersecretary of Commerce for International Trade, also reflected on the domestic implications of the Glenn sanctions. He argued that unilateral sanctions imposed by Washington in the relative absence of comparable sanctions by other nations could have negative implications, as suppliers and investors from other countries would quickly fill the vacuum in the Indian economy created by the loss of U.S. business.[13] Moreover, he also doubted if the relative insularity of the Indian economy would allow the U.S. economic sanctions to have the intended effect.[14]

The prohibitions were not so comprehensive in nature to preclude all the trade and commerce with India and Pakistan, yet, considerably affected U.S. domestic economic interests. The Glenn Amendment implied withdrawal of U.S. government credit assistance related to trade and investment purposes in the target countries. Consequently, in the absence of credit financing by the U.S. government, the ability of several U.S. entities to pursue projects in India and Pakistan was curtailed.[15] Within a month of the punitive measures, the U.S. Congress faced a conflict between the sanctions and the interests of American farmers. The sanctions curtailed $90 million of export financing for American farmers to participate in the mid-July wheat auction in Pakistan.[16] The target country, Pakistan, was a leading buyer of American white wheat and the third largest overseas purchaser of all U.S. wheat.[17] With the blocking of American participation, there were concerns that Pakistan would procure wheat from other countries, viz., Canada, Australia, or France. Moreover, the sanctions meant blocking $300 million worth of credit assistance in the following year also.[18] Thus, the sanctions impinged on the interests of American farmers. Faced with the plight of the U.S. wheat-growers, the Senate, without the usual committee review, passed a Wheat Relief Bill, and it was signed into law on July 14, 1998. This amended the Arms Export Control Act to exclude agricultural commodities from sanctions and thereby allowed financial assistance to enable participation of the

American farmers in the wheat auction.[19] Robert Hathaway captures the irony: "No one [in the Congress] displayed anger at India or Pakistan for violating long-standing international norms against testing. Instead the debate was all about helping the U.S. farmer, about not losing or penalising American wheat growers."[20]

Additionally, concerns were raised regarding the fallout of the sanctions on the already economically and politically feeble Pakistan. The Pakistani government was considerably dependent on foreign aid which constituted an enormous portion, about six to eight percent, of its budget. There were apprehensions that Islamic fundamentalism might step into the void created by political and economic destabilization. And, there was a lingering fear that an impoverished Pakistan might sell nuclear technology to the Middle East.[21] Furthermore, South Asia had hitherto been neglected in the U.S. foreign policy; therefore, Washington had little understanding of the region's geopolitical dynamics. The Clinton administration realized that, apart from nuclear nonproliferation, the United States had several economic and political interests in the South Asian region that required stability of the regimes.[22]

Subsequently, the U.S. Congress passed the India-Pakistan Relief Act of 1998, (Brownback Amendment I) which authorized the president to provide a one-year exemption from the Glenn Amendment to India and Pakistan. On October 21, 1998, President Clinton signed the Brownback Amendment into law and waived the sanctions for a period of one year. This eased the sanctions on government-backed financing and credit guarantees for U.S. companies engaged in business with the targeted countries, India and Pakistan. Also, restrictions on multilateral financial loans and credits to both countries were also lifted; thereby enabling a rescue package from the International Monetary Fund for Pakistan.[23]

Regarding the swift removal of the sanctions, a nuclear nonproliferation scholar remarks, "You can see it is the U.S. Congress' fault how quickly the sanctions were lifted."[24] But it was not only Congress that was interested in the removal of the sanctions, even the executive branch was eager to have the authority to waive sanctions. As diplomatic negotiations with the target countries intensified, the State Department wanted to use the removal of sanctions as an incentive to enhance its own bargaining power with the Indian and Pakistani governments. In this context, U.S. Secretary of State Madeleine Albright sought flexibility in the sanctions.[25] On June 14, 1998, in an interview with CNN, Albright complained that the Glenn Amendment provided no scope for incentives. She remarked, "The very tough sanctions that have been put into place against India and Pakistan is [sic] the Glenn Amendment which has no waiver authority and no flexibility. It's all sticks and no carrot . . . *sanctions that have no flexibility, are just blunt instruments and diplomacy requires us to have some finesse*" (emphasis added).[26] Similarly, Karl Inderfurth requested a waiver from Congress for "greater flexibility" so as to be able to "tailor our approach, influence events, and respond to developments." He affirmed that the waiver would be used after substantial progress had been achieved on nonproliferation objectives.[27] He also elaborated that it would be applied only under specific conditions: first, to prevent "serious negative or unintended" consequences of the sanctions such as threat of financial collapse that may lead to chaotic economic conditions or political instability (the reference was obviously to Pakistan); and, second, to ensure that the sanctions have an equivalent effect on both countries and one country is not placed in a disadvantaged position.[28] Acceding to the request of the executive, in October 1999, the U.S. Congress adopted Brownback Amendment II. This was a significant step as it granted the U.S. President authority to waive all sanctions on both India and Pakistan, not only those under the Glenn Amendment but also under the provisions of the Pressler and Symington Amendments which had restricted economic and military funding to Pakistan since 1990.[29] The legislation also emphasized that "broad applications" of export controls were detrimental to U.S. interests, and therefore urged the executive branch to apply specific and selective export controls only on agencies and companies in India and Pakistan that directly contributed to the weapons of mass destruction and missile programs, and to prohibit the export those items of U.S. origin that would contribute to such programs.[30] Thus, Congress not only favoured removal of the sanctions, it also favoured selective export controls to reduce the impact of the restrictions on U.S. interests.

The sanctions were not sufficient to pressurize India into making major commitments to nuclear regime, nor did Washington "consider increasing the magnitude of the sanctions" to achieve its nonproliferation objectives.[31] Moreover, the sanctions did not even last long enough to make an impact on India. On the contrary, the apprehensions about the deteriorating economic condition of Pakistan forced the Clinton administration not only to remove the sanctions quickly, but also to support a $5.5 billion bailout package from the International Monetary Fund.[32] Furthermore, in order "to prevent Islamabad from slipping into default," President Clinton returned $324.6 million, in cash, to Pakistan.[33] This was the payment obtained from Pakistan for the F-16 aircraft that had been embargoed by the Pressler Amendment since 1990; previously, Washington had neither returned the payment nor delivered the combat aircraft. Now, in addition, the administration granted Pakistan $140 million as compensation.[34] These payments put Pakistan in a far better financial position in the post-1998 test environment than it had been before the nuclear tests. It received huge economic aid as well as money that had been blocked for several years. Randy J. Rydell comments that the total amount Pakistan received "far exceeds the 4 billion the U.S. provided in military and economic aid to Pakistan between 1981 and 1990."[35]

Thus, the rapid removal of sanctions exposed a lack of strong political will both in the U.S. Congress as well as the White House. The majority of the sanctions were removed without eliciting any substantial nuclear nonproliferation commitment from India or Pakistan. Initially, the United States was intent on setting an example for the potential proliferators. But by the end of 1999, as Robert Hathaway remarks, the Congress and the executive moved "*nonproliferation to the back burner and renounced with dizzying speed the sanctions on India and Pakistan*" (emphasis added).[36] Senator Glenn, the author of several nuclear nonproliferation measures in the U.S. law, lamented that sanctions had already failed in their purpose, "which was to prevent a test in the first place."[37]

TALBOTT-SINGH DIALOGUE

Immediately after the Pokhran II nuclear tests, India launched energetic diplomatic efforts to clarify its position that the tests were necessitated by its deteriorating security environment, and to emphasize that there was no "revisionist agenda."[38] As part of that effort, India requested a dialogue with Washington. Notwithstanding the anger within the administration, the Indian invitation to talk was swiftly accepted by the White House. The Indian nuclear tests drew the attention of the Clinton administration to the languishing nonproliferation issues with India. Strobe Talbott aptly referred to the Pokhran II explosions as "attention-grabber and action-enforcer."[39] After the initial phase of reactions and sanctions, Washington felt an urgency to comprehensively review its policy toward nuclear India, thus, a "more reflective process began."[40]

On June 12, 1998, barely a month after the nuclear tests, a high-level U.S.-India dialogue began.[41] It consisted of 14 bilateral meetings over the next year and a half. The U.S. delegation was led by the then deputy secretary of state, Strobe Talbott. Since the beginning of the Clinton administration, Talbott had been involved in nuclear nonproliferation issues in South Asia. From the Indian side, Jaswant Singh, deputy chairman of the Indian Planning Commission, joined the talks as a special emissary of the prime minister.[42] The Talbott-Singh talks turned out to be an unprecedented dialogue between the two nations whose relationship hitherto was aptly characterized by Selig S. Harrison as a "dialogue of the deaf."[43]

The Talbott-Singh dialogue was held in an "opaque environment,"[44] yet, soon there was a discernible change in Washington's tone. After a few initial rounds, Karl Inderfurth stated, "we are making progress in *defining the principles* that will underpin U.S. relations with India"[45] (emphasis added). The purpose of these talks, he emphasized, was to explore for a "common ground." He stated that the attempt was, "to build on areas of agreement and find some ways to manage differences where we do not agree."[46] In contrast to its earlier punitive approach, the United States was not singularly focused on dictating nuclear nonproliferation objectives, rather, it was keen to encourage a positive environment and facilitate talks that would achieve broader American objectives with India. Thus, the dialogue covered a broad spectrum of United States-India relations, from political, defence, economic, and technological relations, to regional and international developments.[47]

NUCLEAR BENCHMARKS

Based on resolutions of the U.N. Security Council, the G-8 and P-5 on the South Asian nuclear tests, Washington outlined four nuclear benchmarks as the primary terms of reference for the Talbott-Singh dialogue.[48] The success in achieving these nuclear objectives was related to the removal of the sanctions. Washington categorically reiterated the "crucial and immutable guideline" that it does "not and will not concede . . . that India and Pakistan have established themselves as nuclear weapon states."[49] The benchmarks for the Talbott-Singh dialogue basically outlined obligations for India: to (i) sign and ratify the CTBT; (ii) sign the FMCT and refrain from production of fissile material until the treaty enters into force; (iii) accept limitations on the development and deployment of missiles and aircraft capable of carrying weapons of mass destruction, that is, define a minimum required deterrent; and (iv) tighten export controls on sensitive materials and technologies.[50]

Next, it is important to examine to what extent the Clinton administration was successful in achieving these relatively modest and diluted nuclear nonproliferation goals during the highly acclaimed Talbott-Singh talks.

Evidently, in the initial phase of the Talbott-Singh talks, India had expressed willingness to sign the CTBT but sought some incentives in return.[51] Due to the opaque nature of the talks there is considerable ambiguity about the concessions being negotiated in lieu of India's signatures on the CTBT. A former Indian diplomat, J. N. Dixit, maintains that the Indian representative, Jaswant Singh, was briefed to garner maximum strategic advantage for India's signature on the CTBT, such as removal of technological embargoes imposed since 1974 or recognition of India as a major power.[52] In September 1998, Indian Prime Minister Vajpayee at the U.N. General Assembly expressed willingness to sign the CTBT by the date of its entry into force, albeit not unconditionally.[53] Madeline Albright, too, in her testimony to the Senate Foreign Relations Committee, noted the progress made in the Indo-American talks. She confirmed that India had agreed to adhere to the Comprehensive Test Ban Treaty by September 1999, to join negotiations for fissile material production cutoffs, and to tighten its export controls over sensitive technologies.[54]

Washington maintained silence on the nature of the incentives being offered to India. In this context, Talbott affirms that "access to nuclear technology was, in the Clinton administration, not on the table, since India was staying outside the NPT."[55] Nonetheless, a prominent Indian scholar Kanti Bajpai avers that even though Washington had publicly denied the idea of a deal, the fact that Washington engaged in the high-level dialogue suggests that "in reality it was [already] reconciled to some sort of bargain before it embarked on the talks."[56]

While the negotiations for a "mutually acceptable price"[57] to elicit India's signatures on the CTBT were progressing, several developments, both within India and the United States, doomed the plan to failure. First, the disclosure regarding New Delhi's willingness to sign the CTBT created concerns within India regarding the possibility of a secret deal with the Clinton administration. Simultaneously, the coalition government led by Vajpayee lost its majority and the vote of confidence. The Indian parliament was dissolved and the Vajpayee government was reduced to a caretaker government. Therefore, both politically and constitutionally it lost the credibility to take decision on a significant issue like signing the CTBT.[58] Second, and ironically, the CTBT was rejected in the U.S. Senate. John D. Holum realized Washington's loss of bargaining power on the issue of the CTBT with India. He confessed, "The CTBT can help head off a nuclear arms race in South Asia. . . . Persuading them to formalize their testing moratoria through the CTBT is a major goal of the international community. *But it is not easy asking them* [India] *to give up a legal right to test when we retain it*" (emphasis added).[59] Thus, the United States did not make any progress on this issue in its deliberations with India.

Regarding the second benchmark, the production of fissile material, India expressed its readiness to participate in the Conference on Disarmament in Geneva for the formulation of a Fissile Material Cut-off Treaty (FMCT).[60] The objective of the FMCT was to cut-off the production of fissile material designed for utilization in nuclear weapons. India was willing to make efforts for the early conclusion of a non-discriminatory FMCT that "will end the *future* production of fissile material for weapons purposes" (emphasis added).[61] Nonetheless, India outrightly rejected the U.S. request for an immediate moratorium, as this entailed an instantaneous cut-off of the production of fissile material and India felt it did not have enough fissile material to meet its security needs.[62]

Logically speaking, the issue of capping the fissile material stockpile was inevitably linked to India's minimum deterrence needs. As Michael Krepon argues, "A cut-off in fissile material production for weapons and constraints on missile programs were unachievable as long as India could not be sure about its requirements for deterrence against China as well as Pakistan."[63] In this context, Richard Celeste, the U.S. ambassador to India, insisted that New Delhi articulate in concrete terms its measure of a minimum credible deterrent as well as be transparent regarding the delivery systems being used and the locations of the nuclear devices.[64] Although, India had consistently expressed the need for a minimum nuclear deterrent, but, hitherto had not quantified its deterrence needs nor adopted a nuclear doctrine.[65] Nevertheless, India perceived this as America's attempt to gain a "supervisory function" in the highly sensitive issue of nuclear defence.[66] India responded that its right to minimum credible deterrent was "nonnegotiable"[67] and dismissed the U.S. demand as insignificant. Subsequently, Celeste clarified that the intention behind seeking the physical quantification was only to ensure that the proposed deterrent was not perceived as an "open-ended threat" by India's neighbors. He further stressed that India need not reveal sensitive security-related information.[68] Similarly, allaying the apprehensions of the Indian side, Talbott elaborated that the United States does not intend to dictate India's defence posture, but, it was essential for India to reconcile "the two adjectives 'credible' and 'minimum'" in its deterrence concept. He remarked that Washington just required an assurance that New Delhi was not seeking "an open-ended arms competition, but only the minimum necessary to ensure Indian security."[69] This implies that in the post-Pokhran II scenario, the United States recognized and accepted India's need for a "minimum deterrent" based on its security requirements. This, indeed, was a distinct shift in the Clinton administration's initial nuclear approach of "cap, rollback, and eliminate."

In August 1999, responding to Washington's persuasion, India's national security advisor, Brajesh Mishra, released the *Draft Report of India's Nuclear Doctrine*. It dwelled on India's key nuclear policy objectives and specified: the proposed nuclear force architecture; issues of command and control of nuclear forces; related research and development; and its position on arms control and disarmament issues.[70] Therein India defined its strategic needs to be a "large, complex, and potentially open-ended nuclear arsenal."[71] Washington's insistence on making India quantify its deterrence requirements was seemingly well-intentioned; it aimed to enable verifiable limits on the scope and the extent of weaponisation in order to maintain stability in the highly volatile South Asian region between the two hostile nascent nuclear powers. Yet it proved to be, as Krepon avers, "ill-advised."[72] By quantifying its deterrence needs, India inevitably progressed toward institutionalization of nuclear weapons as a significant component of its national security doctrine as well as arsenal.

Finally, the fourth benchmark, export controls, was not a controversial issue between the two nations. India indicated that its export control policies on nuclear and missile technologies were already in line with international standards and that further nuclear nonproliferation measures would be undertaken.[73] In this context, Anupam Srivastava, a prominent specialist on WMD export controls, remarks, "It [India] has enacted and long maintained tighter controls than most countries, certainly more than the P-5 [nuclear weapon] states, over exports of weapons of mass destruction, components, and related technologies."[74]

SHIFTING NUCLEAR GOALPOSTS

The Talbott-Singh talkathon was inconclusive. Initially, sanctions were linked to progress on the nuclear front, yet, based on different political-economic considerations, most of the sanctions were swiftly waived. The Clinton administration failed to elicit any substantial commitment from India on the specified nuclear objectives and, instead, ended up shifting the nuclear goalposts with respect to India. First, even a cursory reading of the new nuclear benchmarks reveals a subtle yet substantial change in the American nuclear nonproliferation policy toward India; the U.S. approach changed from "cap, rollback, and eliminate" to the maintenance of nuclear restraint. Samantha Ravich opines, "the benchmarks were created with the mindset that the rollback of India's weapons program was a possibility."[75] I contend that in the post-Pokhran II era, the United States did not consider it pertinent to insist on rollback and elimination of nuclear weapons, rather, Washington simply persuaded India to exercise nuclear restraint in order to prevent accidental nuclear fallout in South Asia.

Second, and most significant, the oft-proclaimed objective of the Clinton administration, that is, adherence of India to the NPT as a nonnuclear weapon state (NNWS), was conspicuously absent from the nuclear benchmarks. The Clinton administration seemingly reconciled itself to the fact that India possessed nuclear weapons and there was no possibility of a rollback. In fact, in an email exchange with the author, Strobe Talbott conceded that the dialogue and the "benchmarks . . . *were not about the rollback but about moving forward in a way that reconciled the interests of both sides*" (emphasis added).[76] Henceforth, India's adherence to the NPT—as a nonnuclear weapon state—became a nonissue in the nuclear narrative between the U.S. and India.

Third, the Clinton administration failed to enlist India's commitment to the significant treaties of the nonproliferation regime. India was able to evade signing the CTBT as it was rejected by the U.S. Senate and thereby, Washington lost its bargaining position. Also, the FMCT was still languishing in the Conference on Disarmament. Therefore, no agreement could be reached and India was not bound to accept restrictions on the production of fissile material.

Fourth, undoubtedly, the Clinton administration refused to accord a *dejure* recognition of India's status as a "nuclear weapon state" as defined by the NPT. Nonetheless, I propound that these benchmarks revealed a tacit acceptance of India's nuclearization, along with its specified requirement for a "minimum nuclear deterrent." Initially, the Clinton administration had insisted on nonweaponization of the nuclear option and non-deployment in South Asia. The post-1998 test scenario reflected a change in the U.S. stance in that it now recognized "India's right to build a credible minimum deterrent."[77] In January 2000, Strobe Talbott, in an interview with a prominent Indian news daily *The Hindu*, stressed that the United States "fully" recognizes that it is "*the sovereign right [of India] to make decisions on what sort of weapons and force posture are necessary for the defense of India and Indian interests*" (emphasis added).[78] Based on the condition that the deterrent posture be transparent as well as acceptable to the United States so as to prevent any miscalculation or accidental nuclear war on the subcontinent. Nonetheless, this acceptance of India's need for a nuclear deterrent reflected a distinct modification in U.S. nuclear nonproliferation policy; this has gone largely unrecognized. The Clinton administration, despite modifying the objectives and stance of its nuclear nonproliferation policy, failed to effectively deal with the post-proliferation challenge of nuclear India, the anomaly.

(IN)SIGNIFICANCE OF THE DIALOGUE

Although, the dialogue failed to bring India within the nuclear nonproliferation regime, yet, the Talbott-Singh dialogue cannot be considered a total failure. In an interview with the author, Ambassador Pickering emphasized that the dialogue process proved for the first time that "India and the U.S. could have a somewhat intellectual and philosophical dialogue about nuclear issues," instead of the earlier reactive and emotionally charged monologues.[79] Furthermore, the interlocutors claimed that the purpose of the talkathon was "reconciliation," i.e., to bridge the hitherto divergent perspectives and achieve harmonization of bilateral interests on regional and international issues.[80] Emphasising the significance of the dialogue, Jaswant Singh stated, these were "*the longest lasting, the most productive, and, potentially, the most useful talks* the United States and India have had in the past many decades" (emphasis added).[81] The dialogue created a better understanding between the two states and enhanced the U.S. perceptions of the geopolitical dynamics in the South Asian region. This was manifest in the support extended by the United States during the 1999 India-Pakistan Kargil crisis. Earlier, in the 1971 Indo-Pakistan War Washington had stationed its nuclear submarine in the Arabian Sea in support of Pakistan. In 1999, due to a better awareness of the political equations and the grim realities in South Asia, the United States stood beside India to thwart intervention of Pakistani troops in the Indian Kashmir. This endorsement of the "sanctity of the Kashmir divide"[82] proved to be a turning point in U.S.-India relations. As Stephen Cohen, aptly states, "For the first time, during the Kargil crisis the U.S. sided with India. *India was flabbergasted*."[83] He elaborates further, "It was a very important U.S. effort to destroy the parallelism in the U.S. policies and attitudes towards India and Pakistan. There was a real preference for India."[84] Earlier, the United States had always approached New Delhi within an India-Pakistan context, grouping the two countries together in its South Asian policy. Thus, the Kargil war demonstrated a big change in the decades-old approach of Washington, not only toward India, but toward South Asia in general. In fact, it can be considered as the beginning of the dehyphenation of India-Pakistan in the consideration of South Asian matters; this policy was developed further by the successive Bush administration.

For India, Washington's support during the Kargil crisis was, indeed, a positive signal that elevated its "political confidence" in the United States.[85] This positive trend was reinforced during President Clinton's long-awaited visit to India in March 2000. This long overdue visit had been initially planned as part of the Strategic Dialogue, launched in 1997, but was cancelled in the aftermath of the 1998 nuclear tests. Interestingly, during the Talbott-Singh dialogue, the presidential visit was used as a bargaining chip to get Indian signatures on the CTBT. Yet, in the absence of success on the nuclear front, Clinton went ahead with his trip.[86] It was the first visit of a U.S. president in seventeen years and was regarded as the "capstone of the major series of efforts"[87] to rejuvenate America's relationship with India.

Throughout the Talbott-Singh dialogue, both sides realized that there were boundless opportunities for cooperation. President Clinton on his state visit to India institutionalized a high-level, multi-tiered, and multi-faceted dialogue.[88] The "contours of détente" between the United States and India had begun to take shape during the Talbott-Singh dialogue and were laid out in the joint statement, *India-U.S. Relations: A Vision for the 21 st Century*.[89] The joint statement claimed, "At the dawn of a new century, President Clinton and Prime Minister Vajpayee resolve to create a closer and qualitatively new relationship between the two countries."[90] Several collaborative forums were also established, such as the U.S.-India Financial Economic Forum, the United States-India Commercial Dialogue, and the U.S.-India Working Group on Trade; in addition, the two nations agreed to cooperate on energy and the environment and pledged to set up a United States-India Science and Technology Forum. These steps taken by President Clinton were clear indications of a broadening and deepening of the United States' relationship with India. The softening of President Clinton's attitude toward nuclear India was clearly evident in his address to the joint session of the Indian parliament. He stated:

> Only India can determine its own interests. Only India can know if it truly is safer today than before the [Pokhran II] tests. Only India can determine if it will benefit from expanding its nuclear and missile capabilities, if its neighbors respond by doing the same thing. Only India

> knows if it can afford a sustained investment in both conventional and nuclear forces while meeting its goals for human development. These are questions others may ask, but only you [India] can answer.

In contrast to his earlier condemnation of the Pokhran II nuclear tests, President Clinton not only expressed the hope to completely bridge the nuclear nonproliferation divide with India, rather also desired to build a United States-India coalition against proliferation. He stated, "And let us turn our dialogue into a *genuine partnership against proliferation*. If we make progress in narrowing our differences, we will be both more secure, and our relationship can reach its full potential" (emphasis added).[91]

Thus, the Clinton administration created an upward swing in its bilateral relationship with India, but failed to make nuclear India adhere to the nonproliferation regime. During the Clinton era, there was considerable shifting of the nuclear goalposts and the nuclear nonproliferation objectives were reduced to what was possible, achievable, and consistent with the broader U.S. security and foreign policy objectives in South Asia. Moreover, the Talbott-Singh dialogue cleared the acrimony on several languishing nuclear issues and created space for the next administration to bridge the nuclear divide with India. Thus, the Clinton administration laid the groundwork for the subsequent shift in U.S. nuclear nonproliferation policy toward India.

NOTES

1. This chapter draws upon material reprinted by permission of Taylor & Francis LLC (http://www.tandfonline.com) from Bhatia, Vandana, "Non-proliferation Policy of the Clinton Administration toward India: Shifting of Nuclear Goalposts?" *Comparative Strategy* 32(3): 261–82.
2. Christine Fair, "India and the U.S.: Embracing a New Paradigm," in *Indian Foreign Policy in a Unipolar World*, ed., Harsh Pant (London: Routledge, 2009), 132.
3. Richard Haass, Testimony before the Senate Task Force on Economic Sanctions, Senate, 105th Congress, 2nd Session, Washington D.C., September 9, 1998. Available at http://www.brookings.edu/testimony/1998/0909sanctions_haass.aspx?rssid=sanctions (accessed March 10, 2009).
4. Strobe Talbott, U.S. Deputy Secretary of State, "U.S. Diplomacy in South Asia: A Progress Report," Address at the Brookings Institution, Washington D.C., November 12, 1998.
5. *Fact Sheet: India and Pakistan Sanctions*, USIS Washington File, June 18, 1998.
6. Thomas Graham Jr., "South Asia and the Future of Nuclear Non-Proliferation," *Arms Control Today* (May 28, 1998): 5.
7. *Fact Sheet: India and Pakistan Sanctions*, USIS Washington File, June 18, 1998.
8. Richard N. Haass, *Economic Sanctions: Too Much of a Bad Thing*, Brookings Policy Brief Series, no. 34 (Washington D.C.: Brookings Institution, June 1998). Available at http://www.brookings.edu/papers/1998/06sanctions_haass.aspx?rssid=sanctions (accessed March 10, 2009).
9. Haass, testimony, September 9, 1998.
10. Ibid.

11. Ambassador David L. Aaron, Testimony of the Undersecretary of Commerce for International trade, Hearing on India-Pakistan Nuclear Proliferation, Subcommittee on Asia and the Pacific, House Committee on International Relations, 105th Congress, 2nd Session, Washington D.C., June 18, 1998. Available at http://www.fas.org/spp/starwars/congress/1998_h/98061806_npo.html (accessed May 2, 2009).

12. Ibid. Amb. Aaron also informed that "U.S. exports to India in 1997 increased nine percent over 1996, and increased 81 percent between 1991, when India began its economic liberalization program and last year [1997]."

13. Ibid.

14. Ibid.

15. Ibid.

16. Sridhar Krishnaswami, "Trading Sanctions for Flexibility," *Frontline* 15, no. 16 (August 1–14, 1998), 45.

17. Richard Cronin, Barbara Leitch LePoer, Jonathan Medalia and Dianne Rennack, *India-Pakistan Nuclear Tests and U.S. Response,* CRS Report for Congress (Washington D.C.: Congressional Research Service, updated November 24, 1998),CRS-21; Robert M. Hathaway, "Confrontation and Retreat: The U.S. Congress and the South Asian Nuclear Tests," *Arms Control Today* (January-February 2000). Available at http://www.armscontrol.org/act/2000_01–02/rhjf00 (accessed March 8, 2009).

18. Krishnaswami, "Trading Sanctions for Flexibility," 26.

19. Dianne E. Rennack, "India-Pakistan: Current U.S. Economic Sanctions," CRS Report (Washington D.C.: Congressional Research Service, February 11, 2002), CRS-2.

20. Hathaway, "Confrontation and Retreat."

21. Dinshaw Mistry, "Diplomacy, Sanctions and the U.S. Nonproliferation Dialogue with India and Pakistan," *Asian Survey* 39, no. 5 (September/October 1999): 757.

22. Hathaway, "Confrontation and Retreat."

23. Rennack, "Current U.S. Economic Sanctions," CRS-2.

24. Interview with a non-proliferation scholar, anonymity requested, Washington D.C., February 2009.

25. Madeleine Albright, in her remarks to the press, stated, "Sanctions that have no waivers and do not provide any flexibility make it very difficult to carry out a foreign policy that allows us to do the kinds of things we are trying to do." Secretary of State, Madeleine K. Albright *Press Remarks on India and Pakistan,* Office of the Spokesman, U.S. Department of State, Washington D.C., June 3, 1998.

26. Madeleine K. Albright, Interview by Wolf Blitzer, Late Edition, CNN, June 14, 1998, *Transcript: Secretary of State Albright's CNN Interview,* Office of the U.S. Spokesman, U.S. Department of State, June 15, 1998. In the same interview, she also mentioned, "the Glenn Amendment as it is currently written—doesn't allow for any incentives. There is no way to induce those two countries, from our perspective, to get better behavior. So what happens is we launch [the sanctions]—we have all the sticks or the sledge hammers and then other countries can go in and pick up the contract." Albright meant that while the U.S. imposed unilateral sanctions, other countries would rush to benefit from the opportunities abdicated by Washington.

27. Karl F. Inderfurth, Statement of the Assistant Secretary of State for South Asian affairs, Subcommittee on Near Eastern and South Asian Affairs, Senate Foreign Relations Committee, July 13, 1998. Available at http://www.fas.org/spp/starwars/congress/1998_h/98071303_npo.html (accessed March 8, 2009).

28. Ibid.

29. See, Cronin et al; Hathaway, "Confrontation and Retreat."

30. Hathaway, "Confrontation and Retreat."

31. Mistry, "Diplomacy," 757.

32. Howard Diamond, "U.S. Waives Many Test-Related Sanctions on India, Pakistan," *Arms Control Today* (November/December 1998). Available at http://legacy.armscontrol.org/act/1998_11–12/ipnd98.asp (accessed March 8, 2009).

33. Ibid.

34. Mistry, "Diplomacy," 761; Hathaway, "Confrontation and Retreat."

35. Randy J. Rydell, "Giving Nonproliferation Norms Teeth: Sanctions and the NPT," *Nonproliferation Review* 6, no. 2 (Winter 1999): 15.

36. Hathaway, "Confrontation and Retreat"

37. Senator Glenn, "Nuclear Weapons and Sanctions," *Congressional Record* 144, 105th Congress, 2nd Session, July 6, 1998, p.S-7350.

38. C. Uday Bhaskar, "Systemic Compulsions in India-U.S. Relations," in *India-U.S. Relations: Addressing the Challenges of the 21st Century*, ed., N.S Sisodia, Peter R. Lavoy, Cherian Samuel and Robin Walker (Delhi: Magnum Books, September 2008), 26; Brajesh Mishra, Principal Secretary to the then Prime Minister of India, held parallel dialogues with British and French counterparts; though these talks were not as intensive and prolonged as with the United States.

39. Strobe Talbott, in an email response to the questionnaire submitted by the author, April 20, 2009.

40. Kanti Bajpai, "India-U.S. Foreign Policy Concerns: Cooperation and Conflict," in *Engaging India: U.S. Strategic Relations with the World's Largest Democracy*, ed., Gary K. Bertsch, Seema Gahlaut and Anupam Srivastava (New York: Routledge, 1999), 202.

41. Washington also undertook a parallel series of dialogue with Pakistan, but the US-Pakistan dialogue is beyond the scope of this book.

42. After his election to the Indian Parliament, Jaswant Singh was inducted into the Cabinet as the Foreign Minister of India (December 1998–July 2002).

43. Selig S. Harrison, "Dialogue of the Deaf: Mutual Perceptions and Indo-American Relations," in *Conflicting Images*, ed., Sulochana Raghavan Glazer and Nathan Glazer, (Glen Dale, MD: Riverdale, 1990).

44. Bhabani Mishra, "India-U.S. Relations: A Paradigm Shift," *Strategic Analysis* 29, no. 1, (January-March 2005): 84; Also see, Sukumar Muralidharan, "On to the Next Round," *Frontline* 16, no. 3 (January 30–15 February, 1999). Available at http://www.hindu.com/fline/fl1603/16030970.htm (accessed March 21, 2009).

45. Inderfurth, testimony, July 13, 1998.

46. As quoted in, Chidanand Rajghatta, "American Sanctions Will Go Soon, Says Inderfurth," *The Indian Express (Mumbai)*, August 31, 1998.

47. J.N. Dixit, "Indo-U.S. Relations: Delhi Dialogue and After," *Rediff News*, February 11, 1999. Available at www.rediff.com/news/1999feb/11dixit.htm (accessed March 10, 2009). The U.S. delegation consisted of Karl Inderfurth; Vice-Chairman of the U.S. Joint Chiefs of Staff Committee General Joseph Ralston; Assistant Secretary in Charge of Disarmament Robert Einhorn; a representative from the National Security Council dealing with South Asia; and Matthew P. Daley, who had served as deputy chief of mission at the U.S. Embassy in India, 1993–1997.

48. Initially, it seems the dialogue included other nuclear issues which were subsequently dropped. Indian Prime Minister Vajpayee, in his Statement to the Parliament, noted that "after six rounds of talks, Indo-U.S. discussions narrowed down to four issues": the CTBT, the Fissile Material Cut-off Treaty, export controls, and defence posture. See, A. B. Vajpayee, *Bilateral Talks with United States*, Statement of the Prime Minister in the Parliament, December 15, 1998, in *Strategic Digest* 24, no. 1 (January 1999): 3.

49. Talbott, "*Progress Report*," November 12, 1998.

50. Ibid. Regarding the strategic restraint, Talbott also remarked, "In keeping with their (India and Pakistan) stated desire to define their security requirements at the lowest possible levels, we have urged India and Pakistani counterparts to consider strategic measures–a package of prudent constraints on the development, flight testing and storage of missiles and also on the basing of nuclear capable aircraft."; Also see, Strobe Talbott, "Dealing with the Bomb in South Asia," *Foreign Affairs* 78, no. 2 (March–April 1999): 110–22.

51. "CTBT Issue: India 'Eager' to Secure Some Concessions," *The Hindustan Times* (New Delhi), July 5, 1998; Also see, "India May Sign NPT, CTBT if Conditions Met," *Times of India* (New Delhi), June 8, 1999. Reportedly, India sought waiver from the restrictions on transfer of dual-use technologies and partial removal of sanctions.

52. Dixit, "Indo-U.S. Relations."

53. Prime Minister Atal Bihari Vajpayee, Address to the 53rd United Nations General Assembly, New York, September 24, 1998. He stated, "India, having harmonized its national imperatives and security obligations and desirous of continuing to cooperate with the international community is now engaged in discussions with key interlocutors on a range of issues, including the CTBT. We are prepared to bring these discussions to a successful conclusion, so that the entry into force of the CTBT is not delayed beyond September 1999." Also see, Muralidhar Reddy, "India May Sign CTBT Next Year," *The Hindu* (Chennai), November 26, 1998.

54. Madeline Albright, prepared statement of the Secretary of State, Hearings before the Committee on Foreign Relations and the Subcommittee on International Operations of the U.S. Senate, *Fiscal Year 2000 Budget and Embassy Security for a New Millennium*, Senate, U.S. Congress, 106th Congress, 1st Session (February 24, 1999), 18. Albright mentioned, "Following last May's [1998] nuclear tests, we worked with India and Pakistan to prevent a nuclear arms race. Both agreed to adhere to the CTBT by year's end [1999], join negotiations for a fissile materials production cutoff and tighten export controls."

55. Talbott, email, April 20, 2009 (pls. see note. 39).

56. Bajpai, "Cooperation and Conflict," 203.

57. Ibid.

58. "CTBT signing by September Unlikely: PM," *The Times of India* (Mumbai), 1 May 1999.

59. Senior Advisor for Arms Control and International Security, John D. Holum, *Remarks to the Foreign Policy Association*, New York, February 16, 2000. Available at www.state.gov/www/global/arms/remarks/holum/holum_fp.html (accessed March 10, 2009).

60. Shri Jaswant Singh, External Affairs Minister of India, Speech to the 54th Session of the United Nations General Assembly, New York, United Nations, September 22, 1999. He mentioned, "Notwithstanding India's readiness to engage in constructive negotiations on a treaty to prohibit the future production of fissile materials for nuclear weapons and nuclear explosive devices, the Conference on Disarmament in Geneva has so far, sadly, been unable to register any forward movement."

61. Ibid.

62. O. P. Sabherwal, "Real Hurdles in Indo-Pak Talks," *The Tribune* (Chandigarh), January 20, 1999.

63. Michael Krepon, "Engaging India," Review of *Engaging India: Diplomacy, Democracy and the Bomb*, Strobe Talbott, *Arms Control Today* 34 (September 2004). Available at www.armscontrol.org/act/2004–09/bookreviews (accessed March 10, 2009).

64. "U.S. Wants India to Specify its Nuclear Deterrent Needs," *Asia Times Online*, January 8, 1999; Also see, "Nukes: Mind Your Own Business, U.S. Told," *Economic Times*, January 7, 1999. Richard Celeste's remark that created a furore in India was: "How many missile systems and warheads does India need to have a minimum nuclear deterrent?"

65. In this context, Ashley Tellis wrote, "India still does not know what its force-in-being will look like when it is eventually completed. . . . The nuclear deterrent New Delhi desires is still several years and possibly up to two decades from completion." Ashley Tellis, *Nuclear Posture: Between Recessed Deterrent and Ready Arsenal* (Santa Monica, CA: RAND, 2001), 759.

66. Sukumar Muralidharan, "On to the Next Round," *Frontline* 16, no. 3 (January 30–15 February 1999). Available at www.hindu.com/fline/fl1603/16030970 (accessed April 05, 2009).

67. C. Raja Mohan, "China Slams India's Nuclear Talks," *The Hindu* (Chennai), 18 January 1999.

68. K.V. Krishnaswamy, "Celeste Defends Demand on Deterrence," *The Hindu* (Chennai), January 23, 1999.

69. Strobe Talbott, as quoted in, C. Raja Mohan, "Early Solution to Nuclear Issues Will Help: Talbott," *The Hindu* (Chennai), January 14, 2000.

70. Draft Report of National Security Advisory Board (NSAB) on Indian Nuclear Doctrine, Ministry of External Affairs, Government of India, India, August 17 1999.

71. Ashley J. Tellis, *India's Emerging Nuclear Doctrine: Exemplifying the Lessons of the Nuclear Revolution* (Seattle: National Bureau of Asian Research, 2001), 2.

72. Krepon, "Engaging India."

73. Dixit, "Indo-U.S. Relations."

74. Anupam Srivastava, "Indo-U.S. Strategic Dialogue: From Sound Bytes to Sound Decisions," *Bharat Rakshak Monitor* 2, no. 4 (January–February 2000). He further states, "But strangely, the country [India] has shied away from a clearer dissemination of the stringent controls that it has voluntarily imposed over a range of wherewithal and related know-how. Partly as a consequence to this approach, it has neither received the considerable economic benefits and strategic leverage that such transfers would have yielded, nor did it receive international recognition for its responsible behavior."

75. Samantha F. Ravich, "Nuclear Nonproliferation and the Cases of Russia, China and India," in *The Challenge of Proliferation: A Report of the Aspen Strategy Group*, ed., Kurt Campbell (Washington D.C.: The Aspen Institute, February 2005), 107.

76. Talbott, email response, April 20, 2009 (pls. see note 39).

77. Mohan, "Early Solutions."

78. Ibid.

79. Interview with Ambassador Thomas Pickering, March 2009.

80. Rajghatta, "American Sanctions Will Go Soon"; Also see, Strobe Talbott, *Address at India International Center*, 30 January 1999, New Delhi.

81. Jaswant Singh, Interview by Amberish K. Diwanji, "India in Neither in the First, Second or Third World, India is a World in Its Own Right," *Rediff On The Net*, May 11, 1999. Available at http://www.rediff.com/news/1999/may/11bomb.htm (accessed January 26, 2009).

82. Krepon, "Engaging India."

83. Interview with Stephen Cohen, specialist on South Asian affairs, February 2009.

84. Ibid.

85. Mishra, "India-U.S. Relations," 84; also see, Strobe Talbott, *Engaging India: Diplomacy, Democracy and the Bomb*, (Washington D.C.: Brookings Institution Press, 2004), 154–69.

86. As a reflection of change in approach toward South Asia, President Clinton made a six-day visit to India, with only a five hour stopover in Pakistan. He also visited Bangladesh during this trip and thus, became the first American president to visit that country.

87. Pickering, interview, March 2009.

88. It included regular bilateral summit meetings and an Annual Foreign Policy Dialogue to be held between the U.S. secretary of state and the external affairs minister of India to improve mutual understanding of bilateral, regional, and international security matters. *India-U.S. Relations: A Vision for the 21st Century,* Joint India-U.S. Statement, March 21, 2000. Available at http://www.indianembassy.org/indusrel/clinton_india/joint_india_us_statement_mar_21_2000.htm (accessed January 26, 2009).

89. Fair, "Learning to Think," 49. In the joint statement, both leaders proclaimed that: "In the new century, India and the United States will be partners in peace, with a common interest in and complementary responsibility for ensuring regional and international security. We will engage in regular consultations on, and work together for, strategic stability in Asia and beyond. We will bolster joint efforts to counter terrorism and meet other challenges to regional peace. We will strengthen the international security system, including in the United Nations and support the United Nations in its peacekeeping efforts."

90. Joint India-U.S. Statement, March 21, 2000.

91. Clinton, "Joint Session of Indian Parliament," March 22, 2000.

FIVE

Reorientation of the Nonproliferation Regime

Re-Imagining India

As discussed in the previous chapter, that in the aftermath of the Pokhran II nuclear tests, the United States revised its punitive approach toward India, the defacto nuclear weapon state, and initiated nuclear bargaining. Yet, it failed to bridge the nuclear divide with India. President Clinton lacked the strategic vision as well as the determination to resolve the nuclear issues with India. His approach, embedded in Cold War thinking, proved to be ad hoc and reactionary. The Bush administration came to power in the year 2001 with the vision of strengthening relations with India and picked up the hitherto unresolved nuclear agenda. The nuclear pact with India is considered an extension of the qualitative transformation of U.S.-India relations during the Bush era. It is generally regarded that President Bush intended to develop a U.S.-India strategic partnership against China, and therefore, signed the civilian nuclear cooperation pact with India. This implies that the Bush administration compromised nonproliferation objectives to achieve foreign policy objectives. Nonetheless, I argue that such explanations are contentious and reflect a knowledge deficit regarding the rationale for the U.S.-India nuclear agreement. In an interview with the author, Philip Zelikow stated, "One of the misunderstandings about this [U.S.-India nuclear pact] is that we made this decision to balance the power of China. And that may have been a motivation for some people who supported the agreement but it was not a motivation for us [the decision-makers], i.e, President Bush, Secretary Rice, Robert Zoellick, or me."[1]

In this chapter, I critically analyze the Bush administration's approach toward nuclear nonproliferation regime, and its attempt to reset the anomalous relation with India. In this regard, this chapter explores: What was the approach of the Bush administration toward the nuclear nonproliferation regime (NPR) and how it contributed to re-imagining of India? What was the administration's approach toward nuclear energy, with regard to India? What did the strategic partnership with India entail? What was the significance of the strategic trade measures—High Technology Cooperation Group (HTCG) and the Next Steps in Strategic Partnership (NSSP)?

This chapter is divided into five sections. The first section is an attempt to understand the strategic partnership with India. The second section examines Bush's nuclear prism and the reorientation of the nuclear regime. It also focuses on the re-imagining of India as a potential partner in curtailing proliferation of weapons of mass destruction (WMD). The third section highlights the renewed emphasis on nuclear energy and recognition of India's inevitable requirement for nuclear energy. The fourth section focuses on the U.S.-India strategic trade measures, the High Technology Cooperation Group, and the Next Steps in Strategic Partnership which created, hitherto absent, mutual trust and confidence building in advanced technology transfers. I contend that the nuclear deal between the United States and India was a product of the reorientation of the nuclear nonproliferation regime which not only necessitated rather also created space for engaging India. The Bush administration realized the potential of India as a potent force in strengthening the nonproliferation regime. Unlike previous administrations, the Bush administration affirmed India's legitimate civilian nuclear energy requirements and was open to exploring ways to balance U.S. nonproliferation objectives with the inevitably growing energy needs of India. Through a series of bilateral high technology commerce initiatives, based on the innovative approach of reciprocal obligations, Washington convinced India to strengthen its domestic laws as well as its export controls. Accordingly, India's positive steps aroused confidence in the Bush administration that encouraged them to proceed to gradually lift technological barriers. Subsequently, the Bush administration was able to achieve the hitherto seemingly impossible task of balancing its nuclear nonproliferation goals with India's quest for advanced dual-use technologies. Concomitantly, it was able to accommodate the ever elusive nuclear India, i.e., the anomaly within the nuclear regime.

SECURITY COOPERATION

As discussed previously, the Clinton administration launched the U.S.-India relationship into an upward trajectory; this trend was carried further during the Bush era. But, as the Bush administration reoriented the bilateral relationship, it was not an asymmetrical transition. India too juxtaposed its nonalignment policy and showed considerable support for its "natural ally,"[2] now also called a "civilizational ally."[3]

Soon after coming to power, the Bush administration began contemplating removal of the sanctions imposed on India in 1998.[4] In June 2001, the U.S. ambassador-designate to India, Robert Blackwill argued that the U.S. strategy of imposing sanctions against India had not worked and suggested a brisk removal. He thought the best way to achieve the U.S. nonproliferation objectives was to build a "broad, comprehensive, and robust relationship with India."[5] In August 2001, a senior administration official indicated the "almost certain lifting of American economic and military sanctions imposed on India."[6] The decision to remove sanctions was delayed as the administration was contemplating "the question of how and whether to also lift sanctions on Pakistan." Nonetheless, the launch of the Global War on Terror (GWOT) after the terrorist attacks in the United States on September 11, 2001 (hereafter 9/11) increased the geopolitical significance of Pakistan and "expedited" the decision to lift the sanctions against it.[7]

On September 22, 2001, President Bush issued an executive order to lift all remaining nuclear related sanctions against India and Pakistan.[8] Welcoming removal of the sanctions, the Indian finance minister, Yashwant Sinha, remarked that it was a minor issue as the sanctions had already spent themselves. He asserted, "as far as the Indian economy was concerned, except for certain defense supplies, sanctions had no meaning."[9] Nonetheless, it was indeed a positive step for ending acrimony in the bilateral relationship. Furthermore, in the aftermath of the 9/11 attacks India had immediately offered to assist Washington in any possible manner. India itself had been a victim of terror for several years and the Global War on Terror vindicated its long standing claim that terrorist camps flourished in the Afghan-Pakistan sector.[10] The 9/11 incidents caused the United States to revamp its strategy in South Asia. In this context, McMillan argues, "We [the U.S.] were changing the way we looked at Pakistan, the way we looked at India. We were looking for allies and partners wherever we could find [them]."[11] At the summit meeting of President Bush and Prime Minister Vajpayee on November 9, 2001, the process of reorienting the bilateral relationship was unleashed. It culminated in several path-breaking measures that enabled the two countries to realign their divergent interests.

STRATEGIC PARTNERSHIP

"Strategic partnership" was a relatively new term employed by the Bush administration to signify the relationship it intended to develop with

India. With no proper definition and lack of historical precedent, the term was largely misunderstood. Viewed narrowly in the Cold War perspective the strategic partnership was mistaken as an alliance to maintain the Asian geopolitical balance of power, specifically directed against China. On the contrary, the Bush administration wanted to enlist India's support at a global level for the shaping of the future world order. In the words of Nicholas Burns:

> As Washington thought about how best to contend with the greatest Globalization's challenges—international drug and criminal cartels trafficking in women and children, climate change and especially the rise of terrorism and its potential intersection with the Weapons of Mass Destruction—it became clear to most of us in the U.S. government that we needed to combine forces with powerful emerging countries such as India (Brazil, Indonesia, and South Africa) to respond to these threats.[12]

Thus, the U.S. strategic partnership with India was not intended as an alliance directed against any single country, its object was to enhance joint capabilities to deal with the multitudinous and complex threats of the post–9/11 world. Kenneth Juster defines "strategic partners" as "two major global powers in the world effectively collaborating on and addressing some of the strategic issues that we are or will be facing throughout the 21st century."[13] It was not meant to be a formal alliance. That is, India was not expected to take *diktat* from the United States nor did the latter expect a quid pro quo from the former. As Blackwill affirmed, the United States and India are natural allies because of the long term comprehensive national interests and "not because of any current or future organizational connection." He emphasized, "There will be no formal alliance between the two countries." Yet, "this does not mean that Washington and New Delhi will always agree on specific policies or tactics. That will not happen."[14] This was clearly evident in 2003 with the launch of the U.S.-led war against Iraq. Despite the burgeoning defense cooperation involving joint military exercises, India refused to contribute its troops to the U.S. mission because the Iraqi invasion did not have a mandate from the United Nations. Although Washington desired India to join, India's refusal to do so did not affect the bilateral relationship.

The Bush administration marked a significant departure from the previously held U.S. perception of India as "a persistent nonproliferation problem that required an American imposed solution."[15] Washington had traditionally viewed India in the narrow South Asian context, now it saw India as a player in the Asian and global balance of power.[16] The inevitable rise of India as a global power was emphasized in the influential report of the U.S. National Intelligence Council, *Mapping the Global Future.* Highlighting the tectonic changes that were manifesting, it stated, "The likely emergence of China and India . . . as new major global players—similar to the advent of a united Germany in the 19th Century and a powerful United States in the early 20th Century—will transform the geopolitical landscape."[17] This would, interalia, "have the potential to render obsolete the old categories of East and West, North and South, aligned and nonaligned, developed and developing."[18]

Not surprisingly, within a year of the beginning of the Bush administration there was a significant revival of Indo-U.S. security cooperation. The foundations were laid under the leadership of Secretary of De fence Donald Rumsfeld, who saw great potential in defense cooperation with India. Soon after the sanctions were removed, in November 2001, Rumsfeld visited India to discuss with George Fernandes, his Indian counterpart, the hitherto prohibited issues of arms sale and the revival of defense cooperation.[19] Thereafter, U.S.-India security cooperation and dual military interaction has been unprecedented in "scale, scope, range, and frequency of joint exercises."[20] Lalit Mansingh, the then ambassador to the United States, claimed it was the "most visible manifestation of our new [strategic] relationship."[21] Subsequently, in December 2001 the defunct Defense Policy Group (DPG) was revived. In a joint statement of the Defense Policy Group, the two sides affirmed the significance of the defense relationship to "assist both countries to counter threats such as the spread of weapons of mass destruction, international terrorism, narcotics trafficking, and [sea] piracy."[22] The DPG had been established in 1995 during the Clinton era with a scope limited to the promotion of mutual understanding through joint exercises and high-level visits.[23] However, until 1997, the two countries had undertaken only five joint exercises of the armed forces; but, since the revival of the group the armed forces held "mutually beneficial combined exercises"[24] every single year.[25] The purpose behind these exercises was to build U.S.-India military synergy through interoperability in difficult terrains and inhospitable climes as well as to enhance communication and coordination.[26]

Within the broader parameters of the DPG, in 2002 a Security Cooperation Group (SCG) and a Joint Technical Group (JTG) were established to negotiate the significant issue of military arms transfer, joint research and development (R&D), and the production of defense technology.[27] Anupam Srivastava observes that, in a series of assessments since 2002, the Pentagon realized that if the firewalls regarding dual-use technologies were removed, the joint U.S.-India co-production of defense weapons systems could benefit both countries.[28] Stressing the significance of the sale of military transfers to India, Blackwill remarked,

> Of course we should sell advanced weaponry to India. The million-man army actually fights, unlike the post-modern militaries of many of our European allies. Given the strategic challenges ahead, the United States should want the Indian armed forces to be equipped with the best weapons systems, and that often means buying American.[29]

Significantly, the 2001 DPG meeting recognized that both India and the U.S. have been targets of terrorism, therefore, defense cooperation for counterterrorism purposes is crucial.[30] Thomas Pickering aptly reflects that prior to 9/11 the United States was oblivious of India's persistent problem of terrorism. He remarks, India "faced serious terrorist problems and had been facing them for many years whether they were insurgencies in Assam or . . . banditry in Andhra Pradesh or, in fact, a series of very devastating bomb explosions in Mumbai 1993."[31] It was only as a consequence of 9/11 that the United States became aware of the terrorism issues in South Asia. Yet, he further clarifies that it was only in the aftermath of the November 2008 Mumbai attacks that U.S.-India counterterrorism cooperation was considerably strengthened.[32] The Mumbai terrorist acts made the United States realize the enormity of the threat faced by India, the lone stable democratic nation in the South Asian region.

Thus, the U.S.-India comprehensive security cooperation, termed as a strategic partnership contrary to the general perception, was based on the convergence of interests. It included the conduct of joint military exercises, counterterrorism cooperation, improvement of the defense-supply relationship, and defense coproduction. The DPG served as a significant forum for high-level policy dialogue and formulation of initiatives to achieve mutual security interests.

BUSH'S NUCLEAR PRISM

The Bush administration has been criticized for its relative indifference to traditional measures of bilateral and multilateral strategic arms control and nuclear nonproliferation. Critics argue that the Anti-Ballistic Missile (ABM) treaty was sidelined, "the CTBT [Comprehensive Test Ban Treaty] was left comatose, Strategic Arms Reduction (START-3) was allowed to lie, and the Nuclear Nonproliferation Treaty (NPT) was largely ignored."[33] Yet, the critics fail to realize that during the Bush era the issue of proliferation of weapons of mass destruction had acquired new dimensions that mandated a change in approach to emerging threats.

Since the disintegration of the Soviet Union there were concerns regarding the proliferation of nuclear technologies, weapons, and transfer of nuclear know-how into wrong hands intent on exploding "dirty bombs."[34] Subsequently, the potential nexus between rogue states and terrorist groups created additional apprehensions. In the post–9/11 era, the threat of nuclear trafficking and terrorism acquired certain urgency. This does not mean that the proliferation threats simply shifted from state proliferators to nonstate actors. Rather, the threats associated with the proliferation of nuclear materials have become multidimensional in nature. As Lewis Dunn remarks, "The nations of the world confront today multiple proliferation challenges. Indeed, these challenges may well be more severe than at any time since the dawn of the nuclear age in 1945."[35] In January 2001, the Baker-Cutler Task Force Report highlighted the threat of nuclear terrorism. According to this report, "*the most urgent unmet threat*" to the United States' national security is the "*danger that the weapons of mass destruction or weapons-useable material in Russia could be stolen and sold to terrorists or hostile nation-states and used against American troops abroad or citizens at home*" (emphasis in original).[36] In addition, there were reports that al-Qaeda leaders responsible for the 9/11 attacks were actively seeking nuclear, chemical, and biological weapons to use in attacks in the United States and other places. After the launch of the Global War on Terror and the stationing of troops in Afghanistan, there was confirmation of the plans for development of "rudimentary nuclear weapons . . . in an al-Qaeda safe house in Kabul."[37] Thus, it was emerging that terrorist groups are intent to escalate the jihad (a holy war waged by Muslims against infidels) to the next level (related to the 9/11 attack on the United States) by relying on explosions of crude bombs.

The Bush administration was quick to realize that the threat of nuclear proliferation was "diverse, unpredictable, dangerous, and increasingly difficult to counter."[38] Previously, state-sponsored weapons programs were the primary proliferation concerns, but now, "the acquisition of weapons of mass destruction by nonstate actors and terrorist groups" was "an equally significant threat."[39] Due to the increasing complexity of WMD threats, President Bush highlighted the vulnerability of America. He stated:

> The greatest threat before humanity today is the possibility of secret and sudden attack with chemical or biological or radiological or nuclear weapons. In the past, *enemies of America required massed armies and great navies, powerful air forces to put our nation, our people, our friends and allies at risk.*[40] (emphasis added)

Bush acknowledged that the threat from WMD existed during the Cold War as well but, earlier, the hostile states could be countered through deterrence. The possession of a credible deterrent ensured the enemy would rely on nuclear weapons as "weapons of last resort."[41] In the contemporary era, for the fanatics and terrorists these are the weapons of "first resort—the preferred means to further their ideology of suicide and random murder." Chemical, biological, radiological, and nuclear weapons are easier "to acquire, build, hide, and transport" than conventional weapons. Therefore, Bush rightly emphasized that this necessitated a "change in thinking and strategy."[42] Nuclear weapons, once valued as weapons of deterrence, are considerably ineffective against the contemporary Hydra (many headed) form of terrorism and the lurking threat of dirty bomb explosions. In addition, the NPT-centric regime is focused on curtailing the proliferation of nuclear technology to states and as such there is a paucity of measures to deal with the emergent challenges of the "second nuclear age."

Discovery of the "nuclear Wal-Mart" that had flourished since 1987 and was engaged in black marketing of sensitive dual use technologies confirmed the fears regarding illicit nuclear trafficking. This nuclear racket was spearheaded by A. Q. Khan, the father of Pakistan's nuclear weapons program, who also functioned as "the director of the network, its leading scientific mind, as well as its primary salesman."[43] It took several years for the American and British intelligence services to penetrate this network and a primary factory in Malaysia was found to be engaged in building parts of a nuclear centrifuge and supplying it worldwide.[44] This directed attention to two interrelated problems that abetted illicit nuclear trafficking: The first was "onward proliferation" whereby "one proliferator supplies another," thus forming a chain of proliferators; the second was the "subcontract" or outsourcing of the manufacture of nuclear related technologies.[45] Due to the absence of export laws in Malaysia, nuclear centrifuge reactors were being manufactured in its territories and subsequently shipped to several places around the world enroute to Libya.[46] This highlighted the ineffectiveness of traditional measures to deal effectively with the changing nature of proliferation threats.

The Bush administration, cognizant of the vitiated nuclear scenario, realized the dire need to supplement the NPT-centric regime with innovative measures to enhance interdiction and enforcement capabilities to curb newer threats of illicit WMD proliferation. The increased emphasis on pursuing a proactive approach toward curtailing the spread of WMD technologies was reflected in the National Security Strategy to Combat Weapons of Mass Destruction (2002). It stated that the Bush administration would seek to "enhance the capabilities of our military, intelligence, technical, and law enforcement communities to prevent the movement of WMD materials, technology, and expertise to hostile states and terrorist organizations."[47] This marked a distinct shift toward NPT-plus measures.

In 2004 in a significant speech at the National Defense University, Washington, DC, President Bush elaborated his multi-pronged strategy to deal with a wide range of WMD proliferation threats. He emphasized "active nonproliferation, counter proliferation, and missile defenses" as measures necessary to complement the traditional nonproliferation methods.[48] Active nonproliferation can be understood as measures for securing sensitive materials within the borders of legitimate recipients or supplier states. In this context, President Bush outlined the following protocol: first, the supply of civilian nuclear technologies will be restricted to states that sign the IAEA Additional Protocol; second, a special committee will be created from IAEA boards to focus intensively on verification and safeguards; third, IAEA board positions will be denied to states under investigation for illicit nuclear activities, such as Iran; fourth, domestic and international laws will be strengthened to enact strict export controls to contain the proliferation of dual-use technologies; finally, the Nuclear Suppliers Group (NSG) provision will be modified to include the adoption of full-scope safeguards by the recipient before the sale of uranium enrichment and reprocessing technologies.[49] Through these measures President Bush aimed to strengthen the nonproliferation regime by introducing internal reforms in the IAEA and export controls. Conforming to the active nonproliferation measures, the Bush administration engaged India in high-tech commerce (2002–2005), alongside, seeking the latter's conformation to domestic and international technological restrictions. Subsequently, through the July 2005 agreement, the United States was able to induce India to adopt IAEA safeguards for civilian facilities.

Counterproliferation emerged as a central component of the Bush nuclear scheme to curb WMD proliferation. Counterproliferation measures had previously been adopted but they had low priority in the U.S. strategy.[50] The Clinton administration defined counterproliferation as the "full range of military preparations and activities under the Department of Defense (DoD) to reduce threats from [nuclear] delivery systems."[51] Departing from nuclear orthodoxy, in a *sui generis* approach, the Bush administration instituted several measures to curb the danger of nonstate actors smuggling weapons of mass destruction and related technologies. These included programs such as the Proliferation Security Initiative (PSI),[52] the Container Security Initiative (CSI), and the Megaports Initiative[53] promoted by the U.S. security and enforcement agencies through cooperation with friendly states. The CSI was launched in 2002 by the U.S. Customs and Border Protection, under the aegis of the Department of Homeland Security, to identify and screen containers for suspicious materials. That is, it became mandatory at foreign ports to identify and inspect all containers before they are loaded onto the vessels bound for the United States.[54] The PSI was a U.S.-led multilateral initiative to interdict and "search planes and ships carrying suspect cargo and to seize illegal weapons or missile technologies."[55] Subsequently, President Bush called for broadening the scope of the PSI, that is, moving beyond simply interdiction of shipments and transfers to take law enforcement actions such as, "to shut down the [illegal] labs, seize their materials, [and] freeze their assets."[56]

In April 2004, the Bush administration spearheaded efforts for a unanimous adoption of U.N. Security Council Resolution (UNSCR) 1540. Under Chapter VII of the U.N. charter, UNSCR 1540 makes it mandatory for states to criminalize the proliferation of WMD and related technologies, to institute domestic measures to strengthen their export controls, and to secure sensitive items. The resolution does not specifically mention PSI or CSI initiatives, but indirectly supports these measures. Paragraph 3 of UNSCR 1540 requires states "to enforce effective measures to establish domestic controls to prevent the proliferation of nuclear, chemical, or biological weapons and their means of delivery, including by establishing appropriate controls over related materials."[57] In accordance with the provisions of UNSCR 1540, India in mid-2005 adopted domestic legislation to further strengthen its export controls regarding sensitive items.[58] Viewed in conjunction with the PSI and the CSI, this resolution demonstrated a change in the U.S. approach in encouraging cooperative actions to thwart nuclear trafficking and nuclear terrorism.

During the Cold War, bilateral arms control was a high priority for the United States as it sought to curtail the offensive arms race with its arch nuclear rival the Soviet Union. The ABM treaty, signed and entered into force in 1972, prohibited both the United States and the Soviet Union from "deploying nationwide defenses against strategic ballistic missiles."[59] With the demise of the Soviet Union there was a gradual decline in arms control measures. Although the Bush administration unequivocally expressed disinterest in arms control measures, yet this lower priority can actually be traced to the Clinton administration. In this context, Saunders comments, "Despite greater potential for arms control to produce substantive accomplishments in the post Cold War period . . . the Clinton administration did not initiate a single successful arms control treaty."[60]

Futhermore, in May 2001, President Bush unequivocally declared the 1972 ABM treaty was no longer relevant to the changing nuclear nonproliferation scenario, and it was time for the United States "to move beyond the constraints of the 30-year-old treaty."[61] The rationale offered by the Bush administration was that Russia was no longer a predominant threat, yet the United States had to shield itself from potential missile attacks from rogue states or nonstate actors. Thus, the administration advocated building a missile defense system to protect against "missiles in the hands of these states, states for whom terror and blackmail are a way of life."[62] President Bush received considerable criticism for withdrawing from the ABM treaty and initiating the NMD program, but this trend toward NMD had been developing within Washington during the previous administration as well. Actually, after the demise of the Soviet Union, in accordance with the Law of State Succession, the fate of the ABM treaty became unclear.[63] Yet, the Clinton administration emphasized that the treaty was in force and in 1997 signed a Memorandum of Understanding with the Russian Federation, Belarus, Kazakhstan, and Ukraine. But this memorandum was not submitted to the Senate for approval. Second, within the United States there was a growing inclination toward the limited National Missile Defense (NMD) and Congress supported the proposal. The Clinton administration provided conditional approval to NMD based on the considerations of technological readiness, assessment of rogue state missile threats, related costs, and arms control factors.[64]

RE-IMAGINING INDIA: A "RESPONSIBLE" PARTNER

With the increasing dialogue and comprehensive cooperation, Washington began to realize that India, despite being outside the regime, had maintained a high standard of nonproliferation. This perception was strengthened by the knowledge that illegal proliferation activities had been occurring in the South Asian region since the mid-1980s, yet India was not involved in any such activities. In fact, as a senior official at the Nuclear Regulatory Commission remarked, "India has been miscast as a proliferator. India may have created a program for itself but there is very little evidence that India has ever done anything to proliferate beyond its borders." Thus, India fits with the western image of a "nonproliferator."[65] On the other hand, Pakistan was "caught red–handed" with the A. Q. Khan network that was not only engaged in fetching technology for Pakistan, it was also passing nuclear technology around the world. Similarly, North Korean nuclear technology ended up in the Middle East because the North Koreans were in dire need of money.[66] Several high-ranking officials in the Bush administration shared the perception that India, despite being nonparticipant in the NPT regime, had adhered to nonproliferation norms.[67] Kenneth Juster, undersecretary for industry and security, stated, India "had an excellent record of not being involved in proliferation activities."[68] Similarly, Nicholas Burns avers, "The nonproliferation system was very weak; a large country, India, was outside whereas there were others inside the system that were cheating—like North Korea and Iran."[69] Burns emphasizes, India "was not an outlaw. It had not broken any treaty [NPT] because it had not signed any treaty."[70]

Furthermore, the Bush administration engaged in curtailing WMD proliferation by instituting NPT–plus measures such as NMD, the PSI, and the CSI, and sought India's cooperation. Moreover, India, due to its growing technological prowess, geographical location, and economy, could play a significant role in the new security architecture. President Bush emphasized the need to replace arms control treaties that had lost their relevance. India, given its disdain for the NPT and CTBT, was enthusiastic for Bush's innovative framework for a new post–Cold War nuclear edifice that is, replacing previous discriminatory treaties with a cooperative security regime, based on missile defense and counter-proliferation. Thus, adoption of the new measures by the Bush administration created space to engage India as a partner in nonproliferation.

The decision of the Bush administration to withdraw from the ABM treaty and build a missile defense system drew strong global reactions.[71] Richard Armitage, the deputy secretary of state (2001–2005) undertook the mission to explain the new strategic framework—including nonproliferation, counterproliferation, missile defense, and reduction of the U.S. nuclear arsenal —to key allies and friendly nations. In this context he visited India. Although India advised the United States not to unilaterally abandon the 1972 treaty, it welcomed the reduction of the U.S. arsenal as well as the shift toward a more cooperative defense framework.[72] Following a meeting with Armitage, Jaswant Singh affirmed, "What we are endeavouring to work out together is a totally new security regime for the entire globe."[73] India was exceptionally pleased that the United States considered it vital enough to send its undersecretary for defense, Richard Armitage, to discuss the issue.

In the midst of the worldwide scepticism of Bush's nuclear approach, "India's quick and enthusiastic support"[74] was a surprising development. In stark contrast to the deeply embedded anti-Americanism, this was an unprecedented position taken by India on the issue of missile defense. The support extended by the Vajpayee government to Washington's plan of NMD created some initial displeasure in India; however, following a countrywide debate on the issue a solid consensus emerged. The idea of missile defense appealed to India for several reasons. First, as Sandhya Singh remarks, "A defensive umbrella in which a tracking satellite can find and neutralize enemy missiles in mid-air is no small protection for a country [India] physically surrounded by civilizationally hostile forces."[75] Second, India saw NMD as a supplement to its nuclear doctrine of "no first use," as a missile defense shield would curb any temptation of hostile forces to strike first.[76] Finally, NMD was consistent with India's decades-old quest for technological advancement. As C. Raja Mohan avers, "the development of the missile defense appears an inevitable technological trend and a country like India has to invest in it."[77]

Thus, Washington realized India could be "really helpful" in the establishment of new security architecture.[78] In 2002, a joint statement of the Defense Policy Group meeting reflected the eagerness of both the countries to collaborate on NMD. Both sides "reaffirmed the contribution that missile defenses can make to enhance cooperative security and stability."[79] Subsequently, bilateral senior level talks were held and missile defense was incorporated in the Next Steps in Strategic Partnership as an invaluable component of the "quartet" of issues on which the two countries sought to cooperate (discussed later in this chapter).

India and the Proliferation Security Initiative (PSI)

Besides being a nonproliferator, India had specific capabilities that made it attractive as a significant partner for curbing the threat of weapons of mass destruction. First, due to its technological prowess, India could substantially cooperate in the joint development of "new systems of tagging, tracking, and surveillance." Second, India's prime location in the Indian Ocean region and its blue water naval capabilities were considered beneficial, especially "in the vital task of safeguarding the seas from nuclear trafficking."[80] Recognizing Indian naval prowess, Nicholas Burns remarked, "India's robust navy travels the sea-lanes linking the

Middle East and Africa with East Asia and we are working with it to expand the surveillance of suspect cargo vessels and real-time communication."[81] Due to India's predominance in the Indian Ocean region, the effective functioning of the PSI without Indian involvement was "unthinkable."[82] On several occasions U.S. officials expressed interest in the participation of New Delhi in the U.S.-led Proliferation Security Initiative (PSI) to interdict nuclear trafficking on the high seas. Colin Powell stated, "We would like to see India participate in the PSI . . . we are going to increase the dialogue with respect to possible Indian participation."[83]

Initially, India had certain apprehensions about the implications of joining the Proliferation Security Initiative. First, the PSI was a U.S.-led effort without United Nations or any international legal sanction.[84] Second, the PSI required members to allow *impromptu* checks of their own ships and aircraft. Third, there were apprehensions regarding the considerable strain and "material degradation" of the vital assets of the Indian armed forces during interdiction operations. Fourth, India already had politically sensitive relations with its neighbours, therefore, this initiative involved a considerable political risk that a dispute might escalate into a military conflict.[85] For instance, one of the reasons that led to the 1962 Chinese attack on India was the fact that India offered shelter to Tibetan refugees—including the Dalai Lama—who were fleeing persecution by Chinese authorities. Finally, India considered the retention of certain states as "core members" in the PSI as discriminatory. The function of the core group was to define the basic principles of interdiction for the PSI and to expand its membership. Significantly, in 2005, the United States disbanded the PSI core group in order to allay India's concerns.[86] Subsequently, India agreed to engage with the United States in discussions regarding ways to cooperate in the PSI.

India and the Container Security Initiative (CSI)

The Bush administration was also keen to seek India's cooperation in the CSI. As emphasized by Nicholas Burns, "We also urge India to participate in the Container Security Initiative and to unleash its proven expertise in information technology to meet a new generation of threats in cyberspace."[87] In May 2005, following talks regarding cooperation on the issue, India agreed to join the CSI.[88] It offered to make its largest port, Jawaharlal Nehru Port, also known as *Nhava-Sheva* and run by the Jawaharlal Nehru Port Trust (JNPT), compliant to the CSI. As India is an export driven economy, it was in India's economic interests to ensure the safety of maritime trade infrastructure as well as goods. In the absence of CSI compliant screening procedures in India, the cargo originating from India enroute to the United States would have to be shipped to other CSI complaint ports such as Colombo, Dubai, or Singapore. This would translate not only into an increase in expenses for goods of Indian origin, but also into a loss in revenue due to diversion of foreign goods to other ports.[89] It was not an easy decision for India as it had reservations regarding the posting of the U.S. Customs and Border Patrol in its ports. The Container Security Initiative stipulates that all the shipping cargo bound for the United States is to be checked by U.S. customs officials at the port of origin. Moreover, India perceived that, in order to be effective, the CSI should not be U.S.-specific, rather, it should be a global initiative to protect the global flow of goods. As terrorists threaten global maritime trade, and container cargo can be used to transport potentially dangerous goods, India logically felt it was essential to ensure the security of containers originating from any port and bound for destination anywhere in the world. Sureesh Mehta, an admiral in the Indian Navy, remarked that safeguarding cargo bound only for the United States did not constitute "a foolproof system." Emphasizing the need to revisit maritime security, he remarked, the "CSI should be an integral part of a country's security system and not be U.S.-specific. Whenever a container leaves a port, each country concerned should certify it as safe."[90] The Lashkar-e-Tayyeba attacks in Mumbai (India) in November 2008 further reinforced the threat from the seas and the need to strengthen maritime security worldwide.

Thus, the urgency to deal with the threats of nuclear terrorism and trafficking led to reorientation of the nuclear regime. India—hitherto a nuclear pariah and a target of the nonproliferation regime—was no longer considered a "country of proliferation concern" to Washington.[91] Rather, it was recast as a responsible partner in curbing the newer complex threats of nuclear terrorism and trafficking.

NUCLEAR RENAISSANCE AND INDIA

During the Bush era there was renewed emphasis on nuclear energy to reduce dependence on oil and natural gas from foreign sources. America's dependence on foreign crude oil was deemed detrimental to U.S. security. President Bush remarked that it was synonymous with "putting our [America's] national energy security in the hands of foreign nations, some of whom do not share our interests."[92] Thus, President Bush regarded it accorded priority to make America self-sufficient in the energy sector. His plan for U.S. "national energy independence" envisaged 1,300 new power stations, both conventional and nuclear, to be built over 20 years to keep pace with the growth in energy demand, interalia.[93] No nuclear reactor had been built in the United States since the near-miss in 1974 at the Three Mile Island nuclear power plant in Pennsylvania.[94] Besides safety concerns, other factors such as high capital costs, environmental concerns, nuclear waste management, and threats of proliferation had stalled further development of nuclear power stations.[95] Thus, this was a significant attempt by the Bush administration to resuscitate the U.S. nuclear power industry.

Globally, too, the steady growth of energy requirements, especially with the rise of China and India, coupled with concerns regarding climate change, spurred a "nuclear renaissance." It is often claimed that "technology has made nuclear power safer, cleaner, and more efficient."[96] Nevertheless, the spread of nuclear technology increases risk for nuclear proliferation. Cognizant of the inherent challenge to balance the growing needs of nuclear energy with U.S. nonproliferation goals, President Bush pledged to build international cooperation in harnessing nuclear energy as an alternative source of power. This led to a search for new approaches to the nuclear fuel cycle "to avoid the spread of enrichment and reprocessing facilities" and, thereby, to curb the weaponization of civilian nuclear technology.[97] In this context, President Bush expressed interest in supporting the energy quest of the rising Asian powers. He remarked:

> I am going to work with developed nations, our friends, allies, to help developing nations, countries like China and India to develop and deploy clean energy technology. . . . As well we will explore ways we can work with like-minded countries to develop nuclear technologies that are safe, clean, and *protect against proliferation*. With these technologies, with the expansion of nuclear power, we can relieve stress on the environment and reduce the global demand for fossil fuels.[98] (emphasis added)

U.S.-India Nuclear Safety Cooperation

In 2003, the Bush administration not only revived the hitherto suspended nuclear safety cooperation with India, but also expanded it to the widest extent possible within the sphere of U.S. domestic laws and international commitments toward nonproliferation. As part of this dialogue, the U.S. National Regulatory Commission (NRC) was engaged with its Indian counterpart the Atomic Energy Regulation Board (AERB) to ensure the regulation and safety of nuclear reactors in India.

Interestingly, the U.S.-India nuclear safety dialogue had begun during the Clinton administration in 1994. But in the aftermath of the 1998 nuclear tests it was indefinitely suspended. During the interview with the author, a senior official at the NRC affirmed, "in many ways my agency has been at the forefront in this paradigm shift [U.S.-India nuclear cooperation] going back to the mid-90s."[99] The NRC began taking interest in Indian nuclear safety standards after a fire at the Narora Atomic Power Station (NAPS) located near the capital city, Delhi. On March 31, 1993, a fire broke out in the turbine generator of the 235 MW reactor at NAPS and raged for almost 12 hours. There was no damage to the reactor building and all the safety systems functioned normally.[100] The then executive director of the AERB, S. V. Kumar, affirmed that "no plant workers [were] killed or injured and there was no radiation hazard either to the staff or the public." Fortunately, when the fire disabled the reactor's primary and secondary cooling systems the back-up cooling system prevented a complete meltdown of the reactor.[101] Recalling the incident, the NRC official stated, although "the fire was quite dangerous, the operators at the site were extremely capable, knowledgeable, and nothing worse happened as they were able to contain it."[102] Nonetheless, it created concerns within the NRC because earlier, in March 1975, the United States had also experienced a major fire in its Brown's Ferry nuclear plant in Tennessee.[103] This incident emphasized the need to strengthen the safety regulations at nuclear power plants, to prevent future fire accidents and to ensure public health and safety. Thus, after the NAPS incident, the NRC felt an urgent need to engage India in discussions regarding the safety of its nuclear program. The fact that India had developed its nuclear program in isolation reinforced the necessity to ensure its alignment with international safety standards. The NRC took the position that "nuclear safety issues should be cast out from other nonproliferation concerns, as an accident can be problematic for public health and safety."[104] Due to President Clinton's strong commitment to the nonproliferation objectives, and given India's non-adherence to the NPT, the NRC official recalls, "The dialogue with the executive was not easy. It was a bumpy road." Finally, the NRC was allowed to begin a limited dialogue with India on the issues of nuclear safety. In the fall of 1994 a delegation of Indian regulators came to the United States and discussions began on several important general topics of nuclear safety. The NRC also encouraged India to join the International Convention on Nuclear Safety, which it did in 1994.[105]

Although the conversation had begun, due to the inherent distrust in the bilateral relationship "it took several years for the dialogue to really get going."[106] The Indians perceived that the NRC intended to highlight the weaknesses of their nuclear program. When India conducted nuclear tests in 1998 the interaction on nuclear safety issues was indefinitely suspended.[107] Charles Ferguson, formerly physical scientist, Office of Nuclear Safety, Bureau of Nonproliferation, U.S. Department of State (2000–2002), reveals that in the aftermath of Pokhran II, "the nonproliferation bureau was 'adamantly opposed' to any nuclear related work with India even in the area of civilian nuclear safety."[108] Also, the Indian nuclear scientists were denied visas to the United States until the sanctions were in place.[109]

At the time of suspension, there were three main ongoing projects. The first was related to the Tarapur nuclear reactor based on U.S. design technology. There were some cracks in the shrout of the nuclear reactor core. The Indian experts required U.S. assistance to develop cameras, to investigate possible damage to the reactor, and to ensure that the reactor was safe. The second project aimed to ensure that fire codes in Indian nuclear plants met international standards so that a fire incident would not "knock out the whole reactor, the safety system, or the electrical cable line." The last project was on emergency operating procedures.[110]

In November 2001, during the Indian prime minister's visit to Washington, these nuclear safety projects were revived and both sides expressed strong desire to engage more closely in the sphere of civilian nuclear cooperation. Ferguson opines, "*That was the decisive visit which led to the current* [*nuclear*] *deal*" (emphasis added).[111] The following year, India acceded to the Convention on the Physical Protection of Nuclear Material. Subsequently, nuclear cooperation became an invaluable component of the "trinity of issues" of the High Technology Cooperation Group (discussed later in the chapter).

In February 2003, a fifteen-member American delegation led by the chairman of the U.S. Nuclear Regulatory Commission, Dr. Richard A. Meserve, visited India. Besides resuming cooperation in nuclear safety issues, the purpose of the visit was to identify specific areas for collaboration in peaceful applications of nuclear energy and space research.[112] The NRC was committed to the stance that a "dialogue with India is more important than banning India from the dialogue, at least on the very minimal on the nuclear safety front."[113] This position was not only respected but greatly enhanced during the Bush administration. Consequently, the bilateral nuclear safety dialogue between the NRC and the AERB was expanded beyond the previous issues of fire safety, emergency operating procedures, and design issues, to include two other areas: risk-informed regulation and licence renewal for nuclear reactors.[114] That is, the purpose of the dialogue now included regulation of a safe nuclear program in India. Moreover, since 9/11 the threat of terrorist attacks on nuclear installations had become a concern, therefore, the physical safety of nuclear reactors was included in the U.S.-India discussions. Measures to enhance "the security of nuclear power plants and the security of nuclear materials which may be in use in agriculture, medical uses, or oil well logging" were introduced to avoid their misuse or their falling into the wrong hands.[115] In March 2002 India acceded to the Convention on the Physical Protection of Nuclear Material.

Thus, during the Bush administration, the U.S.-India nuclear safety dialogue was not only revived but was significantly expanded based on (i) increased reliance on nuclear power for both countries, (ii) ensuring the safety of nuclear reactors in India, and (iii) protection against the threat of terrorist acts.

RECOGNITION OF INDIA'S NUCLEAR ENERGY NEEDS

The revival of the nuclear safety cooperation with India served as a significant confidence-building measure and assured both the countries that they had a mutual interest in providing safe and reliable nuclear energy. Gradually, despite their contradictory approaches to nuclear weapons, this nuclear safety dialogue led to finding a common ground.

The Bush administration became aware of the necessity to move beyond current safety and regulatory issues; because India's economic growth was creating a "voracious appetite for electricity."[116] In a report by the Aspen Strategy Group it was emphasized, "A broader U.S.–Indian energy dialogue can be an important tool in strengthening the overall relationship."[117] Moreover, it was believed that if India's nuclear industry remained isolated it might be difficult for it to achieve sustainable energy. David Victor stated, "As long as India's nuclear industry remains isolated, it is hard to see that India will build more than the occasional reactor as the cost basis for nuclear equipment will be too high and fuel needed for such reactors will not be available."[118]

Indian officials and scientists voiced similar energy concerns at several international fora. Within India, there were debates about whether the Indian nuclear program would be able to meet its projected energy requirements. The chairman of India's Atomic Energy Commission (AEC), Anil Kakodkar, underlining India's commitment to nonproliferation, made a plea for the removal of technological embargoes imposed on India. He stated, "We have a commitment and an interest in contributing as a partner against proliferation . . . we must shed the baggage inherited from the past which restricts the flow of equipment and technologies related to the peaceful uses of nuclear energy."[119] That is, the world needs to recognize that India can assist to curb proliferation and toward this end, the technological embargoes should be reconsidered.

Significantly, in July 2005, a mere couple of weeks before the scheduled visit of Prime Minister Manmohan Singh to the United States, the chairman of the AERB, A. Gopalkrishnan, for the first time drew public attention to the shortage of fuel for the Indian nuclear reactors. Calling for international cooperation in the supply of nuclear fuel, A. Gopalakrishnan criticized the silence maintained by the Indian government as well as the Indian Department of Atomic Energy (DAE): "it has been a major problem for the officials of NPCIL [Nuclear Power Corporation of India Limited] and the Nuclear Fuel Complex (NFC) for some time."[120] Contrary to the common perception, he emphasized that the urgent need for India, was not to build nuclear reactors, rather arranging fuel supply for the nuclear reactors, existing as well as yet to be built.[121] Cognizant of the U.S. domestic laws and international, technological embargoes, Gopalkrishnan proposed that Washington support could at least support the removal of NSG objections so as to enable India to import the critically needed uranium, i.e., nuclear fuel from other countries.

Interestingly, India's growing nuclear energy needs were being recognized at the international level, too. Several nations, especially France and Russia, were looking forward to nuclear cooperation with India and desired a modification of the NSG Guidelines—prohibited member states from supplying nuclear assistance and materials to any country that has not accepted full-scope safeguards, e.g., India. In May 2003, Russia raised the issue of easing the restrictions at the NSG meeting in Busan, South Korea. Subsequently, a public statement was issued by Russia. It stated, "We believe that the activities of the NSG should not of course create obstacles for international cooperation in this field of peaceful purposes of atomic energy and take into account new realities in this field in an adequate and timely manner." [122]

STRATEGIC TRADE: CONFIDENCE BUILDING

Despite the strengthening of the bilateral relationship, since the Clinton administration, the issue of technology transfers remained sensitive. To recall, the peaceful nuclear test explosion by India in 1974 had created concerns regarding the potential military uses of civilian nuclear technology transferred to the developing nations. It had also led to a rift between India and the United States (and Canada) regarding the use of the CANDU nuclear reactor and the U.S.-origin fuel for the nuclear explosion which were intended for India's civilian program.[123] Thereafter, the United States had instituted technological controls to restrict dual-use technologies to India; consequently, both countries suffered from decades of distrust and divergent objectives. The United States, due to India's refusal to accede to the NPT-centric regime, was concerned about the end-usage of Indian technology as well as its export to third parties. India, on the other hand, viewed the United States in colonial terms as an unreliable supplier and responsible for setting up a "technological apartheid" regime. For three long decades, U.S.-India were unable to bridge their divergent objectives.

During the Bush era, Indian officials were eager for the easing of U.S. restrictions so that India would have greater access to sensitive technology, and on several occasions they expressed their desire for the lifting of the technological embargoes imposed since 1974. The Indian government was "focusing narrowly" on the liberalization of U.S. restrictions on the export of nuclear and missile-related technology.[124] For instance, Brajesh Mishra, in his speech at the Council of Foreign Relations, emphasized India's nonproliferation self-restraints as well as his hope for a deeper engagement in the arena of advanced technology. He stated,

> I have been saying very candidly that a trinity of issues—high technology commerce, civilian nuclear energy cooperation, and collaboration in space can take the Indo-U.S. relationship to a qualitatively new level of partnership. India has consistently followed responsible policies on nonproliferation of nuclear and missile technologies and has strict export control regimes for dual-use technologies.[125]

In a marked departure from the previous administrations, President Bush accorded legitimacy to India's quest for the technological advancement necessitated by its flourishing economy. The Bush administration also realized that a "deeper cooperation" in the trinity of issues could be the "leading edge" of the bilateral relationship.[126] Bush explored ways in which Washington could engage in high technology trade consistent with its own nonproliferation objectives. At a historic summit meeting in November 2001, President Bush and Prime Minister Singh highlighted their commitment to stimulate high technology commerce. They agreed to begin a dialogue to evaluate processes by which transfer of dual-use and military items could be undertaken within a framework of "greater transparency and efficiency."[127] This was an unequivocal expression of the desire on both sides to engage in strategic trade and explore ways to proceed within a framework of the broader interests of both countries. Thus, the advent of the Bush administration and its empathy with India's technological aspirations reoriented the "context of the bilateral nuclear dialogue."[128]

Nonetheless, Colin Powell, the then secretary of state, in an interview with the *Washington Post*, emphasized that although the United States respected India's demands for advanced technology and intended to do whatever it could to satisfy them; there were certain red lines regarding nonproliferation that Washington could not cross. The United States envisaged "glide path"—a three phase plan whereupon India would undertake measures to control nonproliferation and would strengthen domestic export control laws and the United States would reciprocate by lifting technological restrictions.[129] Subsequently, Washington began to define the criteria and "structure a process" for enhancing a synergic trade relationship in dual-use technologies, to ensure the appropriate usage of the sensitive items. Juster elaborates, it included "developing 'habits of cooperation' on issues of mutual concern and, even more important, developing mechanisms for institutionalizing that cooperation."[130] Meanwhile, the Indian government also submitted several unofficial papers with ideas on how to realize the goals set in the November 2001 joint statement.[131]

High Technology Cooperation Group (HTCG)

Based on the Bush-Vajpayee commitment to engage in high-tech trade commerce, Condoleezza Rice and Brajesh Mishra held sustained talks and published the results as the Rice-Mishra Paper. It laid out a "set of clearly defined objectives to be negotiated by the two bureaucracies in a reasonable time frame."[132] The Rice-Mishra Paper emphasized the need to explore ways to address American national security interests regarding nonproliferation and India's desire for advanced technologies. This provided the foundation for the High Technology Cooperation Group to address the bilateral challenges in high technology commerce.[133]

In November 2002, Kenneth Juster, the U.S. undersecretary for industry and security in the Department of Commerce[134] visited India and held talks with Kanwal Sibal, the Indian Foreign Secretary, regarding the establishment of a High Technology Cooperation Group (HTCG). The Juster-Sibal talks represented a "determined political effort" to tackle Indo-U.S. divergence over nonproliferation and advanced technology transfers—issues that had been lingering for several decades.[135] The proposal was reviewed by the Indian government and a joint press release was issued on November 13, 2002, for creation of an HTCG comprising senior representatives of the relevant departments of both the governments.

On February 5, 2003, the HTCG met and signed the Statement of Principles which enumerated the reciprocal obligations of the two countries.[136] The Statement of Principles emphasized the commitment of both countries to prevent proliferation of sensitive technologies and the "shared goal" of strengthening export control systems through laws, regulations, and enforcements. In order to gain authorized transfers of dual-use items and technologies India was required to fulfill certain obligations. It had to adopt a "mutually satisfactory system of assurances regarding end-use, diversions, transfers, and retransfers within and outside India, re-export, and, where necessary, physical protection from and access to controlled items by third parties."[137] The purpose of these measures was to "increase transparency and accountability" to ensure legitimate end-usage of technology of U.S. origin, and to curb proliferation of sensitive technologies.[138] The United States pledged to reciprocate by lifting restrictions in a phased manner consistent with its national security and foreign policy objectives and international commitments.[139] Significantly, the HTCG valued the role the private sector could play in encouraging high tech commerce. Accordingly, in July 2003, the HTCG in conjunction with the Confederation of Indian Industry (CII), the Federation of Indian Chambers of Commerce and Industry (FICCI), the National Association of Software and Service Companies (NASSCOM), and the U.S.-India Business Council (USIBC) sponsored a public-private forum on "Financing Innovation" in Washington. The forum focused on further growth of bilateral commercial cooperation in four emerging areas of technology—information technology, life sciences, defense technology, and nanotechnology.[140]

Thus, through the HTCG, commerce in dual-use goods was carried out in a framework that protected the national security and foreign policy interests of the United States while fulfilling India's technological demands. Commenting on the success of the U.S.-India phased technology transfers, Raja Mohan remarked, "More progress on the subject [technology transfers] has taken place over the last couple of years than in the previous three decades."[141] It also proved to be a confidence-building exercise to explore ways in which bilateral high tech commerce could be increased further. That is, the HTCG was not seen as the endpoint, rather, as the beginning of strategic trade with India.[142] In the words of Kenneth Juster, for Washington "it was a significant confidence building measure" and an unusual development in the U.S.-India relationship.[143] The phased technology transfers allowed the United States and India, for the first time ever, to engage in strategic trade without apprehensions and acrimony.

Next Steps in Strategic Partnership (NSSP)

The HTCG not only made considerable progress in initiating strategic trade, but also structured a process based on "reciprocal obligations." This, in turn, created a unique and innovative pathway to enhance the trade in sensitive areas related to nuclear and missile technology. Simultaneously, it reinforced the need for commitment from both sides; that is, for the United States to ease restrictions, and India, for its part, to strengthen its technology regulations. Consequently, as Juster asserts, "that's when our [U.S.] government developed the Next Steps in Strategic Partnership (NSSP) framework."[144] In September 2003, Steve Hadley, the deputy secretary of state, accompanied by Juster, visited India to present NSSP proposals to the Indian government in meetings with Brajesh Mishra, the Indian national security advisor.[145] The meetings represented a significant attempt by Washington to "progressively eliminate the punitive sanctions" in order to facilitate trade in strategic technologies with India while respecting its own international commitments and domestic obligations regarding nonproliferation.[146] During the interview by the author, Daniel Markey, a south Asia expert, noted, "NSSP was pretty good, it basically said what things the U.S. can do to get the nuclear issue off the table with India without changing the laws, without negotiating the treaties [NPT and CTBT]."[147]

After a series of negotiations the NSSP was announced in January 2004. It initiated a three stage process of reciprocal measures to build confidence and to enable U.S. exports of "increasingly sensitive items" to India. The NSSP created some consternation within India as it was seen as the alignment of Indian export controls according to U.S. interests. In this context, Juster, one of the key architects of NSSP, relates that the breakthrough was possible when "we were able to overcome many of

India's technical concerns."[148] Furthermore, allaying India's concerns, he clarified that the motive behind encouraging India to strengthen controls was not intended as a zero-sum game—to extract concessions—rather, it was based on reciprocity. The requisite measures undertaken by India would enhance the confidence of the United States to increase the level and scope of technology exported to India: "In short, the NSSP can and should be a "win-win" process for both countries."[149]

The NSSP initiated cooperation in the "quartet" of issues—civilian nuclear activities, peaceful space programs, appropriate environments for high technology trade, and missile defense. However, it is important to note that, even at the stage of NSSP, civilian nuclear activities were restricted to nuclear regulatory and safety issues.[150] Like the HTCG, the NSSP strengthened the realization that the United States and India, inter-alia, have a common interest in preventing the proliferation of weapons of mass destruction. Thus, Washington could confidently proceed to facilitate high technology trade with India, as the latter would not divert the technologies to third parties. The NSSP turned these interests into concrete actions to be undertaken by both countries "consistent with each country's laws and international obligations."[151]

At the completion of the NSSP (phase I), in response to India's measures regarding enhanced export controls, the United States further eased restrictions on the export of dual-use items to India. The following issues were addressed: (i) The Indian Space Research Organization (ISRO)—India's premier scientific institution—was removed from the Department of Commerce Entity List. This measure removed a major irritant in the furthering of Indo-U.S. strategic ties and was a long-pending Indian request, as it was affecting India's space program. This measure facilitated several dual-use items to be exported to the ISRO without a licence and served as a positive sign to encourage American investment in the Indian civilian space sector; (ii) Licensing requirements were reduced for low-level dual-use items (known as EAR99 and XX999 items) exported to ISRO subordinate entities that were still on the Entity List. This change in licensing policy enabled a reduction of approximately 80 percent in the applications for dual-use exports to ISRO subordinate entities. (iii) A presumption of approval policy was established for all dual-use items of U.S. origin, except those controlled by the Nuclear Suppliers Group, to the "balance of plant" portion of nuclear plants under IAEA safeguards; this enabled the expansion of civilian nuclear cooperation between the United States and India.[152]

Following the successful conclusion of phase I of the NSSP, the second phase was launched in October 2004. According to Juster, "we then started to make real progress in Phase II of the NSSP and we soon had the transition to the second term of the Bush administration."[153] Closely involved in negotiations with his Indian counterpart in instituting mechanisms for cooperation between the two hitherto estranged nations, Juster avers, "The NSSP was a critical step in the transformation of the relationship" and claimed it to be a "milestone" in the U.S.-India strategic relationship which further paved way for "even greater engagement in a number of key areas in which cooperation has previously been limited or nonexistent."[154] Thus, these measures constituted a diplomatic triumph that led to an increased flow of dual-use goods into Indian civilian space and nuclear activities. Concomitantly the NSSP was also a significant confidence building measure that affirmed that the United States and India could bridge their hitherto divergent interests in a mutually beneficial way. Nonetheless, the realization also dawned that there was still a long way ahead to realize the full potential of the relationship. That is, the NSSP was "very ambitious but was also constrained."[155]

SIGNIFICANCE OF THE HTCG AND THE NSSP

The perception that the U.S.-India nuclear deal was a mere spill-over effect of the qualitative transformation of the bilateral relationship ignores the significant series of strategic trade measures undertaken by the two countries. The purpose of these measures, as Anupam Srivastava avers, was to improve "firewalls" between India's defense and civilian sectors. Thereafter, the success in both, the HTCG and the NSSP, paved the way for the Joint Statement of July 18, 2005, i.e., the nuclear agreement between the United States and India.

Significantly, it can be ascertained that the 2008 nuclear agreement ensued from HTCG and NSSP, but it is naive to believe that it was an automatic progression. The Bush administration recognized, "a vibrant high-technology trade relationship" would be the "key component" for "fundamentally transforming U.S.-Indian relationship." Yet, there is considerable evidence that the U.S. did not envisage trade in nuclear reactors to India at the beginning of the HTCG or the NSSP. This counters the general perception that the U.S.-India nuclear agreement was a consequence of a no-holds-barred approach, especially to nuclear issues, of the Bush administration toward India. In 2003, C. Raja Mohan, a prominent Indian scholar, categorically stated,

> New Delhi will not be able to get its entire wish list on technology acquisition cleared by Washington. Specifically, India has been long interested in buying the nuclear reactors to augment its civilian nuclear program. *But Washington does not seem prepared at this stage to make India exempt from the internationally agreed rules on nuclear reactor sales. It is not prepared to go beyond cooperation on research on nuclear safety and the supply of nonnuclear equipment to nuclear stations.*[156] (emphasis added)

Nonetheless, the HTCG and the NSSP confirm that through mature sustained high-level dialogue with India, the Bush administration was able to encourage India to institute controls on both internal and external end-usage of technology and to allay U.S. fears of proliferation. The U.S.-India discourse became a "grown up dialogue rather than finger pointing at a bad child [India's] attitude that came about in the 1970s."[157]

This chapter reviewed the significant reorientation of the nuclear regime during the Bush administration. The NPT, targeting mainly state-actors, was not equipped to deal with the contemporary threats of nuclear trafficking and terrorism. There was a discernible need to supplement the nuclear nonproliferation regime with measures to cater to the post–9/11 global nuclear order. Contrary, to general perception, President Bush expanded the functional scope of the nuclear nonproliferation regime through adoption of interdiction measures such as PSI and CSI to deal with threats of nuclear trafficking and terrorism. The Bush administration vigorously supported IAEA safeguards and the strengthening of international export controls to overcome loopholes in the treaty that had been framed five decades ago. Cognizant of the vitiated nuclear order, Washington realized that India was not only a benign proliferator rther could also serve as a partner in curtailing the complex threats of the post–9/11 global nuclear order. Furthermore, the series of strategic trade measures, mainly proposed by the United States—the High Technology Cooperation Group and the Next Steps in Strategic Partnership—enabled the United States to strike a balance between New Delhi's desire for advanced technology and Washington's concerns regarding legitimate nuclear uses in a controlled environment and the possibility of a technology spill-over in India's military sector or across India's borders. These measures enabled the two countries to lay a strong foundation of mutual trust and confidence building before taking the leap toward a nuclear agreement.

NOTES

1. Interview with Philip Zelikow, March 2009. Zelikow served in several capacities during the Bush administration, especially significant was his role as a Counsellor to the Secretary of State, Condoleezza Rice.

2. Also see, Robert D. Blackwill, "The India Imperative," *The National Interest* no. 80 (Summer 2005): 12; Also see, Malini Parthasarthy, "India, U.S. Natural Allies: Vajpayee," *The Hindu*, September 9, 2000. In 2000, Shri Atal Bihari Vajpayee, former prime minister of India, proclaimed the United States and India as "natural allies." Since then, the term "natural allies" has been often been employed by the leadership of the two countries.

3. Sandhya Singh, "US: A Civilizational Ally," *The Pioneer*, May 8, 2001.

4. Alex Wagner, "Bush Waives Nuclear-Related Sanctions on India, Pakistan," *Arms Control Today* (October 2001). Available at http://www.armscontrol.org/act/2001_10/sanctionsoct01 (accessed April 29, 2009). Even within the U.S. Congress support for the removal of sanctions was becoming strong. In an address to the Brookings Institution, senator Sam Brownback, chairman of the Near East and South Asia, subcommittee of the Senate Foreign Relations Committee, urged the Bush administration to remove the sanctions imposed in the aftermath of the 1998 nuclear tests. Brownback argued that the United States and India, besides the enlarging technical cooperation,

need to increase defense and security cooperation as they faced a common threat in China. Similarly, Senator Joe Biden wrote to the Bush administration expressing support for the withdrawal of sanctions on India—in appreciation of India's relatively good behavior in exercising restraint on nuclear related technologies—thus, setting an example for Pakistan. Moreover, Biden argued, "Economic sanctions on India serve to stigmatize rather than stabilize. If we show our goodwill by removing this irritant, India will respond with reciprocal acts of goodwill in nonproliferation and other areas." Jane Parlez, "U.S. Ready to End Sanctions on India to Build Alliance," *The New York Times*, August 27, 2001; Aziz Haniffa, "Sanctions Against India, Pakistan May be Lifted Simultaneously," *The Tribune* (Chandigarh) September 8, 2001. Even in 2001, reports were emanating of the Chinese assistance to the Pakistani missile program, see, "China helps Pak to Make Missiles: CIA," *The Tribune*, September 9, 2001.

5. Robert Blackwill, as quoted in, Sridhar Krishnaswami, "Sanctions Strategy has not Worked: Blackwill," *The Hindu*, June 28, 2001.

6. As quoted in, Parlez, "U.S. Ready to End Sanctions."

7. Wagner, "Nuclear-Related Sanctions"; R. Ramachandran, "Out of the Blacklist," *Frontline* 18, no. 21 (October 13–26, 2001).

8. Ibid. Originally, 200 entities were sanctioned in the wake of India's May 1998 nuclear tests. In October 2001, the U.S. Department of Commerce reduced the number of blacklisted Indian agencies to sixteen that were prohibited from doing business with their U.S. counterparts. It included some significant entities like, the Defense Research & Defense Organization (DRDO), the Atomic Energy Commission (AEC), the Indian Space & Research Organization(ISRO), Bhabha Atomic Research Center (BARC), Sriharikota Space Center the Vikram Sarabhai Space Center amongst others. Sanctions that continued on Pakistan included: Military Coup Sanctions, Section 508 of the Foreign Assistance Act of 1961; and Missile Sanctions, Chapter 7 of the Arms Export Control Act, required by the U.S. membership in the Missile Technology Control Regime (MTCR), a voluntary regime of thirty-three states that seek to limit missile proliferation. Nonetheless, on September 28, 2001, President Bush in another determination (No. 2001–31) sanctioned a funding of $50 million for Pakistan ascertaining it to be important to America's security interests. This special funding, as Ramachandran remarks, "seems to nullify all the democracy related sanctions imposed after the October 1999 coup."

9. Yashwant Sinha, as quoted in, Rahul Bedi, "Lifting of Sanctions a 'Sweetner' for Siding with U.S.," *The Telegraph*, September 24, 2001. George Fernandes, the former Indian defense minister, commented that the withdrawal of sanctions is not significant unless it includes, "the restrictions imposed on items of dual-use technologies and the exchange of scientific know-how."

10. Initially, when the United States chose Pakistan as its "non-NATO ally" in the GWOT, it created a certain pessimism in New Delhi regarding the impossibility of upward momentum in the bilateral relationship with Washington. As C. Rajamohan states, "Nevertheless, while India enthusiastically courted Washington after September 11, the United States chose reluctant Pakistan as its partner against Taliban." C. Raja Mohan, "The Paradigm Shift Toward South Asia," *The Washington Quarterly* 26, no. 1 (Winter 2002–03): 144; also see, Bhabani Mishra, "India-US Relations: A Paradigm Shift," *Strategic Analysis* 29, no. 1 (January-March 2005).

11. Interview with Joseph McMillan, Senior Research Fellow, National Defense University, February 2009.

12. Nicholas R. Burns, "America's Strategic Opportunity with India," *Foreign Affairs* 86, no. 6 (November/ December 2007): 134.

13. Interview with Kenneth Juster, February 2009.

14. Blackwill, "India Imperative," 14.

15. Ibid., 9.

16. C. Rajamohan, "Indo-US Relations: The Trend Lines," in *India-U.S. Relations: Addressing the Challenges of the 21st Century*, ed., N.S Sisodia, Peter R. Lavoy, Cherian Samuel and Robin Walker, (Delhi: Magnum Book, September 2008), 18.

17. National Intelligence Council, *Mapping the Global Future: Report of the 2020 Project*, (Washington D.C.: Director of National Intelligence, December 2004), 9.

18. Ibid., 9–10. The report highlights the rise of these new powers is a "virtual certainty," yet, there is uncertainty over how these states would interact—whether cooperatively or competitively—in the global order. Nonetheless, it recommends that the United States can play a significant role in influencing the future role of these states.

19. See, Wade Boese, "US-India Discussing Arms Deals, Military Ties," *Arms Control Today* (December 2001). Available at http://www.armscontrol.org/act/2001_12/indarmsdec01 (accessed April 26, 2009).

20. Ashok Sharma, *Indo-US Strategic Convergence: An Overview of Defence and Military Cooperation*, CLAWS Papers, (New Delhi: Centre for Land Warfare Studies, November 2, 2008), 17.

21. Ambassador Lalit Mansingh, "Accomplishments and Challenges in the New Era of Cooperation," Keynote address at the Sigur Centre for Asian Studies, The Elliot School of International Affairs, George Washington University, Washington D.C., April 1, 2004.

22. *Joint Statement, Third Meeting of the U.S.-India Defense Policy Group*, December 3–4, 2001. Available at http://avalon.law.yale.edu/sept11/joint_010.asp (accessed February 15, 2009) (hereafter: *DPG Joint Statement, 2001*).

23. Sharma, "Indo-U.S. Strategic Cooperation," 13.

24. Indian Ministry of Defense, *Annual Report 2002–03*, Government of India, New Delhi, 2003, 9. (hereafter, *Annual Report 2002–03*)For instance, "*Balance Iroquois*" and "*Cope India*" are series of the U.S.-India joint military exercises which were held for several years.

25. Sharma, "Indo-U.S. Strategic Cooperation," 16.

26. *DPG Joint Statement, 2001,* specified the intention of holding military exercises including: training for combined humanitarian airlift; combined special operations training; small unit ground/air exercises; naval joint personnel exchange and familiarization; combined naval training exercises between the U.S. marines and corresponding Indian forces; Accordingly, joint military exercises were held at all levels—ground, sea, and air—in challenging environments, besides, joint patrolling in the significant straits of Malacca to Arabian Sea. Also see, Mansingh, "New Era of Cooperation." He notes, the armed forces of the U.S. and India "have carried out operations in the tropical heat in May 2002, in the freezing climes of Alaska in Oct 2002, in dense jungles in Mizoram in February 2003 and in the Pacific Island of Guam in June 2003." In October 2003, the U.S. Special Forces along with India's mountain divisions exercised together in Ladakh—in the state of Jammu and Kashmir—at the heights of 18,000-20,000 feet.

27. *Annual Report 2002–2003*, 9; Also see, *Joint Statement on US–India Defense Policy Group Meeting,* 2002, U.S. Department of Defense, News Release, 2678–02, May 23, 2002. Available at http://www.defenselink.mil/news/May2002/b05232002_bt267–02.html (accessed March 15, 2009) (hereafter, *DPG Joint Statement, 2002*). The purpose of the SCG was to advance a U.S.-India defense supply relationship by assisting in the licensing and sales of the weapon systems and components. The JTG, on other hand, was established for the purposes of joint production of defense technologies; Also see, Sharma, "*Indo-U.S. Strategic Convergence*," 15. Ever since Washington cut-off fuel supply for India's Tarapur nuclear reactor, New Delhi regarded the U.S. as an unreliable supplier. This perception was accentuated in the aftermath of the 1998 sanctions as these affected Light Combat Aircraft project started during the Reagan administration. Besides, India could not get the spare parts of certain carriers—like *Sea King* helicopters and fighter aircrafts—even though these were not of U.S.-origin.

28. Anupam Srivastava, "The Strategic Context of India's Economic Engagement with China," *Indian Journal of Economics and Business*, Special Issue on China and India (September 2006): 4. In view of the growing strategic interests, the United States and India signed a historic defense agreement in June 2005, that enabled, "Washington to

supply the state-of the art combat systems, and engage in co-production and collaboration of sophisticated weapons systems with India."

29. Blackwill, "The India Imperative," 11.

30. *DPG Joint Statement, 2001.*

31. Interview with Ambassador Thomas Pickering, March 2009.

32. Ibid.

33. Manpreet Sethi, "NPT RevCon 2010: An Oppurtunity to Refocus Priorities," *Strategic Analysis* 34, no. 2 (March 2010): 246.

34. The term "dirty bombs" refers to the crude nuclear bombs.

35. Lewis Dunn, "Today's Global Proliferation Challenges: Some Thoughts on Potential Indo-U.S. Cooperation," *India-U.S. Relations: Addressing the Challenges of the 21st Century*, ed., N.S Sisodia, Peter R. Lavoy, Cherian Samuel and Robin Walker (New Delhi: Magnum Books, September 2008), 71. Dunn lists the current global nuclear proliferation challenges as: Preventing spread of nuclear weapons in Northeast Asia and the Middle East; prohibiting access to WMD technologies by the terrorist groups; enhancing the legitimacy and effectiveness of global nonproliferation institutions; managing the proliferation risks arising from the spread of nuclear power; rejuvenating global nuclear disarmament agenda; and avoiding the next use of nuclear weapons (72).

36. Howard Baker and Lloyd Cutler, *A Report Card on the Department of Energy's Nonproliferation Programs with Russia* (Washington D.C.: Secretary of Energy Advisory Board, U.S. Department of Energy, January 10, 2001). Available at http://www.seab.energy.gov/publications/rusrpt.pdf (accessed February 15, 2009).

37. Kenneth Juster, Undersecretary of Commerce, "September 11 and U.S. Nonproliferation Policy," speech at the Ninth Asian Export Control Seminar, Tokyo, Japan, 26 February, 2002. Available at www.bxa.doc.gov/PRESS/2002/JusterJapanSpeech02_2602.html (accessed March 25, 2009).

38. Ibid.

39. Ibid.

40. The White House, Office of the Press Secretary, Fact Sheet, *President Announces New Measures to Counter the Threat of WMD*, George W. Bush, Speech at National Defense University, Fort McNair, 11 February, 2004. (hereafter, President Bush, February 11, 2004). Available at http://www.whitehouse.gov/news/releases/2004/02/20040211–4.html (accessed March 26, 2009).

41. Ibid.

42. Ibid.

43. Ibid.

44. Ibid. The illegal nuclear network was detected when "a shipment of advanced centrifuge parts manufactured at the Malaysia facility" was identified and followed. In Dubai, the shipment transferred to *BBC China*, a German-owned ship. After the ship crossed the Suez Canal, it was intercepted by the German and Italian authorities. For more details of the Khan nuclear network, see, Sara Kutchesfahani, "Case Study: The Khan Network," in *Nuclear Safeguards, Security and Nonproliferation: Achieving Security with Technology and Policy,* ed., James Doyle (Burlington, MA: Butterworth-Heinmann Homeland Security Series, July 2008); Christopher Clary, "A.Q. Khan and the Limits of the Nonproliferation," *Disarmament Forum*, no. 4 (2004).

45. Todd E. Perry, "The Growing Role of Customs Organizations in International Strategic Trade Controls," *Nuclear Safeguards, Security and Nonproliferation: Achieving Security with Technology and Policy,* ed., James Doyle, (Burlington, MA: Butterworth-Heinmann Homeland Security Series, July 2008), 550.

46. Ibid.

47. *National Strategy to Combat Weapons of Mass Destruction* (WMD), Homeland Security Presidential Directive 4 (Washington D.C.: The White House, December 2002), 2.

48. President Bush, February 11, 2004.

49. Ibid.

50. Vinod A. Kumar, "Counterproliferation: India's New Imperatives and Options," *Strategic Analysis* 31, no. 1 (January-February 2007): 26.

51. Zachary S. Davis and Mitchell Reiss, *U.S. Counterproliferation Doctrine: Issues for Congress,* 94–734 ENR (Washington D.C.: Congressional Research Service, September 21, 1994), 8.

52. The White House, *Proliferation Security Initiative: Statement of Interdiction Principles,* Fact Sheet (Washington D.C.: Office of the Press Secretary, September 4, 2003). Available at http://www.state.gov/t/isn/c27726.htm (accessed April 05, 2009). The Statement of Interdiction Principles (SOP), September 4, 2003, identifies specific steps for effectively interdicting proliferation-related shipments; Also see, *Factsheet: Proliferation Security Initiative Support Cell,* United States Strategic Command, Available at http://www.stratcom.mil/fProliferation_Security_Initiative_Support_Cell (accessed April 05, 2009). The factsheet notes, "The PSI is not led or 'chaired' by a single country, rather, it's united by a common purpose and designed to support flexible, fast action and coordination among partner nations to counter WMD proliferation." For details on PSI, see, Mark Shulman, *The Proliferation Security Initiative as a New Paradigm for Peace and Security,* Strategic Studies Institute (Carlisle, PA: U.S. Army War College, April 2006).

53. The Megaports Initiative, undertaken by the National Nuclear Safety Administration (NNSA) was launched in 2003, and aims at cooperating with other countries to screen cargo at major seaports. The initiative provides radiation detection equipment and trains personnel to check for nuclear or other radioactive materials.

54. U.S. Customs and Border Protection is an important component of the Department of Homeland Security concerned with the trade and travel to the United States. For more information check its webpage, http://www.cbp.gov/xp/cgov/about/.

55. The White House, *Remarks by the President to the People of Poland,* Press Release, Office of the Press Secretary Washington D.C., 31 May, 2003 (hereafter, President Bush, May 31, 2003).

56. President Bush, February 11, 2004.

57. *Text of the UN Resolution 1540, S/RES/1540,* Adopted by the Security Council at its 4956th meeting, 28 April 2004, 3. Available at http://daccessdds.un.org/doc/UNDOC/GEN/N04/328/43/PDF/N0432843.pdf?OpenElement (accessed April 16, 2009).

58. Kumar, "India's New Imperatives," 26–28.

59. The Anti-Ballistic Missile Treaty at a Glance, Available at http://www.armscontrol.org/factsheets/abmtreaty (accessed January 9, 2009); Text of the Anti-Ballistic Missile Treaty available at http://www.state.gov/www/global/arms/treaties/abm/abm2.html (accessed January 9, 2009).

60. Philip C. Saunders, "New Approaches to Nonproliferation: Supplementing or Supplanting the Regime," *The Nonproliferation Review* (Fall-Winter 2001): 124.

61. The White House, Office of the Press Secretary, "Remarks of the President to Students and Faculty at National Defense University." May 21, 2001. (hereafter, President Bush, May 21, 2001). Available at www.whitehouse.gov/news/releases/2001/05/20010501–10.html (accessed March 15, 2009).

62. Ibid.

63. Douglas J. Feith and George Miron, *Memorandum of Law: Did the ABM Treaty of 1972 Remain in Force After the USSR Ceased to Exist in December 1991 and Did it Become a Treaty Between the U.S. and the Russia Federation,* written testimony submitted to the hearing by the U.S. Senate Foreign Relations Committee, 106th Congress, 1st Session, 106–339, May 25, 1999; Also see, as G. Miron, "Memorandum of Law: Did the ABM Treaty of 1972 Remain in Force After the USSR Ceased to Exist in December 1991 and Did it Become a Treaty Between the U.S. and the Russia Federation?" *American University International Law Review* 17, no. 2 (2002): 337. Feith and Miron argue that the ABM treaty had lapsed with the disintegration of the Soviet Union.

64. Craig Cerniello, "NMD Bill Clears Congress as Senate Re-examines ABM Treaty," *Arms Control Today,* April/May 1999. Available at http://www.armscontrol.org/act/1999_04–05/nmdam99 (accessed December 26, 2010).

65. Interview with a senior official at the Nuclear Regulatory Commission (NRC), anonymity requested, March 2009. Although it cannot be ignored that India has built the nuclear weapons program for itself, yet, as the NRC official argues, India has consistently affirmed that "as soon as the nuclear weapon states live up to their promise under the NPT; it would be happy to come under the NPT fold. This is not an unreasonable thing to request. Because, a fundamental bargain underlying the NPT is: *we nuclear powers will disarm and you the nonnuclear states will not arm.*"

66. Ibid.

67. In 2003–2004 some allegations had surfaced that the Indian nuclear scientist Dr. Y.S. R. Prasad, who retired as the Chairman of India's Nuclear Power Corporation in the year 2000, was later, employed by the Iranian Government. Prasad allegedly visited Iran on several occasions without obtaining clearances from the Indian government. Later, the Iranian government forwarded the details on the employment of Dr. Prasad to the International Atomic Energy Agency (IAEA) Then, the IAEA requested the Indian government to debrief Dr. Prasad. The Indian government argued that Dr. Prasad, a retired nuclear scientist, an expert in nuclear power engineering, worked only on Iran's Bushehr nuclear project which is under International Atomic Energy Agency safeguards. For details, see "The Indian Scientist also Involved in Nuclear Proliferation to Iran," *Frontier Star* (NWFP, Pakistan) February 8, 2004; Manoj Joshi, "Indo-Iran Ties May Hurt Good Friend, U.S." *Times of India* (New Delhi), February 22, 2004.

68. Juster, interview.

69. Burns, interview.

70. Zelikow, interview.

71. The White House, Office of the Press Secretary, *ABM Treaty Fact Sheet*, press release, 13, Dec 2001. Available at www.state.gov/t/ac/rls/fs/2001/6848.htm (accessed December 6, 2010).

72. *The Visit of the U.S. Deputy Secretary of State Richard Armitage to New Delhi*, press release issued by Ministry of External Affairs, Government of India, May 11, 2001. Available at http://www.indianembassy.org/press_release/2001/may/may_11.htm (accessed March 15, 2009).

73. As quoted in Satindra Bindra, "India Backs Missile Shield," May 11, 2001. Available at http://archives.cnn.com/2001/WORLD/asiapcf/south/05/11/india.armitage.pakistan.zhu.01/index.html.

74. C. Raja Mohan, "A Paradigm Shift Towards South Asia?" *The Washington Quarterly* (Winter 2002–03): 144.

75. Singh, "A Civilizational Ally."

76. C. Rajamohan, "Vajpayee, Bush Explore Tie-up in Missile Defence," *The Hindu* (Chennai), September 23, 2003.

77. Ibid.

78. Interview with Daniel Markey, specialist on South Asia, February, 2009.

79. *Joint Statement on US–India Defense Policy Group Meeting*, May 23, 2002. US Department of Defense, New Release, 2678–02. Available at www.fas,org/terrorism/at/docs/2002/USIndiaDefensePolicyGroup.htm (accessed April 21, 2009).

80. Samantha F. Ravich, "Nuclear Nonproliferation and the Cases of Russia, China and India." in *The Challenge of Proliferation: A Report of the Aspen Strategy Group*, ed., Kurt Campbell (Washington D.C.: The Aspen Institute, February 2005), 108.

81. Nicholas Burns, "America's Strategic Opportunity with India," *Foreign Affairs* 86, no. 6 (November/ December 2007): 141.

82. Amit Kumar, *India and the U.S.-led WMD Non-Proliferation Initiatives*, Pugwash India Research Articles, 29 March 2008. Available at www.indianpugwashsociety.org/article_detail.asp?aid=62 (accessed on December 6, 2010).

83. Siddarth Varadarajan, "U.S. for Indian Hand in Proliferation Initiative," *Times of India*, March 18, 2005.

84. Moreover, as Sharon Squassoni points out, PSI has no "international secretariat, no offices in federal agencies established to support it, no database, no reports of

successes or failures, and no established funding." Sharon Squassoni, *Proliferation Security Initiative*, CRS Report for Congress, (Washington D.C.: Congressional Research Service, updated September 14, 2006), CRS-3.

85. Deepa Ollapally, *"U.S.-India: Ties that Bind,"* The Sigur Centre Asia Papers, The (Washington D.C: Elliott School of International Affairs, George Washington University, 2005); Also, see, Amit Kumar, *"Non Proliferation Initiative"*; Reshmi Kazi, "Proliferation Security Initiative and India," *Peace and Conflict* 7, no. 7 (October 2004).

86. Squassoni, "Proliferation Security Initiative," CRS-2.

87. Nicholas Burns, "Strategic Opportunity," 141.

88. Vijay Sakhuja, "Container Security Initiative: Is India Serious About its Maritime Trade," no. 1748 (New Delhi: Institute of Peace and Conflict Studies, May 19, 2005). Available at http://www.ipcs.org/article_details.php?articleNo=1748 (accessed March 25, 2009) The four main criteria for making a port CSI-compliant, include: Establishing security criteria to identify high-risk containers; pre-screening containers before they arrive at U.S. ports; using technology to pre-screen high-risk containers; and, developing and using secure containers. In the past, India, too, has been a victim of the transport of potentially dangerous goods to its ports. In October 2004, ten persons in Delhi were killed in a blast caused by live shells in metal scrap in shipping containers imported from war infested zones in West Asia. See, Gurpreet S. Khurana, "India and the Container Security Initiative," *IDSA Strategic Comments* (July 17, 2007). Available at www.idsa.in/publications/stratcomments/GurpreetKhurana170707.htm (accessed March 26, 2009).

89. Sakhuja, "Container Security Initiative."

90. "N-Weapons Could Be Brought Through Sea: Navy," *Indian Express* (New Delhi), February 18, 2009.

91. Mark J. Valencia, *The Proliferation Security Initiative: Making Waves in Asia*, Adelphi Paper no. 376 (London: International Institute for Strategic Studies, 2005), 65.

92. "Bush Unveils Energy Plan," *BBC News*, May 17, 2001. Available at http://news.bbc.co.uk/2/hi/business/1336544.stm (accessed March 26, 2009).

93. Ibid. Other proposals included: increased oil exploration in an Arctic wildlife reserve; an easing of regulations on oil refining; coal extraction; and the building of new nuclear power plants.

94. Stephen Evans, "US Attraction to Nuclear Power," *BBC News*, May 15 2001. Available at http://news.bbc.co.uk/2/hi/americas/1330256.stm (accessed March 26, 2009).

95. C. Raja Mohan, *Impossible Allies: Nuclear India, United States and the Global Order*, (New Delhi: India Research Press, 2006), 134.

96. The White House, Office of the Press Secretary, *Fact Sheet: Promoting Energy Independence and Security*, Washington DC, April 27, 2005. Available at http://georgewbush-whitehouse.archives.gov/news/releases/2005/04/20050427–9.html (accessed April 01, 2009). It emphasized the significance of the nuclear power and listed several initiatives being pursued by the Bush administration, including: construction of new nuclear power plants; launch of the *Nuclear Power 2010 Initiative*, a seven-year effort by government and industry to design and license the first new nuclear plants; and international collaboration on the Generation IV Initiative to develop a safer, more cost-effective, and more proliferation-resistant source of nuclear electricity and hydrogen.

97. Dunn, "Global Proliferation Challenges," 77.

98. The White House, Office of the Press Secretary, "President Discusses Energy at National Small Business Conference," Washington D.C., April 27, 2005; Available at www.whitehouse.gov/releases/2005/04/20050427–3.htm (accessed April 01, 2009).

99. Senior NRC official, interview.

100. The Department of Atomic Energy, *Annual Report 1993–94*, (New Delhi: Government of India, 1994), 9; Also see, "Turbine in Nuclear Power Station Catches Fire," *Associated Press*, March 31, 1993.

101. "Fire Damage Will Take Months to Fix," *Nucleonics Week*, April 8, 1993; Also see, Brahma Chellaney, "Backup Cooling System Averted Indian Reactor Meltdown," *United Press International*, April 4, 1993.

102. Senior NRC official, interview.

103. Ferguson, interview. He informed that a fire at the Brown Ferry-1, nuclear reactor occurred on March 20, 1975. The fire broke out when a worker was using a lighted candle to check for air leaks from a temporary seal—made of highly combustible polyurethane foam coated with a flame retardant paint—before putting a permanent seal. The fire quickly spread from the cable spreading room into the reactor building. The fire burned out of control for seven and half hours destroying over 1600 electrical cables including 628 safety-related cable systems. Also, see, *NIRS Investigation Finds That "New" Browns Ferry-1 Reactor Still Doesn't Meet Fire Protection Regulations Its 1975 Fire Caused*, Press Release, Nuclear Information and Research Service, NIRS, June 20, 2007.Available at http://www.nirs.org/press/06–20–2007/1 (accessed April 06, 2009); *Cable Fire at Brown's Ferry Nuclear Plant*, NRC Bulletin, BL-75–04A, Nuclear Regulatory Commission, Washington D.C., April 3, 1975.

104. Senior NRC official, interview.

105. The Department of Atomic Energy, *Annual Report 1994–1995*, (New Delhi: Government of India, 1995), 8.

106. Senior NRC official, interview.

107. Ibid.

108. Charles Ferguson, email, May 15, 2008.

109. Anjana Pasricha, *India, U.S. Resume Cooperation on Nuclear Safety*, Voice of America News, February 27, 2003. Available at http://www.voanews.com/english/archive/2003–02/a-2003–02–27–17-India.cfm?moddate=2003–02–27 (accessed, February 18, 2009).

110. Ferguson, interview.

111. Ferguson, email. Later, during the interview, Ferguson also informed that prior to the state visit of PM Vajpayee, in early 2001 the U.S. State Department had refused the visit of some Indian nuclear safety scientists who were coming to attend a Conference on Nuclear Safety, being organized by the World Association of Nuclear Operators (WANO). Despite the tremendous pressure exerted by WANO—its a worldwide organization engaged in peer review to ensure safety of nuclear power plants—the administration refused to make any concession, to allow the Indian scientists to visit the U.S. For more information about World Association of Nuclear Operators, please visit the organization's website. http://www.wano.org.uk/.

112. "U.S. Nuclear Regulator Impressed with Indian Safety Standards," *National News*, March 03, 2003. Available at http://news.indiamart.com/news-analysis/us-nuclear-regulator-2134.html (accessed March 25, 2009); Also see, Beth Duff-Brown, "*American Scientists Praise India's Safety Regulations*," Associated Press, February 27, 2004. The chairman of the U.S. Nuclear Regulatory Commission, Richard Meserve, praised India for the safety measures at the nuclear power plants.

113. Senior NRC official, interview.

114. Ferguson, interview; Senior NRC official, interview; Risk Informed regulation refers to an approach of the NRC "which incorporates an assessment of safety significance or relative risk." Available at http://www.nrc.gov/reading-rm/basic-ref/glossary/risk-informed-regulation.html.

115. Senior NRC official, interview.

116. David J. Victor, "Nuclear Power for India is Good for Us All," *International Herald Tribune*, March 16, 2006.

117. Ravich, "Nuclear Nonproliferation," 110.

118. David J. Victor, *The India Nuclear Deal: Implications for Global Climate Change*, Testimony to the U.S. Senate Committee on Energy and Natural Resources, U.S. Senate, Washington D.C., July 18, 2006.

119. "Barriers to Safe N-Energy Must Go," The *Hindu*, 18 September 2003.

120. A. Gopalkrishnan, "Indo-U.S. Cooperation: A Non-Starter," *Economic and Political Weekly*, July 2, 2005. He also said, " The DAE may argue that depleted uranium available from the spent-fuel reprocessing plants will supplement our limited natural uranium stocks, but in reality this will not lead to any substantial alleviation of the problem."

121. Ibid.

122. Amit Baruah, "Iraq Dominates PM's Talks with Leaders," *The Hindu*, June 1, 2003; "France, Russia Seek Cooperation in 'Peaceful Uses of Nuclear Energy,'" *The Hindustan Times*, June 1, 2003.

123. Kenneth Juster, "Stimulating High-Technology Cooperation with India," speech at the 28th Annual Meeting of the US-India Business Council, New York, June 2, 2003.

124. Juster, interview.

125. Brajesh Mishra, "India, United States and the New World Order: Prospects for Cooperation," speech of India's National Security Advisor at the Council on Foreign Relations, New York. May 7, 2003. Available at http://mea.gov.in/speech/2003/05/07spc01.htm (accessed April 06, 2009).

126. John H. Gill, "Regional Concerns, Global Ambitions," in *Strategic Asia 2003–2004: Fragility and Crisis*, ed., Richard J. Ellings (Washington D.C.: National Bureau of Asian Research, 2003), 201.

127. President Bush and Atal Bihari Vajpayee, *Text of the US-India Joint Statement* issued at the official visit of Prime Minister Vajpayee, 9 November 2001. Available at http://www.indianembassy.org/indusrel/2001/ind_us_js_nov_9_01.htm (accessed April 06, 2009).

128. C. Raja Mohan, "Lowering the Barriers?" *The Hindu*, November 20, 2003.

129. Colin Powell, Interview by Glenn Kessler and Peter Slevin, "Washington Post Reporters Interview Powell," *The Washington Post*, October 3, 2003; Sridhar Krishnaswami, "US, India Close to Agreement on Trinity," *The Hindu*, October 6, 2003; Powell stated: "We have really structured a new relationship with the Indians. . . . There were a basket of issues that they were always asking us about [technology transfers] . . . we nicknamed it 'The Trinity' . . . we have been trying to be as forthcoming as we can . . . but we also have to protect certain red lines that we have with respect to proliferation, because it's sometimes hard to separate within space launch activities and industries and nuclear programs, that which could go to weapons and that which could be solely for peaceful purposes...and also we've had a very productive set of discussions with the Indians over the last, almost two years now about these issues and how close we could get to satisfying these interests without crossing our red lines. And the 'glide path' was a way of bringing closure to this debate."

130. Kenneth Juster, interview by Seema Sirohi, *Outlook India*, January 24, 2005.

131. Juster, interview.

132. Mohan, "Lowering the Barriers."

133. Ibid.

134. Kenneth Juster played a key role in stimulating the strategic trade. He headed the US Bureau of Industry and Security (BIS) which was primarily responsible for administering effective export controls and their compliance with regard to strategic trade, thereby, advancing U.S. foreign policy, national security and economic interests. For details about Bureau of Industry and Security, see, http://www.bis.doc.gov/about/index.htm.

135. Mohan, "Lowering the Barriers."

136. Juster, interview.

137. *Statement of Principles for U.S.-India High Technology Commerce,* Bureau of Industry and Security, U.S. Department of Commerce, Washington D.C., February 5, 2003. Available at www.bis.doc.gov/internationalprograms/statementprinciplesindia.htm (accessed March 15, 2009).

138. Mohan, "Lowering the Barriers."

139. "Statement of Principles."

140. Kenneth Juster, "U.S.-India Relations and High-Technology Trade," speech at luncheon hosted by the Federation of Indian Chambers of Commerce and Industry, New Delhi, November 20, 2003. Available at www.bis.doc.gov/news/2003/kennewdelhinov03.htm

141. Mohan, "Lowering the Barriers."

142. Kenneth Juster, "Stimulating High-Technology Cooperation with India," speech at the 28th Annual Meeting of the US-India Business Council June 2, 2003, New York.

143. Juster, interview.

144. Ibid.

145. Juster, interview. He informed that the expectation was to get a prior approval of the NSSP by the Indian government so as to have the NSSP endorsed by President Bush and Prime Minister Manmohan Singh at the UN General Assembly meeting in mid-September 2003. "But Indian government was not prepared to do that yet and wanted to give more thought to this proposal. So we continued to negotiate and work on such a document. The Government of India sent a delegation to Washington DC a few weeks later for further discussions."

146. Mohan, "Impossible Allies," 28.

147. Markey, interview.

148. Juster, interview. "I made a number of trips to India in 2004 and representatives of the Government of India came to Washington D.C. as part of this process. There was also a change of government in India that had an impact on this process. In August 2004, I had series of meetings with India's new joint secretary of the Ministry of External Affairs, helped in part by the Indian National Security Advisor (J.N. Dixit, who soon thereafter, tragically died of a heart attack)."

149. Juster, interview, in *Outlook India.*

150. "United States and India Successfully Complete Next Steps in Strategic Partnership," Factsheet, Department of State, Washington DC, July 18, 2005.

151. Matthew S. Borman, "NSSP: U.S., India Interests in Action," *The Hindu*, October 2, 2004.

152. See, the update on the completion of the NSSP phase I, Bureau of Industry and Security, Department of Commerce. Available at http://www.bis.doc.gov/news/2004/us-indianextstep.htm (accessed April 26, 2009).

153. Juster, interview.

154. Factsheet, "Next Steps in Strategic Partnership."

155. Markey, interview.

156. Mohan, "Lowering the Barriers."

157. Senior NRC official, interview.

SIX

The U.S.-India Nuclear Agreement

Accommodating the Anomaly

For more than three decades post-Pokhran I explosions, the United States instituted export controls to deny India access to advanced dual-use technology. The objective was to halt the advancement of India's nuclear proficiency, both civilian and military. Nonetheless, India, excluded from the nuclear nonproliferation regime (NPR), not only developed and advanced its civilian nuclear program but also crossed the nuclear weapons threshold. This blow to the strategy of technological isolation, pursued by the successive U.S. administrations. Even President Clinton, credited with reinforcing the nonproliferation regime, was unable to reign India within the NPT loop. Post-Pokhran II, the Talbott-Singh dialogue under the Clinton administration did reflect easing of the U.S.-India estrangement, yet the nuclear issues seemed tenacious. Subsequently, in the post–9/11 era, the Bush administration re-imagined India as a "responsible" partner and there was a qualitative improvement in the bilateral relationship. Nonetheless, the dilemma prevailed: how could India's anomalous relationship with the global nonproliferation regime be resolved? This was not only a lingering issue rather was also proving to be increasingly disadvantageous to leave nuclear India in isolation anymore. The then secretary of state, Condolezza Rice, aptly summed up the predicament:

> *The real choice is this: do we want a state that intends to expand significantly its civil nuclear power production in the years ahead to remain outside the international nonproliferation regime? Or do we instead want it to adopt global nonproliferation practices while increasing our insight into its civil nuclear program . . . India could already build additional weapons within the limits of its capabilities if it so desired, with or without this deal.*[1]

The first section of this chapter focuses on the historic decision of the Bush administration to engage in civilian nuclear trade with India. The U.S.-India civilian nuclear agreement generated considerable furor, owing to diverse interpretations—especially, related to the objectives of the Bush administration vis-à-vis the nuclear nonproliferation regime (as discussed in chapter 1). This necessitates the analysis of the terms of the agreement within the context of the nuclear nonproliferation regime. Toward this purpose, the second section employs the "regime theory," to attempt a theoretical analysis of the nuclear nonproliferation regime, and identify its constituent attributes. As a corollary, the third section argues that peaceful nuclear cooperation agreements have been important part of U.S. nuclear nonproliferation policy, enabling the United States to restrict the nuclear behavior of recipient states. Proceeding further, the final section attempts a detailed analysis of the terms of the agreement, and related U.S. domestic legislation, especially the Henry Hyde Act, to analyze the shift in the U.S. nuclear nonproliferation policy. I contend that the U.S.-India nuclear deal was an attempt to accommodate the elusive India within the NPR and thereby, bring New Delhi under global nuclear governance.

THE POLICY DECISION

In April–May 2005, intensive discussions were held within the U.S. State Department on the issue of granting India access to civilian nuclear technology.[2] At the outset, it is important to specify that the plan to resume U.S.-India civilian nuclear commerce was a top-down decision, revealed to the Indian Prime Minister's delegation only during their visit in July. Understandably, it was not a decision that "can be made in public,"[3] as it was related to a highly sensitive nuclear issue and, contrary to the common perception, it was only at a later stage that the Indian government was informed. In an interview with the author, Philip Zelikow remarked, "I do not think they [the Indian government] first understood the gravity of what we were proposing, when it fully dawned upon them . . . their reaction was pleased astonishment."[4] In this context, C. Raja Mohan confirms that India had little inkling of Washington's plans, except for the possibility of a major initiative on nuclear energy cooperation during Manmohan Singh's visit in July 2005. Yet, Indian government officials and nuclear scientists were sceptical.[5] Due to the decades of technological embargoes led by the United States, there was reluctance to see an unprecedented opening in nuclear energy relations with Washington.

On July 18, 2005, Indian Prime Minister Manmohan Singh and U.S. President George Bush issued a joint declaration on civil nuclear cooperation. Significantly, the United States declared India as *"a responsible state with advanced nuclear technology"* that deserves to *"acquire the same benefits and advantages as other such* [nuclear weapon] *states*" (emphasis added).[6] The declaration included path-breaking pledges on both the sides. The United States committed, inter alia, (i) to offer civilian nuclear technologies to alleviate Indian concerns regarding energy security; (ii) to seek to adjust U.S. laws and policies in order to realize the goals of nuclear cooperation; and (iii) to encourage its [supplier] friends to alter existing international regimes in order to enable civil nuclear cooperation with India. In reciprocation, India committed to (i) segregate its civilian and military facilities and place its civilian facilities under IAEA safeguards; (ii) honor the voluntary moratorium on nuclear testing; (iii) sign and adhere to an IAEA additional protocol with respect to civilian nuclear facilities; (iv) refrain from transfer of enrichment and reprocessing technologies to states that do not have them and support international efforts to limit their spread; and (v) strengthen its export controls through comprehensive national legislation to curb proliferation of sensitive technologies and harmonize them according to MTCR (Missile Technology Control Regime) and NSG guidelines.[7] The United States also offered to support India's entry in the high-profile nuclear fusion project, the International Thermonuclear Experimental Reactor (ITER). This further confirmed that the Bush administration was intent on opening the floodgates of advanced technology to India.[8]

Subsequently, during President Bush's visit to India in 2006, the two sides finalized a plan for the separation of Indian civilian and military facilities, in pursuit of the joint declaration.[9] They also mutually agreed to "limit the spread of enrichment and reprocessing technologies" and "support the conclusion of a fissile material cut-off treaty."[10] Subsequently, on December 18, 2006, President Bush, in a crucial development, signed into law the Henry Hyde United States-India Peaceful Atomic Energy Cooperation Act (hereafter, Henry Hyde Act).[11] Interestingly, it was passed with strong bipartisan support in the U.S. Congress. The Henry Hyde Act was described as an "enabling legislation"[12] as it created legal space, hitherto blocked by the Nuclear Nonproliferation Act of 1978 (NNPA), for resuming nuclear trade with India—a non-signatory of the NPT and a de facto nuclear weapon state. Nonetheless, Congress attached certain clauses to emphasize the nonproliferation measures, such as: the president must annually certify that India is adhering to the terms of the agreement; India must sign a safeguards agreement with the IAEA and get clearance from the NSG; and, most significantly, the deal will lapse if India conducts further nuclear tests.[13]

On the basis of the earlier agreements (July 2005 and March 2006) and the Henry Hyde legislation, a separate technical agreement, popularly called the Indo-U.S. 123 Agreement, was signed by the two countries.[14] It specified respective obligations of the United States and India. In this regard, India was required to sign a safeguards agreement with the IAEA and seek approval from the NSG. Accordingly, in March 2008, India entered into negotiations with the IAEA to develop a framework for safeguards. Following this, India approached the forty-five nation Nuclear Suppliers Group for approval; after hectic diplomatic negotiations led by the United States, the NSG granted an India-specific waiver. Other prominent members besides the U.S—including France, Russia, Britain, and Canada—had already shown interest in nuclear cooperation with India.[15] On the fulfillment of the conditions—the safeguards agreement with the IAEA and the NSG exemption—the 123 Agreement was introduced in the U.S. Congress. Significantly, the agreement was passed with an overwhelming majority in both the House of Representatives and the Senate. Finally, the U.S.-India Nuclear Cooperation Bill was signed into law by President Bush in December 2008.

Following sections will analyze the U.S.-India agreement in context of the nuclear nonproliferation regime.

NUCLEAR NONPROLIFERATION REGIME: CONSTITUENT ATTRIBUTES[16]

In the theoretical context, Stephen Krasner's conceptualization of a regime is the most widely accepted definition of a regime. According to Krasner, a regime is a set of principles, norms, rules, and decision-making procedures; principles and norms reign supreme and define the latter elements.[17] Critics argue there is considerable conceptual overlap and practical difficulty in discerning largely implicit principles and norms. Levy, Young, and Zurn note that principles "involve goal orientations and causal beliefs at the level of the general policy arena," while, "norms describe general rights and obligations mainly at the level of issue areas."[18] That is, principles can be regarded as the fundamental set of assumptions and objectives underlying a regime in a particular issue area; the norms define and regulate the behavior of participant state actors. Rules are regarded as the most concrete and explicit elements of a regime and are usually enshrined in multilateral or bilateral agreements.[19]

The nuclear nonproliferation regime came into being with the signing of the nuclear nonproliferation treaty in 1968. Prior to the NPT, the Atoms for Peace program represented a rudimentary attempt to encourage civilian nuclear cooperation between technological advanced nations and developing countries. It led to nuclear cooperation between several countries including sales of research reactors and participation of foreign scientists in nuclear research projects. Nonetheless, a major drawback of the nuclear cooperation under Atoms for Peace was that no nuclear nonproliferation assurances were elicited from recipients and the suppliers provided limited technology. The Atoms for Peace program did not constitute a regime because it "had no injunctions, and injunctions are the 'essence' of regimes."[20] Thus, "participating countries were free to pursue military programs in conjunction with externally assisted peaceful ones, as did France; there was no compulsory renunciation of a weapons option."[21] Similarly, the CIRUS agreement between the United States, India, and Canada, signed in mid-1950s—is a classic example of this project. The CIRUS agreement, which contained no stringent nuclear nonproliferation provisions, turned sour as it was alleged that India had diverted the nuclear technology for the 1974 "peaceful" nuclear explosion.[22] Subsequently, there was a growing awareness that the use and transfer of nuclear technology needs to be regulated. Besides NPT, several export control arrangements were set up with the intention "to overcome the deleterious effects of uncontrolled diffusion of nuclear technology but promote its organized use."[23]

Employing Krasner's definition, T.V. Paul defines the nuclear nonproliferation regime as "a set of norms, principles, treaties and procedures through which countries pledge not to acquire nuclear weapons or help in their acquisition by other states."[24] The nuclear nonproliferation regime confronts the potentially dangerous horizontal spread of nuclear technology. The spread of nuclear weapons can be fatal, but the spread of atomic energy and its promotion for peaceful uses is beneficial for humankind. Therefore, the guiding principle of the nuclear nonproliferation regime is: *controlled access to nuclear technology and regulation of the behavior of recipients and suppliers.*[25] Hasenclever, Mayer, and Rittberger, observe that norms "serve to guide the behavior of regime members in such a way as to produce collective outcomes which are in harmony with the goals and shared convictions that are specified in the regime principles."[26] Thus, the non-acquisition of nuclear weapons by additional states (nonnuclear weapon states) and non-transfer of nuclear technology without verification by both nuclear weapon states (NWS) and nonnuclear weapon states (NNWS) can be recognized as the main norms of the nuclear nonproliferation regime.[27]

Based on these guiding principles and norms, a complex web of wide-ranging regulations and decision-making procedures enshrined in several multilateral and bilateral agreements serve as prescriptions for the behavior of participant states. The NPT forms the core of the nonproliferation regime and defines the global nuclear order based on a categorization of states as nuclear weapon states and nonnuclear weapon states. The nuclear bargain underlying the nonproliferation regime is institutionalized through the treaty. NWS are obligated not to transfer nuclear weapons to NNWS, and not to export nuclear materials without international safeguards. The NNWS are obliged to renounce their right to build nuclear weapons, but are assured fullest possible nuclear cooperation—including technology, equipment, materials, and knowledge—within a purview of international safeguards.[28] It is important to note that there is significant emphasis on "horizontal" nonproliferation, i.e., prevention of new nuclear states, which India and other non-aligned states had resisted. The NPT also includes a *joint* obligation, albeit weakly worded, for both categories of states to work toward nuclear disarmament.[29]

The NPT articulates intrusive enforcement and verification measures in the form of nuclear safeguards, mainly for the NNWS. The Nuclear Nonproliferation Treaty lacks an inherent monitoring agency, and therefore, the IAEA, established in 1957, is assigned the responsibility to ensure the peaceful uses of energy in nonnuclear weapon states. The IAEA, through a system of nuclear safeguards, ensures that peaceful nuclear materials are not diverted to military purposes. Besides the NPT, the IAEA also provides verification support to several other nuclear agreements and thus plays an important role in global nuclear governance. Trevor Findlay remarks, the IAEA is "the principal organization embodiment of the nuclear nonproliferation regime."[30] Furthermore, "the international system of safeguards governing nuclear energy cooperation is critical to the continued efficacy of the nonproliferation regime."[31]

In accordance with Article III of the NPT, each NNWS is obliged to accept comprehensive (or full-scope) safeguards at its nuclear facilities. In this respect, NNWSs sign individual agreements with the IAEA and declare their nuclear facilities and inventories of nuclear materials.[32] In the late 1990s, based on lessons learned from the revelations of clandestine nuclear activities in North Korea and Iran, the IAEA adopted strengthened safeguards and designed an additional protocol to be accepted by the states. To ensure a broader assessment of states' nuclear activities, the additional protocol requires "states to report nuclear-related equipment production, imports and exports, fuel-cycle-related research and development, and plans for new facilities."[33] In an attempt to ensure comprehensive coverage of states' nuclear activities, the strengthened safeguards have shifted from a quantitative to a qualitative approach—including remote monitoring, environmental sampling, and information from open sources—to assess states' intentions.[34]

Usually, a particular treaty or agreement comes to be regarded as the sole normative source of the respective regime. But this is a narrow and misleading perspective and it is important to view the regime as a "functional whole, which may be composed of a rather heterogeneous set of (formal and informal) agreements, practices, and institutions."[35] An important point is that, although the NPT constitutes the core of the nuclear nonproliferation regime, it is not synonymous with the regime.[36] In this context, Lloyd Axworthy remarked:

> The nuclear nonproliferation regime is based on, and anchored in, international law and norms, as well as incorporated into international mechanisms. The NPT is fundamental, but the broader regime is a complex system of multilateral and bilateral agreements, arrangements, and mechanism intended to promote and achieve a world without nuclear weapons, sooner rather than later. . . . The regime is in-

> tended to provide a framework to enable the world to make effective use of nuclear capability for peaceful purposes.[37]

That is, besides the NPT, there are hordes of other agreements—multilateral and bilateral—that contain injunctions for participants and thereby, constitute the nuclear nonproliferation regime. The examples include but are not limited to: the Statute of the International Atomic Energy Agency; the additional protocol (IAEA); the *Tlatelolco* and *Rarotonga* nuclear weapons free zone treaties of Latin America and the South Pacific, respectively; and the Partial Test Ban Treaty. Recent additions to the nuclear nonproliferation regime include: the Comprehensive Test Ban Treaty (CTBT); UNSCR 1540 resolution; the Proliferation Security Initiative; the Container Security Initiative, and the Global Initiative to Counter terrorism. In this context, the Fissile Material Cut-Off Treaty is still being negotiated in the Conference on Disarmament. Once it is formulated and signed it will place restrictions on the amount of nuclear fissile material accumulated by nuclear weapon states and defacto-nuclear weapon states.

Export control arrangements form another important constituent of the nuclear nonproliferation regime. As discussed previously, in the aftermath of India's so-called peaceful nuclear explosion, there was a spurt of technological control groups such as the Nuclear Suppliers Group (NSG) and the Zangger Committee. Since then, export controls have become an important constituent of the nuclear nonproliferation regime. These export control arrangements not only ensure supplier restraints, including placement of intrusive IAEA safeguards on the transfer of nuclear technology to nonweapon states, but also "establish guidelines for nuclear commerce that would keep commercial competition from undercutting safeguard obligations."[38] Nuclear nonproliferation regime scholars regard the unilateral policies of key suppliers (e.g., the United States, Britain, Canada) that define the rules of nuclear trade as a significant component of the nuclear nonproliferation regime.[39] Roger K. Smith argues that "Less immediate, but no less critical, rules and decision-making procedures can be found in each country's laws—especially the nuclear suppliers."[40] In this context, since the mid-1970s, the United States has actively strengthened its domestic legislations to thwart the proliferation of nuclear technologies. The most important being: (i) the Arms Export Control Act of 1976; and (ii) the Nuclear Nonproliferation Act of 1978 (NNPA).[41]

CIVILIAN NUCLEAR COOPERATION—AN INSTRUMENT OF U.S. NONPROLIFERATION POLICY

Since the beginning of the atomic era, peaceful nuclear cooperation, that is, "transfer of nuclear technology, materials, and knowledge" between states has been relatively common.[42] In fact, Eisenhower's "Atoms of

Peace" speech ignited a universal interest in harnessing nuclear energy for sustainable development and encouraged advanced nuclear nations to engage in civilian nuclear cooperation with developing countries. Yet, cognizant of the dual potential of "atoms of peace" Eisenhower proposed several measures to restrict militarization of nuclear technology. Similarly, the NPT recognizes the inalienable right of nonnuclear weapon states to civilian nuclear energy and pledges nuclear assistance, but it does not grant unconditional access. Article III of the treaty prescribes acceptance of full-scope IAEA safeguards as the condition for peaceful nuclear assistance to nonnuclear weapon states. These safeguards require verification measures on all nuclear facilities to rule out diversion of nuclear material from civilian to military purposes. Thus, as William Foster, points out:

> Neither uranium enrichment nor the stockpiling of fissionable material in connection with a peaceful program would violate Article II so long as these activities were safeguarded under Article III. Also, clearly permitted would be the development under safeguards of plutonium fueled power reactors, including research on the properties of metallic plutonium, nor would Article II interfere with the development or use of fast breeder reactors under safeguards.[43]

In the last several decades, the nuclear nonproliferation regime has evolved through several export control measures, treaties, and agreements. Yet, this neither hampered large scale nuclear energy programs nor stalled peaceful nuclear cooperation—there are more than 2,000 bilateral nuclear agreements among the states.[44] Several nonnuclear weapon states—Canada, Australia, and Japan—that accepted comprehensive safeguards in accordance with Article III, not only developed advanced nuclear energy programs but also emerged as significant suppliers in the international nuclear order. For instance, "Canada has 27 nuclear cooperation agreements in force, covering 44 states, parties to the Nonproliferation Treaty, both developed and developing, to provide a framework for the fullest possible exchange of nuclear, and other material, equipment, and technology."[45] Even the United States, despite the rigorous measures and safeguards contained in the Nuclear Nonproliferation Act of 1978, has engaged in civilian nuclear cooperation with approximately twenty-two countries—ranging from advanced industrialized countries to developing nations in the Middle East, South America, and Asia, including some that have yet not launched civil nuclear power programs such as Bangladesh, Columbia, Egypt, Morocco, Peru, Thailand, and Turkey.[46] With increasing realization of the benefits of nuclear energy to combat climate change coupled with a paucity of energy resources, the demand for nuclear energy is rising. Consequently, the list of recipients of nuclear technology is expanding at a rapid pace, even among smaller states such as Jordan, Vietnam, Qatar, and Algeria. According to Matthew Fuhrmann, "The global nuclear marketplace is more active today than it has been in at least 20 years. Countries in Latin America, Southeast Asia, the Middle East, and Africa have expressed a desire to begin or revive civilian nuclear programs."[47]

Scholars affirm that nuclear trade has been an important component of U.S. nuclear nonproliferation policy.[48] Washington has often used the incentive of nuclear cooperation to elicit nonproliferation commitments from recipient countries. For instance, in 2009 the United States signed a nuclear cooperation agreement with the UAE, a long term commitment to supply nuclear fuel, and elicited the latter's renunciation of development of enrichment and reprocessing capabilities. Jennifer Weeks argues, "This linkage [between nuclear trade and nonproliferation objectives] was reasonably effective through the mid-1970s, while the United States dominated the international nuclear market." Due to the incentive of nuclear trade with the United States, several countries signed the NPT with full or partial safeguards on their nuclear programs.[49] In the mid-1990s the United States also used this strategy to deal with North Korea's noncompliance with the treaty's provisions. North Korea acceded to the NPT in 1985 but reached safeguards agreement with the IAEA only in 1992. With the beginning of IAEA inspections in June 1992, it was found that Pyongyang's declarations of nuclear facilities and weapons-usable plutonium were incomplete and dishonest. This created a severe crisis between the United States and North Korea and stoked fears of war.[50] Amid the crisis, the Clinton administration engaged North Korea in an agreed framework. Washington offered two light water reactors through a multilateral consortium to meet North Korea's energy needs in return for the latter's commitment to halt operations and eventually dismantle its reactor and reprocessing Yongbon plant, freeze construction of two nuclear reactors, and adhere to the IAEA safeguards.[51] This nuclear agreement "managed to contain Pyongyang's plutonium program for nearly a decade."[52] Fred McGoldrick emphasizes the significance of civilian nuclear cooperation in U.S. nuclear nonproliferation policy. He remarks:

> The U.S. agreements for cooperation in peaceful nuclear energy with other states require strict nonproliferation controls that go beyond those of other suppliers, such as consent rights on reprocessing, enrichment, and storage of weapons-usable materials subject to our agreements. They also provide a framework for establishing invaluable person-to-person and institution-to-institution contacts and collaboration that can help advance our nonproliferation objectives.[53]

The U.S.-India nuclear agreement needs to be viewed in this context. During the senate committee hearings, Condoleezza Rice stated "This initiative aligns India more closely with international nuclear nonproliferation standards."[54]

ACCOMMODATING INDIA WITHIN THE NUCLEAR REGIME

Based on the analysis in the above sections, it is clear: (i) injunctions are the essence of regimes; (ii) the nuclear nonproliferation regime is not restricted to the NPT, rather it is comprised of a matrix of institutions and agreements; and (iii) the United States has utilized the civil nuclear cooperation agreements to promote nonproliferation objectives. Viewed in this context, the U.S.-India nuclear pact "subjects India to political and normative pressures" to accept several nonproliferation obligations of the nuclear nonproliferation regime.[55]

Right from the beginning India had an anomalous relationship with the NPT, which in turn prevented India's inclusion in the nuclear nonproliferation regime. Despite decades of technological embargoes, India indigenously developed nuclear weapons aggravating the challenge for the nuclear nonproliferation regime. For three decades, India had refused to accede to the NPT and therefore, remained outside the entire gamut of the nuclear regime. Philip Zelikow remarks, the nuclear regime is "actually a complex of interrelated norms, habits, original memberships," and a variety of agreements.[56] Since the signing of the NPT in 1970, "decades of legal and regulatory relationships had evolved around the nonproliferation system. *And India was outside them all*" (emphasis added).[57] Nonetheless, Zelikow opines that India, despite being an alien to the nonproliferation regime, was neither harming nor contributing to the strengthening of the system. Rather, India had developed a whole set of attitudes about the nonproliferation system based on "a combination of frustration and surreal resentment and pride that it [India] could do anything it wanted to do without any help from anyone else."[58] This is exemplified in India's civilian and military nuclear program, along with indigenous state-of-the-art space and missile programs, built despite long standing technological embargoes. Nonetheless, there were significant concerns that existing outside the nuclear regime, India could build next generation of nuclear weapons, thereby, causing a South Asian nuclear arms race. Thus, India's attitude as a "resentful outsider" was not beneficial to the nonproliferation system, and reigning India into the nuclear nonproliferation regime was considered to be crucial.

In 2001, the Central Intelligence Agency (CIA), in an unclassified report to the U.S. Congress, highlighted the risks of leaving the defacto nuclear weapon states outside the nonproliferation regime. It emphasized strengthening of national export control laws in defacto nuclear weapon states to reduce a considerable proliferation risk. The report stated that, with the advancement in their domestic capabilities, "traditional recipients of WMD and missile technology could emerge as new suppliers of technology and expertise. Many of these countries—such as India, Iran, and Pakistan—are not members of supplier groups such as the Nuclear Suppliers Group, the Australia Group, and the Missile Technology

Control Regime and [therefore] do not adhere to their export constraints." Also, private companies, scientists, and engineers in these countries could take advantage "of weak or unenforceable national export controls and the growing availability of technology." Thus, the CIA report emphasized the necessity to engage defacto nuclear weapon states, as leaving them in isolation would only weaken the nonproliferation system.[59] This added urgency to the decades old dilemma faced by the United States regarding how to include India within the nuclear nonproliferation regime. It was a foregone conclusion that India would neither rollback its nuclear weapons program, nor sign the NPT. Therefore, the choice was limited: either leave India outside the nuclear regime—that is without any restrictions on its civilian or nuclear weapons program—or accommodate the fact that India has developed the nuclear weapons, in order to regulate India's nuclear behavior and prevent further advancement of its nuclear weapons program. The Bush administration chose the latter option. As Zelikow emphasizes:

> *We were trapped in a conundrum from which there was no solution except to cut the Gordian knot. I think there was no way to just untie the knot strand by strand.* Either India was going to be part of the nonproliferation system or was going to stay in the half-way house. There was no way to bring India into the nonproliferation system unless you grandfather the fact that they already had nuclear weapons.[60] (emphasis added)

In view of India's refusal to accede to the NPT, the Bush administration in a strategic move enrolled India in a specific nuclear cooperation arrangement to foster the latter's adherence to equally significant non-NPT regulations, thereby, prevent further damage to the nuclear nonproliferation regime.

The following detailed discussion of the terms of the U.S.-India nuclear agreement reveals how the United States enlisted India in accordance with the significant injunctions and institutions of the nuclear nonproliferation regime.

Moratorium on Nuclear Testing

In exchange for receiving the nuclear technology, India committed to maintain a moratorium on nuclear testing. The Henry Hyde Act clearly specifies that the nuclear cooperation deal with India will be terminated in the event of a nuclear test conducted by India.[61] Not only the United States, even the members of the Nuclear Suppliers Group could withdraw their waiver leading to a "cut off nuclear supplies."[62] The possibility that any further nuclear testing could lead to termination of the nuclear deal will act as a strong deterrent for India.[63] A. Gopalakrishnan affirms, "no future Indian government will dare to test a nuclear weapon in the face of this potential loss of investment, whatever the deteriorated and outdated status of our nuclear deterrent."[64] Although India was reluctant to sign the Comprehensive Nuclear-Test-Ban Treaty (CTBT), this adherence to the moratorium on nuclear testing will strengthen the nuclear nonproliferation regime and will cap India's nuclear capabilities.

In the absence of this moratorium, any further nuclear testing by India would not only impinge on the success of CTBT but could also plunge South Asia in a nuclear arms race and further destabilize the region. Indian tests would "provide political cover for Pakistan and China" to conduct nuclear tests too.[65] Scholars suggest that "a small number of nuclear tests would permit Beijing to perfect warheads that would allow it to target the United States much more effectively. Thus, Indian testing could lead, through a short sequence of events, not only danger in Asia, but also to very direct risk for the United States."[66]

This commitment to refrain from nuclear testing will prevent India from developing state of the art nuclear weapons. Dinshaw Mistry regards it as a "significant concession [made by India] because most of India's nuclear weapons are believed to be first-generation fission weapons, and India's 1998 thermonuclear test was at best a partial success."[67] Understandably, at some stage India would need further testing to develop thermonuclear weapons, or else its nuclear capabilities will be outdated. Bharat Karnad opines, "this deal amounts to death by stagnation for the Indian nuclear weapons program." He emphasizes that for India to be treated as "a country of consequence," it is important to have a thermonuclear deterrent—"the prime currency of power in the new millennium."[68] Thus, India's renunciation of nuclear testing is perilous. Unlike the United States, New Delhi has neither the data nor the technology to conduct the simulated nuclear tests required to develop a thermonuclear deterrent. The U.S. has test data from about 1,054 nuclear tests along with "a computing ability of 100 teraflops and a gigantic ICF facility to obtain miniature thermonuclear explosions."[69] Arun Shourie, after thorough analysis of the terms of the U.S.-India agreement and related U.S. legislation, concluded that Washington desired that "India [be] drained of its strategic nuclear program, and thus [become] a dependent India."[70] He warned that the United States planned ultimately to "rollback and eventually eliminate the nuclear weapons capability of India."[71]

Controlled Nuclear Fuel Supply

The nuclear agreement lacks lifetime guarantee of nuclear fuel supplies to India for the nuclear reactors built by the United States. A. Gopalkrishnan, former Chairman of the Atomic Energy Regulatory Board of the Government of India, emphasizes that "iron-clad assurances" for nuclear fuel supplies are critical to ensure that all imported reactors would "run for their lifetime at high capacity." Earlier in the case of Tarapur nuclear reactor, India had to suffer because of the suspension of nuclear fuel by Washington. Furthermore, the Henry Hyde Act restricts India from stockpiling more than 2–3 years of nuclear fuel supplies; it also stipulates that the U.S. president will provide annual certification that the nuclear fuel supply supplied to India is not in excess of India's civilian requirements and does not contribute to its military program.[72] This provides enough scope for political manoeuvrings and arm twisting by Washington, if India does not follow its dictates on nonproliferation issues, such as the Fissile Material Cut-Off treaty, negotiations, Proliferation Security Initiative or even Iran's nuclear issue. Thus, in India, there was significant apprehension, that a "nuclear weapon test is not the only event which can lead to a temporary or long-term disruption of supplies through termination or suspension of the deal."[73] That is, in the absence of iron-clad assurances of lifetime fuel supplies for the nuclear reactors could result in temporary or long-term suspensions of nuclear fuel. This could translate into significant economic loss for India,[74] as in addition to the United States, India has signed agreements with several countries, thus, making a huge economic investment. In this context, P.K. Iyengar, an Indian nuclear physicist lamented, "The much-hyped promise of nuclear technology doesn't translate to much in real terms." Instead, "Through the 123 Agreement the U.S. has presented us with a gilded cage. By signing the Agreement, we would voluntarily walk into the cage."[75]

Strengthening of India's Nuclear Export Controls

As a nuclear outlier and member of the nonaligned movement, India viewed the multilateral export control regimes as technological apartheid. For the last several decades India refused to adhere to the regulations of these multinational cartels. Through several laws passed since 1962, India instituted a "unilateral set of controls" to regulate its nuclear exports.[76] But, in the contemporary nuclear era, there were growing concerns that these were not broad and stringent enough to prevent leakage of sensitive nuclear materials and technologies. In this context, Randall Woods points out, "While India's export-control system is fairly well developed by international standards, a case in 2003 in which a private engineering company exported some dual-use items and precursors to Iraq via Shell companies in Jordan and Dubai showed that the legal framework and enforcement system contain some serious gaps." Though the High Technology and Cooperation Group (HTCG) as well as Next Steps in Strategic Partnership (NSSP) "promoted streamlining the export process to stimulate trade," yet there were concerns regarding India's export controls to ensure there was no proliferation of the dangerous technologies.[77] This emphasized an urgency to synchronize India's nuclear export regulations with current international standards to prevent unintentional proliferation of India's nuclear materials and know-how.

In the post–9/11 era, there is increased perception of nuclear terrorism and illicit trafficking as grave dangers to international security. This raises concerns about the vulnerability of nuclear materials and technologies and increased emphasis on strengthening global export controls. Levi and Ferguson averred that, in the absence of any regulations, India could serve as a potential, "source of nuclear weapons or materials, and a partner in interdicting dangerous nuclear traffic."[78] The changed global nuclear scenario necessitated that all states possessing sensitive nuclear materials, especially defacto nuclear weapon states like India and Pakistan, be "brought into compliance" with international export controls.[79] Therefore, several leading nonproliferation scholars recommended that "India and Pakistan . . . immediately and unconditionally bring their export control laws and practices up to the most stringent international standards by establishing databases and border controls to prevent scientists and engineers from proliferating nuclear know-how."[80]

In this context, the U.S.-India nuclear pact, inclusive of measures to synchronize India's export controls, is a significant achievement for the nuclear nonproliferation regime. The 2008 nuclear pact marked a progression from the successful strengthening of India export controls in the HTCG and NSSP agreements. The deal mandated India to align its export regulations with those of Nuclear Suppliers Group (NSG) and the Missile Technology Control Regime (MTCR). Pursuing it further, the Henry Hyde Act requires an annual presidential determination that India has adopted necessary measures to secure sensitive materials and technology. Additionally, under U.S. insistence, India agreed to harmonize its export control lists with the Wassenaar Arrangement and the Australia Group.[81]

In the last decade, the United States, in concert with other prominent states, broadened the scope of the nuclear nonproliferation regime through several initiatives aimed at strengthening nuclear export regulations and ensuring their stringent enforcement. These included: United Nations Security Resolution (UNSCR) 1540, the Proliferation Security Initiative (PSI), the Container Security Initiative (CSI), and the Global Initiative to Combat Nuclear Terrorism (GICNT).[82] Washington sought India's participation in all these initiatives. India implemented UNSCR 1540 and accordingly made statutory and regulatory changes in its export regulations.[83] In June 2005, using UNSCR 1540 guidelines, India adopted a comprehensive WMD legislation, The Weapons of Mass Destruction and their Delivery Systems (Prohibition of Unlawful Activities), to strengthen its export controls and their enforcement. The Henry Hyde Act stipulates that India must join the PSI, but according to the then India's Minister of State for Defence M. M. Pallam Raju, "The PSI is a very good initiative, but we do have other domestic political compulsions. There is some resistance. We are working on that."[84] Meanwhile, India made an important port CSI-compliant and initiated the process of achieving compliance.

Founded in 2006, the objective of the GICNT is to "prevent the acquisition, transport, or use by terrorists of nuclear materials and radioactive substances or improvised explosive devices using such materials, as well as hostile actions against nuclear facilities."[85] India joined the GICNT and thereafter, is actively participating in its "working groups on nuclear detection, nuclear forensics, and response and mitigation."[86]

Thus, the July 2005 nuclear agreement and related U.S. legislation launched the process for gradually integrating India into the nuclear nonproliferation regime.

Adoption of IAEA Nuclear Safeguards

For three decades, since the signing of the NPT, India evaded adoption of comprehensive IAEA nuclear safeguards, terming them as discriminatory. India accepted only facility-specific safeguards on six of its nuclear reactors obtained through international cooperation.[87] Furthermore, in late 1990s, India refused to sign the IAEA Additional Protocol, regarding it as an extension of the discriminatory NPT system.[88] Thus, except for the safeguards on the six nuclear reactors, India's nuclear program was shielded from IAEA inspectors and from the international community.

The July 2005 agreement overcame this deficit, enjoining India to accept IAEA safeguards on its civilian nuclear facilities and sign the Additional Protocol. Before, the implementation of the agreement, the Henry Hyde Act, Section 104 (b) (3), necessitated a presidential determination regarding the substantial progress of India and the IAEA on the Additional Protocol, in accordance with the principles and policies of IAEA specific to India's civil nuclear program.[89] Subsequently, in accordance with its July 2005 commitment as well as the Henry Hyde Act, India separated its nuclear facilities into civilian and strategic units. In August 2008, India signed an agreement with the IAEA and, with approval of the IAEA's Board of Governors, India accepted safeguards on its civilian facilities. The India-IAEA Agreement is an "umbrella agreement" that would serve as a model for India's future nuclear agreements with other countries.[90] In May 2009, India also signed the additional protocol with the IAEA.

In fulfilment of its IAEA related commitment, India declared the list of its civilian nuclear facilities. The majority of India's nuclear reactors, fourteen out of twenty-two, including both existing and future nuclear power reactors, were required to be placed under safeguards by 2014. Condoleezza Rice remarked, "Under this initiative, 65 percent of India's thermal reactors will be brought under safeguards, a figure that the Indian government has said could rise as high as 90 percent as India procures more civil reactors in the next 15 years."[91] Furthermore, India agreed to place all future nuclear reactors, whether breeder or thermal, under IAEA safeguards. These safeguards are permanent, that is, once a facility is placed under safeguards, it cannot be withdrawn. Initially, the issue of permanent safeguards was linked to an unrestricted lifetime supply of nuclear fuel from the United States. Although India did not obtain guaranteed lifetime nuclear supplies, yet, it conceded to the nuclear safeguards in perpetuity. India also identified eight nuclear reactors as strategic and thereby, were placed outside the nuclear safeguards. Dinshaw Mistry comments, "India's nuclear separation plan struck a balance between Washington's position, which was influenced by U.S. domestic lobbies, that India place most of its nuclear facilities under safeguards, and India's position, influenced by its nuclear scientists, of keeping key facilities away from international inspections."[92]

Critics argue that India's acceptance of safeguards is merely symbolic, as India has not accepted full-scope safeguards like the NNWS. Furthermore, India was able to choose which facilities to declare as civilian and place under IAEA safeguards. Also, it is argued that "India's Additional Protocol does not contain most of the Model Protocol's provisions, requiring only that India provide the IAEA with information about its nuclear exports."[93]

In this context, I argue that instead of focusing on what is absent in the U.S.-India nuclear deal, it is important to recognize the nonproliferation commitments obtained from India. First, for three decades there was considerable ambiguity regarding India's nuclear program, including civilian. For the first time, India has accepted international inspections of its civilian nuclear program, this in itself is a significant achievement for the nuclear regime. Second, India has accepted safeguards in perpetuity, that is, even if the nuclear agreement with the United States falls apart, India cannot withdraw its facilities from IAEA safeguards.[94] Third, there are concerns that India has kept eight reactors, mainly its breeder reactors, outside of safeguards. These breeder reactors could be a source for plutonium production.[95] Previously, there was no distinction between India's civilian and military facilities, that is, India could have used all the nuclear reactors for strategic purposes. But, post 2005 agreement, India has only eight strategic reactors. Condoleezza Rice emphasized, "imagine the alternative: Without this initiative, 81 percent of India's current power reactors—and its future power and breeder reactors—would continue to remain outside of IAEA safeguards. The Indian nuclear power program would remain opaque, a nuclear black box."[96]

Subsequently, in 2010, under U.S. influence, India shut down the controversial CIRUS reactor. In this context, Brahma Chellaney remarks, this "will deprive the nuclear military program of almost one-third of its current supply of weapons-grade plutonium."[97] Moreover, India has agreed to participate in the formulation of a fissile material cut-off treaty and to sign it. When India signs the treaty, the production of weapons-usable materials will halt, and India will not be able to use the plutonium from the nuclear reactors identified for strategic purposes. Thus, viewed in conjunction with India's readiness to accept a fissile material cut off, the IAEA safeguards can significantly limit the growth of India's nuclear program. The then IAEA director-general ElBaradei welcomed India's intention to identify and place all its civilian nuclear facilities under IAEA safeguards and sign and adhere to an additional protocol with respect to civilian nuclear facilities. He considered it as "a step forward toward universalization of the international safeguards regime."[98]

Denial of Enrichment and Reprocessing Technologies

Enrichment and reprocessing technologies (ENR) used for producing fuel for nuclear reactors can also be used to produce weapons-usable materials—highly enriched uranium and plutonium—for direct use in nuclear weapons. It is "difficult and challenging" for the IAEA to detect facilities that enrich uranium and plutonium. Furthermore, the production of nuclear fissionable materials not only adds to the risk of state-level proliferation, it also increases the dangers of nuclear theft and illicit trafficking.[99] It is increasingly realized that "restraining the spread of reprocessing and enrichment capabilities must be a fundamental component of any nuclear nonproliferation policy."[100]

The noncompliance issues of North Korea and Iran focused attention on a loophole in the Nuclear Nonproliferation Treaty. That is, nonnuclear weapon state signatories of the NPT can legitimately acquire enrichment and reprocessing technologies and subsequently, legally withdraw from the treaty in accordance with Article X. Jon Wolfsthal remarks that this weakness of the NPT "allows governments, in full compliance with their nonproliferation obligations, to produce and possess enriched uranium or separated plutonium, with few assurances that they will not at some point use the material for less-than-peaceful purposes."[101] In 2004, highlighting the need to evolve strategy for the spread of nuclear power without the threat of proliferation, President Bush stated:

> I propose a way to close the loophole. . . . Enrichment and reprocessing are not necessary for nations seeking to harness nuclear energy for peaceful purposes. The 40 nations of the Nuclear Suppliers Group should refuse to sell enrichment and reprocessing equipment and technologies to any state that does not already possess full-scale functioning enrichment and reprocessing plants.[102]

Although, initially, this proposal was rejected by the NSG, yet the notion to curb the spread of ENR technologies gained wider acceptance.[103]

Viewed in this context, the U.S.-India nuclear pact is quite significant. First, cognizant of India's ENR capabilities and possession of related technologies, Washington elicited a critical nonproliferation commitment from India. In the nuclear pact, New Delhi agreed to not transfer sensitive technologies, particularly enrichment and reprocessing technologies, to nations that do not possess them. In addition, India committed to support international efforts to curb the spread of such technologies. Levi and Ferguson remark, this "reinforces an important but largely moribund Bush administration initiative aimed at closing a loophole in the NPT that allows states to acquire bomb-making technologies under civilian guise."[104] Second, Washington allowed India to reprocess the by-products of U.S.-provided nuclear reactors that constitute "safeguarded nuclear materials" only in a new facility especially built for reprocessing and placed under IAEA safeguards.[105] The insistence on new facility was to ensure full compliance with the IAEA safeguards as designs of older facilities may sometimes not allow full application of advanced nuclear safeguards.

Third, and most significantly, the United States refused to sell enrichment and reprocessing technologies to India. In view of India's limited domestic uranium supplies and extensive thorium supplies, Homi Bhaba, the father of the Indian nuclear program, had envisioned a three-stage, closed fuel-cycle, civilian nuclear strategy for India. In the first phase, the aim was to build a few uranium reactors; then, in the second stage, fast breeder reactors would be built that would use plutonium from the spent fuel of the uranium reactors; finally, in the third stage, thorium based reactors would be built to utilize the spent fuel from the fast breeder reactors. Thus, in every stage, reprocessing of the spent fuel is essential for the Indian program. With the expansion of the Indian program, India would need a large-scale reprocessing technology. It is estimated that "India will need to put up eight to ten times the present reprocessing capacity in the coming years to handle the spent fuel from the increasing number of reactors."[106]

Initially, the July 2005 agreement ambiguously pledged "full-scope nuclear cooperation" with New Delhi. This created expectations in India that the agreement included enrichment and reprocessing technologies. But, this is not the case. Michael Krepon in his article, "Another Contentious Issue" provides evidence that ENR technologies are not part of the deal. Robert Joseph, undersecretary of state, in response to the Senate Foreign Relations Committee in November 2005, stated: "We do not intend to provide enrichment and reprocessing technology to India."[107] The Henry Hyde Act, Article 103 (5), delineates the U.S. policy on ENR technologies: "given the special sensitivity of equipment and technologies related to the enrichment of uranium, the reprocessing of spent nuclear fuel, and the production of heavy water, [we need to] work with the members of the NSG, individually and collectively, to further restrict the transfers of such equipment and technologies, including to India."[108] Similarly, at the April 5, 2006, Congressional hearings, Condoleezza Rice affirmed that "the proposed [123] agreement for peaceful nuclear cooperation will not provide for exports of SNT [sensitive nuclear technologies];

the agreement would have to be amended (and the amendment submitted to Congress for review) to allow for such exports."[109]

Thus, Washington refused to sell ENR technologies to India, in addition, elicited a commitment from India as well, not to sell ENR technologies to countries that do not already possess them. This was a significant step toward strengthening the nuclear nonproliferation regime and limit the expansion of India's civilian as well as its nuclear weapons program. R. Ramachandran, assessing the impact of the deal on India, lamented:

> Having made a huge mistake of entering into the India-U.S. nuclear deal, it would be prudent now to focus on scaling up indigenous reprocessing capacity as a priority. The new facility opened . . . at Tarapur is also of only 100 tonne capacity. What we need are plants with capacities of several hundred tonnes. Given that the gestation period of these new plants is six to seven years, there is adequate time for expanding reprocessing capacity. The flip side, of course, is that these new plants will have to be brought under IAEA safeguards.[110]

Commitment to Fissile Material Cut-off

A ban on the production of fissile materials is extremely critical in the current global scenario. Emphasizing the significance of the Fissile Material Cut-off Treaty (FMCT), William Walker aptly remarked, "Regulating fissile materials is the only plausible way to tackle simultaneously the troublesome [multifaceted] challenges of our era."[111] It will (i) prevent the emergence of additional nuclear weapon states; (ii) curb the possibility of development of crude bombs by nonstate actors; (iii) curtail the nuclear arms race at the global as well as the regional level, especially in South Asia—between India-Pakistan or India-China; and (iv) ensure a proliferation risk free environment for expansion of peaceful nuclear power.[112] Leading nonproliferation scholars agree that phasing out of the fissile material production in India and Pakistan is "the single most effective way for Pakistan and India to limit the nuclear arms race, and to contain the pool of material that could potentially be diverted to terrorists."[113]

In the July 2005 agreement, India agreed to actively engage in the negotiations of a fissile material cut-off treaty. Taking into account, India's history of rejecting the nonproliferation treaties, this was a significant commitment to the nuclear nonproliferation regime. Whether the FMCT prohibits the future production of fissile material or affects the current stockpile, it would "effectively cap the growth of India's nuclear arsenal." Also, India would be unable to use plutonium from any of its eight strategic nuclear reactors for weaponization.[114]

Thus, the above discussion reflects that the U.S.-India nuclear agreement regulates India's nuclear behavior—in accordance with the important regulations and procedures of the nuclear nonproliferation regime—

to cap India's nuclear weapons program and to prevent horizontal proliferation of nuclear materials from India. Broadly speaking, the measures included in the nuclear pact: (i) moratorium on nuclear testing: prohibits development of next generation nuclear weapons; (ii) strengthening of export controls: prevents voluntary or involuntary transfer of nuclear materials and technology; (iii) IAEA nuclear safeguards place India's civilian nuclear program under international scanner; (iv) limited nuclear fuel supply: restricts accumulation of nuclear fuel; (v) denial of enrichment and reprocessing technologies: prevents diversion of peaceful nuclear fuel for weaponization purposes; and (v) fissile material cutoff: restricts accumulation of weapons-usable fissile material, that is, limits the quantity of India's nuclear weapons. Furthermore, before finalization of the agreement, Washington required India to seek approval of the two prominent institutions of the nuclear nonproliferation regime—the IAEA, including its Board of Governors, and the forty member Nuclear Suppliers Group. Thus, rather than a revolutionary change *of* the nuclear nonproliferation regime, it marked an adjustment within the regime, to accommodate India, that for three decades resisted joining the nuclear nonproliferation regime. Although, the nuclear pact does not include stringent measures such as India's signatures on the CTBT or acceptance of full-scope safeguards; yet, the significance of this landmark agreement cannot be denied. It is naïve to think that a country that successfully opposed the nuclear nonproliferation regime for three decades can be integrated in a single attempt. Rather, given India's unique position in the nuclear order and its history of estrangement, India's integration in the nuclear nonproliferation regime will be incremental. This nuclear deal is the first step in accommodating elusive India within the regime, and is a landmark in the progress toward achieving the objective of nonproliferation of nuclear weapons. The measures viewed individually may not seem stringent, but viewed in conjunction with each other they have significant potential to curb India's nuclear capabilities.

NOTES

1. Prepared Statement of Secretary of State, Condoleezza Rice, *U.S.-India Global Partnership*, Hearing before the Committee on International Relations, House of Representatives, 109th Congress, Second Session, April 5, 2006. Available at http://commdocs.house.gov/committees/intlrel/hfa26905.000/hfa26905_0f.htm (accessed March 16, 2012).

2. Interview with Philip Zelikow, March 2009; Several small, yet, highly confidential meetings were held within the State Department. There were divisions within the State department on this issue. The Department of Defense at the highest levels, particularly Donald Rumsfeld and Douglas Feith, supported this idea—they were, presumably, India enthusiasts supporting closer ties with India due to the burgeoning defence cooperation. National Security Advisor Steve Hadley and his deputy J.D. Crouch were uncomfortable about the move due to nonproliferation concerns.

3. Interview with a prominent U.S.-India relations scholar, anonymity requested.

4. Zelikow, interview.

5. C. Raja Mohan, *Impossible Allies: Nuclear India, United States and the Global Order*, (New Delhi: India Research press, 2006), 133. C. Raja Mohan informs that in early July 2005, just before Manmohan Singh's visit to Washington, "besides the statements from formal meetings between senior officials of the two sides, middle level officials from the Indian Embassy in Washington and the Ministry of External Affairs were picking up credible signals from the Bush administration on the possibility during Manmohan Singh's visit of a major initiative on nuclear energy cooperation."

6. On July 19, 2005, during a press briefing, Nicholas Burns, under secretary for political affairs, clarified the position that United States was not recognizing Indian nuclear weapons arsenal. He stated, "Nuclear weapons were not the subject of this agreement. . . . We are simply opening up a channel in order to cooperate on a commercial basis and a technological basis on nuclear power itself and that's a very important distinction." Available at http://www.state.gov/p/us/rm/2005/49831.htm (accessed May 6, 2008).

7. See, *The Indo-U.S. Joint Statement* July 18, 2005, Washington DC. Available at http://www.indianembassy.org/press_release/2005/July/21.htm (accessed May 6, 2008).

8. ITER is a multi-billion-dollar consortium to design and build future generation electricity producing fusion power plants. Soon thereafter, the United States fulfilled its promise and India became the member in December 2005. See, *U.S. Supports Indian Involvement in International Thermonuclear Experimental Reactor (ITER) Project*. Available at http://www.indianembassy.org/press_release/2005/Dec/5.htm . (accessed May 6, 2008); The other partners are United States, the European Union, the Republic of Korea, Russia, Japan, China and India. Also, see, India Joins Nuclear Fusion Club, BBC News 6 December 2005. Available at http://news.bbc.co.uk/2/hi/science/nature/4504668.stm (accessed May 16, 2008).

9. See, Manmohan Singh, *Prime Minister's Suo Moto Statement on Discussions on Civil Nuclear Energy Cooperation with the U.S.: Implications of India's Separation Plan*, Office of the Prime Minister, Government of India, March 7, 2006.

10. *Fact Sheet: United States and India-Strategic Partnership*, Office of the Press Secretary, The White House, Washington DC. Available at www.whitehouse.gov/news/releases/2006/03/20060302–13.html (accessed May 16, 2008).

11. The full text of the act is available at http://www.govtrack.us/congress/billtext.xpd?bill=h109–5682.

12. R. Rajaraman, "The India-US Nuclear Deal: The Perspective of a Nongovernmental Nuclear Scientist," in *Canadian Policy on Nuclear Cooperation with India: Confronting New Dilemmas*, ed. Karthika Sasikumar and Wade L. Huntley (Vancouver: Simons Centre for Disarmament and Non-Proliferation Research, 2007), 55.

13. Raj Chengappa and Saurabh Shukla, "Nuclear Showdown," *India Today*, March 7, 2008.

14. It was called 123 Agreement as it refers to the section 123 of the U.S. Atomic Energy Act. The text of this agreement is available at http://www.state.gov/r/pa/prs/ps/2007/aug/90050.htm.

15. William C. Potter and Jayantha Dhanapala, "The Perils of Nonproliferation Amnesia," *The Hindu*, September 1, 2007; William C. Potter, "India and the New Look of US Nonproliferation Policy," *Nonproliferation Review* 12, no. 2 (July 2005).

16. Some aspects discussed in this section, related to the establishment of the nuclear regime, have already been discussed in detail in a previous chapter. Please refer to chapter 2, for further details on the NPT; CIRUS agreement; Atoms for Peace Project; India's Opposition to NPT; and nuclear export control arrangements.

17. Stephen D. Krasner, "Structural Causes and Regime Consequences: Regimes as Intervening Variables," *International Organization* 36, no. 2 (Spring 1982): 185–88.

18. Marc A. Levy, Oran R. Young and Michael Zurn, "The Study of International Regimes," *European Journal of International Relations* 1, no. 3 (1995): 273.

19. Please refer to discussion in the theoretical framework section, introduction chapter.

20. Roger K. Smith, "Explaining the Non-proliferation Regime: Anomalies for Contemporary International Relations Theory," *International Organization* 41, no. 2 (Spring 1987): 266–67.

21. Ibid.

22. Please refer to chapter 2 for a detailed discussion of the CIRUS agreement.

23. Trevor McMorris Tate, "Regime-Building in the Non-proliferation System," *Journal of Peace Research* 27, no. 4 (1990): 410.

24. T.V. Paul, "Systemic Conditions and Security Cooperation: Explaining the Persistence of the Nuclear Nonproliferation Regime," *Cambridge Review of International Affairs* 16, no. 1 (2003): 137.

25. Tate, "Regime-Building," 403.

26. Andreas Hasenclever, Peter Mayer and Volker Rittberger, *Theories of International Regimes* (New York: Cambridge University Press, 2002): 10–11.

27. Kari Mottola, "Whither the Non-Proliferation Regime?" *Current Research on Peace and Violence* 4, no. 4 (1981): 236; Also see, Hasenclever, et al., "Theories of International Regimes," 9–10.

28. Smith, "Explaining the Non-proliferation Regime," 257–58.

29. For further discussion on this aspect, please refer to chapter 2.

30. Trevor Findlay, *Nuclear Energy and Global Governance: Ensuring Safety, Security and Non-proliferation,* (Routledge: New York, 2011), 143.

31. Tate, "Regime-Building," 403.

32. Kenneth Boutin, "93+10: Strengthened Nuclear Safeguards a Decade On," *Vertic Brief* no. 2 (April 2004): 2; Also see, "Integrated Safeguards in the Non-Nuclear Weapon States of the European Union," Technical Sheets, *ESARDA Bulletin,* no. 41 (June 2009): 83.

33. Findlay, *Nuclear Energy and Global Governance,* 146.

34. Oliver Meier, Fulfilling the NPT: Strengthened Nuclear Safeguards, VERTIC Briefing Paper, 00/2, (April 2000): 9.

35. Hasenclever, et al., "Theories of International Regimes," 10: 2f.

36. Kari Mottola, "Whither the Non-proliferation Regime?" *Current Research on Peace and Violence* 4, no. 4 (1981): 235; Also see, Hasenclever, et al., "Theories of International Regimes," 10.

37. Lloyd Axworthy, as quoted in Tariq Rauf, "Toward Nuclear Disarmament," *Disarmament Forum,* (2000): 41.

38. Smith, "Explaining the Non-proliferation Regime," 260.

39. Tate, "Regime-Building," 403.

40. Smith, "Explaining the Non-proliferation Regime," 259.

41. Please see chapter 2 for a detailed discussion.

42. Matthew Fuhrmann, "Spreading Temptation: Proliferation and Peaceful Nuclear Cooperation Agreements," *International Security* 34, no. 1 (Summer 2009): 7.

43. William Foster, former director of the Arms Control and Disarmament Agency, during Senate hearings on ratification of the NPT, 1968, as quoted in Fred McGoldrick, *The U.S.-UAE Peaceful Nuclear Cooperation Agreement: A Gold Standard or Fool's Gold?* Proliferation Prevention Program, Center for Strategic and International Studies (Washington D.C.: CSIS, November 30, 2010), 5.

44. Fuhrmann, "Spreading Temptation," 7.

45. Report submitted by Canada, *Implementation of the Treaty on the Non-Proliferation of Nuclear Weapons,* 2010 Review Conference of the Parties to the Treaty on the Non-Proliferation of Nuclear Weapons, NPT/CONF.2010/9, (March 18, 2010), 4. Available at http://daccess-dds-ny.un.org/doc/UNDOC/GEN/N10/279/58/PDF/N1027958.pdf?OpenElement (accessed March 10, 2012).

46. McGoldrick, "A Gold Standard or Fool's Gold?" 7; Also see, Fred McGoldrick, *New U.S.-ROK Peaceful Nuclear Cooperation Agreement: A Precedent for a New Global*

Nuclear Architecture, Centre for U.S.-Korea Policy, Asia Foundation (November 2009), 1.

47. Fuhrmann, "Spreading Temptation," 40.

48. McGoldrick, "A Gold Standard or Fool's Gold?"; Jennifer Weeks, *Iran and North Korea: Two Tests for U.S. Nuclear Nonproliferation Policy*, Report for American Nuclear Society (La Grange Park, Il, August 30–September 2, 1999). Available at http://belfercenter.ksg.harvard.edu/publication/2015/iran_and_north_korea.html (accessed March 12, 2012).

49. Weeks, "Iran and North Korea."

50. Steven E. Miller, Wael Al-Assad, Jayantha Dhanapala, C. Raja Mohan and Ta Minh Tuan, *Nuclear Collisions: Discord, Reform and the Nuclear Nonproliferation Regime*, (Massachusetts: American Academy of Arts and Sciences, April 2012), 10–11.

51. Henry Sokolski, "Implementing the DPRK Nuclear Deal: What U.S. Law Requires," *The Nonproliferation Review* (Fall-Winter 2000): 146.

52. Miller et al., "Nuclear Collisions," 11. Miller states, "The agreement, however, broke down in 2002, after the revelation that North Korea had been pursuing a secret and illicit uranium enrichment program. In the crisis, that erupted anew, in late 2002, Pyongyang threw out the IAEA, withdrew from the NPT in January 2003, reopened its nuclear facilities, resumed its active pursuit of nuclear weapons, and in October 2006 conducted a nuclear weapons test" (p.11).

53. McGoldrick, "A Gold Standard for Fool's Gold?" 9.

54. Remarks of Secretary of State Condoleezza Rice, *U.S.-India Atomic Energy Cooperation: The Indian Separation Plan and the Administration's Legislative Proposal*, Senate Foreign Relations Committee, April 5, 2006. Available at http://www.foreign.senate.gov/hearings/hearing/?id=d2fe308b-f34d-83ee-1e10–83b3d9e70f8e (accessed March 18, 2012).

55. Findlay, "Nuclear Energy and Global Governance," 151.

56. Interview with Philip Zelikow, March 2009.

57. Ibid.

58. Ibid.

59. *Unclassified Report to Congress on the Acquisition of Technology Relating to Weapons of Mass Destruction and Advanced Conventional Munitions*, July 1 through December 31, 2000 (Washington, DC: Office of the Director of Central Intelligence, 2000), 1.

60. Interview with Philip Zelikow, March 2009.

61. A. Gopalakrishnan, "Assured Fuel Supply is a Mirage," *Deccan Chronicle*, August 5, 2007; P. K. Iyengar, "123 Agreement is a Gilded Cage," *The Asian Age*, August 16, 2007.

62. Paul K. Kerr, *U.S. Nuclear Cooperation with India: Issue for Congress*, CRS Report for Congress, 7–5700, RL-33016, (Washington D.C.: Congressional Research Service, December 15, 2011), 14.

63. A. Vinod Kumar, "A Doctrine at Work: Obama's Evolving Nuclear Policy and What it Bodes for India," *Strategic Analysis* 35, no. 2 (March 2011): 217.

64. Gopalakrishnan, "Assured Fuel Supply." He estimates that, "If in the future, India imports a total of 30,000 MWe of power reactors, our [Indian] capital investment in this alone will be not less than about Rs 300,000 crores. We must add to it fresh additional capital investments of about Rs 1,200,000 crores in electricity-consuming industries and commercial entities that would come up, depending solely on this nuclear electricity. This total investment of Rs. 1,500,000 crores of ours will lie idle if the fuel supplies to these reactors are disrupted."

65. Michael A. Levi and Charles D. Ferguson, *US-India Nuclear Cooperation: A Strategy for Moving Forward*, CSR 16, (Washington D.C.: Council on Foreign Relations, June 2006), 3–4.

66. Ibid.

67. Mistry, "Diplomacy, Domestic Politics," 683.

68. Bharat Karnad, "Nuclear Test is a Must," *The Asian Age*, February 22, 2008.

69. Ibid.

70. Arun Shourie, "'Parity', Did You Say?" *The Indian Express*, August 24, 2006.
71. Arun Shourie, "This is About Energy, Did You Say?" *The Indian Express*, August 23, 2006.
72. Gopalakrishnan, "Assured Fuel Supply."
73. Ibid.
74. Ibid.
75. P. K. Iyengar, "123 Agreement is a Gilded Cage," *The Asian Age*, August 16, 2007.
76. Richard Bruneau, "Engaging a Nuclear India: Punishment, Reward and the Politics of Non-proliferation," *Journal of Public and International Affairs* 17, (Spring 2006), 33.
77. Randall S. Wood, *Non-proliferation Strategies for India and Pakistan in the Aftermath of the May 1998 Tests* (December 2004), 18. Available at http://therandymon.com/papers/nonproliferation.pdf (accessed March 18, 2012).
78. Levi and Ferguson, "US-India Nuclear Cooperation," 12–13.
79. George Perkovich, Jessica T. Mathews, Joseph Circincione, Rose Gottemoeller and Jon B. Wolfsthal, *Universal Compliance: A Strategy for Nuclear Security*, (Washington D.C.: Carnegie Endowment for International Peace, June 2007), 117.
80. Ibid, 159.
81. Rice, "The Indian Separation Plan."
82. Rajiv Nayan, "Integrating India with the Global Export Controls System: Challenges Ahead," *Strategic Analysis* 35, no. 3 (May 2011): 447.
83. Ibid.
84. As quoted in P.S. Suryanarayana, "India Sees No Proxy War with Any Other Rising Nation," *The Hindu*, June 1, 2008.
85. White House Office of the Press Secretary, "Announcing the Global Initiative to Combat Nuclear Terrorism," July 15, 2006. Available at http://www.state.gov/p/eur/rls/or/69021.htm (accessed March 18, 2012). Further information on GICNT is available at http://www.state.gov/documents/organization/145499.pdf
86. Prime Minister's Office, *Nuclear Security Summit National Progress Report: India*, Press Information Bureau, Government of India, New Delhi, March 27, 2012. Available at http://pib.nic.in/newsite/erelease.aspx?relid=81755 (accessed March 16, 2012).
87. Mistry, "Diplomacy, Domestic Politics," 685. These included, two Russian supplied reactors at Tarapur, two Canadian supplied reactors, and two Russian built LWRs under construction.
88. Rajiv Nayan, "The Global Nuclear Non-Proliferation Paradigm and India," *Strategic Analysis* 35, no. 4 (July 2011): 560.
89. Kerr, "Issues for Congress," 15.
90. Nayan, "Non-Proliferation Paradigm and India," 560.
91. Rice, "The Indian Separation Plan."
92. Mistry, "Diplomacy, Domestic Politics," 685.
93. Kerr, "Issues for Congress," 15.
94. Rice, "The Indian Separation Plan."
95. Mistry, "Diplomacy, Domestic Politics," 687.
96. Rice, "The Indian Separation Plan."
97. Brahma Chellaney, "India's U.S.-Influenced Decision to Shut Down Cirus Research Reactor," June 22, 2006. Available at http://chellaney.net/2008/06/22/indias-u-s-influenced-decision-to-shut-down-cirus-research-reactor/ (accessed April 12, 2012).
98. Remarks of Mohammed El-Baradei, *IAEA Director General Welcomes U.S. and India Nuclear Deal*, March 2, 2006. IAEA Press Release , Press Office, Division of Public Information, International Atomic Energy Agency. Available at www.iaea.org/newscenter/pressreleases/2006/prn200605.html (accessed March 18, 2012).
99. McGoldrick, "A Gold Standard or Fool's Gold," 1.
100. Ibid.

101. Jon Wolfsthal, "The Next Nuclear Wave," *Foreign Affairs* (January-February 2005). Available at http://www.foreignaffairs.com/articles/60452/jon-b-wolfsthal/the-next-nuclear-wave?page=show.

102. President Bush, Remarks at the National Defence University, February 11, 2004.

103. Miller et al., "Nuclear Collisions," 22–24; Also see, McGoldrick, "A Gold Standard or Fool's Gold," 2.

104. Levi and Ferguson, "US-India Nuclear Cooperation," 15; Also see, Rajiv Nayan, "Global Export Controls System," 449. In this context, India passed a notification to implement the UNSCR I737, of December 2006, which imposes sanctions on Iran and restricts sale of enrichment and reprocessing technologies to India.

105. Article 6 (iii), US and India Release Text of 123 Agreement, Office of the Spokesman, U.S. Department of State, August 3, 2007.

106. R. Ramachandran, "On Slippery Ground," *Frontline* 28, no. 16, July 30-August 12, 2011. Available at http://www.frontlineonnet.com/fl2816/stories/20110812281611900.htm (accessed March 18, 2012).

107. As quoted in Michael Krepon, "Another Contentious Nuclear Issue," *The Hindu,* July 12, 2011.

108. As cited, Ramachandran, "On Slippery Ground."

109. US-India Peaceful Atomic Energy Cooperation and US Additional Protocol Implementation Act, Report of the Committee on Foreign Relations, Senate, 109–208, 109th Congress, Second Session, July 20, 2006. Available at http://www.gpo.gov/fdsys/pkg/CRPT-109srpt288/html/CRPT-109srpt288.htm (accessed March 18, 2012).

110. Ramachandran, "On Slippery Ground."

111. William Walker, "Cut off the Source," *Bulletin of Atomic Scientists*, (March/April 2006): 68.

112. Ibid.

113. Perkovich, et al., "Universal Compliance," 162.

114. Mistry, "Diplomacy, Domestic Politics," 683–84.

Conclusion

For thirty-five years, India persistently evaded joining the nuclear nonproliferation regime and existed as an anomaly. During this period, the United States employed sanctions and technological controls, yet failed to effectively deal with challenge to the nuclear nonproliferation regime, posed by India. As a corollary, the U.S.-India relationship was significantly impinged due to the disjuncture in their respective approaches to nonproliferation regime. First, though India actively engaged in the deliberations in the Conference on Disarmament, yet, ironically, when the Nuclear Nonproliferation Treaty (NPT) was formulated, India vehemently refused to sign the NPT, calling it discriminatory. Second, in 1974, India conducted a peaceful nuclear explosion (PNE) and placed itself in an ambiguous position, in opposition to the dejure categories of the nuclear weapon states (NWS) and nonnuclear weapon states (NNWS). That is, with the PNE, India demonstrated its technological capability to build nuclear weapons, yet, did not overtly declare its nuclear intentions. Third, continuing its stance on the NPT, India declined to participate in the 1995 review conference and opposed a permanent extension of the treaty. Fourth, akin to NPT, India considered the Comprehensive Nuclear Test Ban Treaty (CTBT) to be discriminatory as well and refused to sign it. Fifth, in defiance of the nuclear nonproliferation regime, in 1998 India conducted nuclear weapons explosions and declared itself a nuclear weapon state. Consequently, post-1998 the challenge for the United States intensified: how to engage nuclear India within the nuclear nonproliferation regime. Initially, the Clinton administration imposed sanctions, followed by intensive dialogue with India, yet, failed to achieve any significant results.

Subsequently, in 2005, the Bush administration's decision to lift a three-decade moratorium on civilian nuclear trade with India, amending U.S. domestic legislation and international export controls, raised significant concerns. This aroused widespread consternation that the Bush administration had acted in contravention of the nuclear nonproliferation regime, as India was a defacto nuclear weapon state and a non-signatory of the Nuclear Nonproliferation Treaty.

The objective of this book was to analyze the significant reversal in the U.S. nuclear nonproliferation policy from censure to nuclear cooperation with India, a non-signatory of NPT and defacto nuclear weapon state. As a corollary, it was significant to examine whether this agreement undermines the nuclear nonproliferation regime. The research methodology for this book included: semi-structured elite interviews and document research. To gain an insight into the determinants of the policy change, the author conducted interviews with the high-level officials of the Clinton and Bush administrations. In addition, interviews were conducted with the policy scholars, at the U.S.-based think tanks and research centers, possessing expertise in nuclear nonproliferation, nuclear energy, and related issues on South Asia and India. Besides, field research was carried out at several institutions in the United States and India; and documents, both primary and secondary were collected. Finally, the research findings—from the documents and interviews—were analyzed within the context of regime theory. Thus, this book overcame the theoretical deficit in the literature.

CHAPTER SUMMARY

Chapter 1, entitled "U.S.-India Civil Nuclear Agreement: Mapping the Debates" examined the varied interpretations in the literature regarding the change in the U.S. nonproliferation policy toward India.

The nuclear cooperation agreement was an unanticipated development between the United States, a leading promoter of the nuclear nonproliferation regime and India, a nuclear outlier and dissentient of NPT. Consequently, there was an upsurge of concerns regarding the reversal in the U.S. nonproliferation policy and its undesirable ramifications on the nonproliferation regime. Divergent interpretations of the rationale for the volte-face in the U.S. nuclear approach emerged amongst the scholarly community. The dominant realist perspectives viewed the nuclear pact as initiation of a U.S.-India "strategic partnership" to create balance of power in Asia, vis-à-vis China. Supporters argued that the nuclear pact was a reward for India's exemplary nuclear nonproliferation behavior and that it created incentives for other challenger states to adhere to the regime. Contrarily, the critics argued that the U.S.-India nuclear deal marked an ominous transition toward counter-enlightenment that would eventually result in unraveling the nuclear nonproliferation regime. That is, it created a pathway for nuclear suppliers as well as non-weapon states to flout the norms of the regime. Nonetheless, the debate was inconclusive and reflected lack of a cogent argument. Furthermore, the literature reviews revealed dearth of credible evidential argument as well as theoretical analysis to provide an impartial understanding of the U.S.-India nuclear pact. Thus, to overcome these lacunae, I was encouraged to undertake an in-depth research, including semi-elite interviews, to understand why, and how, the United States transformed its policy from isolation to engagement toward India—a nuclear defacto state and non-NPT state. In this context, this book examines the triadic relationship between the United States, India and the nuclear nonproliferation regime to determine the rationale for the U.S.-India nuclear rapprochement. That is, whether the U.S.-India nuclear pact undermined the nuclear nonproliferation or represented an attempt to bring India within the global nuclear governance. Toward this objective as well as to overcome the theoretical deficit, I have employed the regime theory to objectively analyze the significance of the U.S.-India nuclear rapprochement.

Chapter 2 provides a historical insight into the U.S.-India estrangement with regard to the establishment of the nuclear nonproliferation regime. It explains that the United States and India had divergent perspectives of nuclear nonproliferation. The United States, keen to prevent emergence of new nuclear states, focused exclusively on preventing horizontal proliferation of nuclear technologies and materials. India, along with other nonaligned states, actively engaged in international negotiations to curb horizontal proliferation and required nuclear weapon states to disarm. The NPT was framed as an instrument to curb horizontal proliferation, with a weakly worded commitment for disarmament. Puchala and Hopkins observe that a regime is shaped by the interests of the actors and may not be representative of interests of all participants.[1] Subsequently, America's mission to curtail horizontal proliferation of nuclear technologies clashed with India's quest and need for advanced technology. India was not ready to renounce its right to access and develop advanced technologies by acceding to the NPT-centric regime. Thus, from a supporter of the cause of nuclear disarmament, India became an anomaly for the NPT-centric nonproliferation regime. Furthermore, with the peaceful nuclear explosion of 1974, India challenged the NPT and ignited a spurt of technological embargoes initiated by Western states. For the next several decades, a stalemate ensued as the international community was unable to figure out how to deal with India.

Chapter 3 describes that in the mid-1990s President Bill Clinton made significant efforts to strengthen the nuclear nonproliferation regime, with an indefinite extension of the Nuclear Nonproliferation Treaty and the signing of the Comprehensive Test Ban Treaty. Unlike previous administrations, in a determined approach Clinton adopted coercive measures to "cap, rollback, and eliminate" India's nuclear capabilities, yet, was unable to prevent the nuclearization of South Asia. The Pokhran II nuclear tests in 1998 represented India's defiance of an increasingly lopsided focus on horizontal proliferation with little progress toward nuclear disarmament. Pokhran II ignited a serious review of the U.S. nuclear nonproliferation policy, hitherto, based on denial and isolation of India, and added critical urgency to deal with this anomaly of the nuclear nonproliferation regime.

Chapter 4 explicates that in the aftermath of India's 1998 nuclear explosions, the Clinton administration imposed sanctions, yet, also engaged India in the first ever sustained nuclear dialogue. Due to change in circumstances, the sanctions were swiftly removed and the Talbott-Singh dialogue failed to gain nonproliferation commitments from India. Nonetheless, in this process there was considerable shifting of the nuclear goalposts vis-à-vis India. Evidently, the post-Pokhran II phase marked a distinct shift in Washington's policy from isolation to nuclear bargaining, yet, the Clinton administration was unable to deal with the challenger of the nuclear nonproliferation regime. This chapter also highlights the lack of measures to deal with post-proliferation situations—a lacunae in the regime that needs to be fixed.

Chapter 5 discusses that during the Bush administration, there was significant reorientation of the nuclear nonproliferation regime, which not only led to the reimagining of India, but also created space to engage India within the regime, as a partner to curb the growing threats of nuclear trafficking and terrorism. The Bush administration realized that, despite an upward swing in the bilateral relationship, the technological restrictions and the resultant mutual distrust were creating obstacles in building a comprehensive relationship with India. In the changed global nuclear scenario, India's continued existence as a defacto nuclear weapon state could prove detrimental to the objectives of nuclear nonproliferation. That is, India, at the receiving end of technological embargoes, could not be expected to play a meaningful role in managing the post-9/11 threats emanating from the nexus of terrorism and WMD trafficking. Cognizant of India's growing nuclear energy needs, the Bush administration utilized the opportunity to engage India. In this regard, the United States launched landmark measures, viz., the High Technology Cooperation Group (HTCG) and the Next Steps in Strategic Partnership (NSSP), thereby, initiating limited nuclear collaboration with India. Ironically, the importance of these strategic measures received little attention in the existing literature. I contend that HTCG and NSSP, imbibing the principle of reciprocal obligations, proved to be the stepping stones for the full-fledged bilateral nuclear collaboration. Proceeding further, the Bush administration, elicited India's acceptance to institute controls on end-usage of technology, and offered full fledged nuclear collaboration. Subsequently, the Bush administration decided to lift the decades old technological embargoes enshrined in its domestic legislation and in the Nuclear Supplier Group's (NSG) guidelines.

Chapter 6 detailed the "principles, norms, rules, and procedures" of the nuclear nonproliferation regime and analyzed the terms of the U.S.-India nuclear agreement in this context. I argue that the NPT forms the core of the nuclear nonproliferation regime but it is not synonymous with the regime. The nuclear nonproliferation regime consists of a heterogenous mix of multilateral and bilateral treaties, agreements, and procedures that regulate the behavior of state actors. Furthermore, it is discussed that the United States employs nuclear cooperation agreements to promote its nonproliferation objectives by regulating the behavior of recipient states. Similarly, the Bush administration did not provide unconditional technological access to nuclear India, but adhered to the principles and norms of the nuclear nonproliferation regime, wherein suppliers set the rules and prescribe appropriate behavior to the recipients of nuclear technology. India had consistently refused to accede to the NPT, and now after becoming a defacto nuclear weapons state, the possibility of India joining the treaty were negligible. Therefore, in a strategic move, the Bush administration made India accede to non-NPT regulations and institutions of the nonproliferation regime, in a strategic bid to engage the recalcitrant India within the global nuclear governance. Accordingly, in exchange for advanced nuclear technology, the initial 2005 U.S.-India nuclear pact made it mandatory for India to align export controls with MTCR and NSG guidelines, to segregate its civilian and military facilities, and to place IAEA safeguards on its civilian facilities. In addition, India accepted a unilateral moratorium on further nuclear testing and signed an additional protocol with the International Atomic Energy Agency. Thus, the change in the U.S. nuclear nonproliferation policy, manifest in the U.S.-India civilian nuclear accord, does not mark unravelling of the regime, rather it marks a specific case modification within the regime to accommodate the anomaly. Thus, the change is progressive rather than retrogressive for the nuclear nonproliferation regime. This is discussed further in the following section.

PROGRESSION V/S REGRESSION

Employing the regime theoretical analysis, this book argues that the U.S.-India nuclear agreement defines a progressive change within the nuclear nonproliferation regime.

Before proceeding with the discussion, I would like to offer a couple of caveats. First, undoubtedly, the U.S.-India nuclear deal was highly controversial, not to speak of the myriad perspectives on the nuclear nonproliferation regime itself; thus, this created ample scope for consternation. Second, this is a qualitative research, that is, in the absence of rigid mathematical and scientific formulae, the argument is subject to different interpretations.

Stephen Krasner, proponent of the regime theory, has provided a distinction between change within the regime and change of a regime. He proposes that changes in principles and norms lead to a complete change of the regime, whereas changes in rules and procedures mark changes within the regime.[2] Once a regime is established, there can be changes in situations, or certain loopholes may emerge, necessitating modifications within the regime. Puchala and Hopkins consider such changes, involving modifications within the regime as evolutionary.[3] In fact, acceptance of such changes attribute dynamism to any regime, otherwise, if a regime does not modify under the changed circumstances, then it would have a high probability to lapse.

Toward this purpose, the reform of the NPT-centric regime has been underway since the end of the Cold War, evidenced by the indefinite extension of the NPT, signing of the CTBT and continued deliberations on the FMCT. The nuclear nonproliferation regime has been in a process of evolution and has moved beyond the NPT. This does not mean the NPT is irrelevant, neither does it mean there is a revolutionary shift. To clarify, the nuclear nonproliferation regime is NPT-centric but the regime is not restricted to the NPT alone, it is a heterogeneous mix of several other agreements, institutions and measures that regulate the behavior of the participants. This process of expansion of the nuclear regime gained momentum in the aftermath of the 9/11 attacks and the heightened risk of nuclear terrorism. The Bush administration introduced landmark initiatives such as the Proliferation Security Initiative (PSI) and Counter Security Initiative (CSI) to enforce stringent interdiction methods to curb trafficking in illicit materials. A series of multidimensional reforms were undertaken to deal with the contemporary issues confronting the regime—the tightening of export controls, strengthening of the IAEA, and broadening of IAEA safeguards, including the additional protocol.

Ironically, the Bush administration came under heavy criticism for reducing the emphasis on the NPT and instituting new counter-proliferation (or interdiction) measures. Contrarily, these multidimensional reforms signified a reorientation of the nuclear nonproliferation regime to deal with the expanded spectrum of nuclear threats from state and non-state actors. If the international community is unable to resolve contemporary challenges, or if these challenges magnify, there is potential for a crisis of the regime. For instance, in the wake of increased demand for nuclear energy, the regime might be unable to contain or manage the proliferation of nuclear technologies. Steven Miller comments, "The expansion and spread of nuclear power could lead to dangers ahead if steps are not taken to ensure that the NPT [centric] regime is able to effectively regulate a more nuclearized world."[4] Thus, the nuclear nonproliferation regime is evolving through "reflexive adaptation."

Andy Knight defines:

> Reflexive adaptation can be characterized as a relatively unconscious response to exogenous or systemic forces. It allows an international organization to adjust structures and processes according to changing demands and does so in a rather ad hoc, creative but largely non-purposive fashion.[5]

Nonetheless, the nuclear nonproliferation regime is currently confronting significant challenges that place it under duress: noncompliance issues, the presence of defacto nuclear states, emergence of non-state actors, nuclear terrorism and trafficking, and a growing demand for nuclear energy.

Steven Miller argues:

> This regime has an oddly schizophrenic history. On the one hand, it has attracted nearly universal membership, its critical importance is routinely acknowledged, and it has proven to be durable and resilient across four challenging decades. . . . On the other hand, it is chronically troubled, beset by crises and setbacks and possible defections, amidst fears for its future and doubts about its adequacy.[6]

Viewed in this context, the Bush administration's attempt to align India with the nuclear nonproliferation engaging defacto nuclear weapons states, like India, marks a progression rather than a retrogression of the nuclear nonproliferation regime. As Joseph F. Pilat emphasizes that the U.S.-India pact was "an effort to address the current problems with the regime by bringing India into the fold to the extent possible."[7]

Within two years of the NPT coming into force, India conducted a "peaceful nuclear explosion," demonstrated its nuclear weapons capability yet maintained ambiguity on weaponization. Thereafter for more than three decades, India existed as an anomaly to the nuclear nonproliferation regime.

It was expected that the strategy of alienation, inclusive of technological embargoes, it would possibly stall India's nuclear civilian and military programs, ultimately forcing it to sign the NPT. Contrary to the expectations, India relying on its technological prowess indigenously developed nuclear energy program, besides advanced its space and missile programs also. In 1998, India ended the ambiguity regarding its nuclear intentions and exploded nuclear weapons. Technically, India became a nuclear weapon state but it was not accorded nuclear weapon status under the NPT. Nonetheless, it marked a severe blow to Washington's strategy of alienation.

Being a defacto nuclear state that neither signed the NPT nor the CTBT, India was outside all sorts of rules and regulations of the nuclear nonproliferation regime, including the IAEA safeguards system. Under the NPT, nonnuclear weapon states are obliged to accept full-scope safeguards, but India had persistently evaded IAEA surveillance. The Bush administration acknowledged that India's case, unlike those of Iran, Iraq, and North Korea, was not of noncompliance with the NPT. Washington realized that keeping India outside the nuclear nonproliferation regime was not serving any purpose, and could be potentially damaging for the regime. Bringing India within some sort of nuclear nonproliferation arrangement would strengthen the regime.

The intensive dialogue and diplomacy between the United States and India that began post-1998 created space for the bridging of the nuclear nonproliferation divide with India. Subsequently, India was allured with the reorientation of the nonproliferation regime, during the Bush administration. Washington accommodated the fact that India is a non-signatory of the NPT and has nuclear weapons. Nonetheless, conditions of the nuclear agreement with India are in accordance with the rules of the nuclear nonproliferation regime, mainly based on supplier controls that would regulate India's nuclear behavior. India had to separate its civilian and strategic nuclear facilities, accept safeguards on its civilian facilities, agree to engage in international negotiations for the formulation of the FMCT, accept continued adherence to the moratorium on nuclear testing, and adopt stricter export controls. For this agreement to be finalized, India had to seek the approval of the two primary organizations of the nuclear nonproliferation regime—the International Atomic Energy Agency and the Nuclear Suppliers Group. Thus, this agreement marks the beginning of the incremental integration of India into the nuclear nonproliferation regime, and ensures adherence of India, non-signatory of the NPT, to the principles and norms of the regime. Bringing India, a challenger, into the regime through engaging India in the non-NPT measures, is beneficial to the cause of nonproliferation. In fact, this creates a path to bridge the divide with other nuclear outliers. Mohammed ElBaradei, the then IAEA director general, welcomed the U.S.-India agreement to embark on full civil nuclear energy cooperation and to work to enhance nuclear nonproliferation and security.

He remarked:

> Out of the box thinking and active participation by all members of the international community are important if we are to advance nuclear arms control, nonproliferation, safety and security, and tackle new threats such as illicit trafficking in sensitive nuclear technology and the risks of nuclear terrorism.[8]

U.S.-INDIA NUCLEAR DIALECTIC: OBAMA ADMINISTRATION

The Bush administration was criticized for signing the nuclear deal with India and held responsible for the drastic change in nuclear nonproliferation policy, with the potential to unravel the global export control regime. Contrarily, based on thorough research, including semi-elite interviews, and utilizing the "regime theory" this book discusses that the nuclear deal was offered to bring India within the nuclear nonproliferation regime. In fact, the post-2008 U.S.-India nuclear dialectic provides evidence that through the nuclear deal Washington intended to align India with the nuclear nonproliferation regime and sought latter's cooperation in strengthening the regime. Furthermore, it was repeatedly argued that the U.S. compromised the nonproliferation objectives at the cost of the realistic goals, to build a strategic partnership with India. This book has challenged the myth of an impending U.S.-India strategic partnership directed against China. Evidently, though the United States and India have continued to strengthen their defence and technology exchange, yet, have not signed any pact against containing China or any other country. The "strategic partnership," viewed in the narrow realist interpretation as an alliance, especially vis-à-vis China, has seemingly died a natural death. Rather, during the U.S. nuclear standoff with Iran, India had refused to follow Washington's dictates without affecting the U.S.-India relationship. Although India complied with the United Nations sanctions against Iran, it refused to be part of the U.S. led sanctions against Iran.[9] Prior to the U.S.-Iran nuclear agreement, in 2014, the Obama administration had categorically warned countries to prohibit trade with Iran. Yet, Washington accepted India's position on Iran and affirmed that it does "not want to jeopardize India's energy security by asking it to reduce its dependence on Iranian oil."[10]

Furthermore, the critics of the Bush administration argued that the U.S.-India nuclear deal would fall apart during the Obama administration due to the latter's strong nonproliferation orientation. Undoubtedly, the Obama administration's approach to nuclear issues differed in several respects, yet they enthusiastically honored the nuclear agreement with India; in fact, pursued a proactive policy of enhancing India's integration in the nuclear nonproliferation regime. That is, rather than backtracking on the path that Bush administration had laid down, President Obama actually proceeded further in full swing. In fact, President Obama attempted to build a global strategic partnership with India, to intensify cooperation on wide range of issues, viz, "ensure a just and stable world order," sustainable development and promotion of democratic values.[11] Moreover, the Obama administration focused its attempts to integrate India into the existing global nuclear architecture. In a joint statement of Manmohan Singh and Barack Obama in November 2010, Washington assured India of its support for India's entry into four multilateral regimes—the NSG, the Australia Group, the Missile Technology Control Regime, and the Wassenaar Arrangement.[12]

Contrary to the perceptions, the Obama administration extended support to the Proliferation Security Initiative and the Container Security Initiative, widely criticized as unilateral imperialist measures of the Bush administration, and sought India's support in these groups. In fact, Obama "seeks to enlarge their scope through cooperative enhancement and institutionalization."[13]

Evidently, there has been a significant shift in India's stance toward the nuclear nonproliferation issues, after its anomalous relationship to the nuclear regime was reset by the Bush administration. Thus, justifying the Bush administration's vision for India to proactively engage in the nuclear regime. As Shyam Saran, special envoy of the then prime minister on nuclear issues, remarked,

> From being an outlier, India is now accepted as a partner in the global nuclear domain. The success of the civil nuclear initiative has engendered a sense of assurance and confidence which enables us to look, proactively and not defensively, at a new global agenda for nuclear nonproliferation and nuclear disarmament.[14]

Earlier, India had refused to sign the CTBT, citing it as discriminatory. Now, India's consideration is whether the CTBT can ensure its national security interests.[15] In the nuclear agreement, India committed to extending the unilateral moratorium on nuclear testing. Over time, this domestic opposition in India to renounce nuclear testing and thus, ease India's acceptance of the CTBT. To date, 183 states have signed and 164 have ratified the treaty. The CTBT will formally enter into force after forty-four designated "nuclear-capable states" (as listed in Annex 2 of the treaty) have deposited their instruments of ratification with the UN secretary-general. Yet of the forty-four specified countries, India, Pakistan, and North Korea still have not signed, and only thirty-six have ratified the treaty. Nonetheless, there has been a noticeable change in India's position. Lauding the Obama administration's moves toward nuclear disarmament, Shyam Saran, states "It is also our conviction that if the world moves categorically toward nuclear disarmament in a credible time-frame, then Indo-U.S. differences over the CTBT would probably recede into the background."[16] In this context, Carl Paddock observes: "Globally, India is now perceived to be inside the tent, a part of the global solution to nuclear nonproliferation issues. So, while the NPT is a no-no for N[ew] Delhi, at least in present form, the CTBT can leave room for manoeuvre."[17]

Furthermore, India is cooperating with the international community on a fissile material control treaty (FMCT) in the Conference on Disarmament. There is little progress in the formulation of a FMCT as the discussions in the Conference on Disarmament are unable to proceed due to procedural and political difficulties—Pakistan has been stalling the negotiations for several years now. Nonetheless, by making its commitment in the July 2005 agreement, "India has closed its options to resist the treaty despite concerns over its implications [due to halting fissile material production] for its strategic program."[18] Thus, the terms of engagement and nuclear dialogue are changing between the United States and India.

The nuclear deal, indeed, has been a "game changer." Through the terms of nuclear deal, the United States has bound India to the nuclear nonproliferation regime, therefore, India cannot escape it commitments. But, the integration of India within the regime will be incremental and it is naïve to expect complete integration overnight. Also, it will neither be automatic nor smooth; there are still some hurdles that have to be crossed. Beginning in 2012, all the export control organizations—Nuclear Supplier Group (NSG), the Missile Technology Control Regime (MTCR), the Australia Group, and the Wassenaar Arrangement—in their plenary meetings began contemplating India's membership.

Earlier, for three decades India had vociferously opposed these export control cartels as technology denial regimes; now, India has been actively seeking greater participation in the global nuclear nonproliferation regime. In a major foreign policy shift, India's foreign secretary, stated: "the logical conclusion of partnership with India is its full membership in the four multilateral regimes."[19] This signifies a crucial change in the nuclear dialectic.

The issue of non-membership of the NPT may haunt India in its attempts to acquire memberships in the export control regimes. This has been the main factor in restricting India's membership of the NSG, especially opposed by China. Sandeep Dikshit remarks, "the fact that the NSG Plenary will consider India's case does not mean membership will be granted automatically. A long road of persuading all the members lies ahead because decisions at NSG are taken unanimously."[20]

Nonetheless, due to the enthusiastic support extended by the Obama administration, in 2016, India was able to gain the membership of the Missile Technology Control Regime (MTCR). To enlist India as a member of the MTCR, is a significant development for the nonproliferation regime. Since MTCR aims to contain the spread of ballistic missile and other unmanned delivery systems that can be used for chemical, biological and nuclear attacks. India, a defacto nuclear weapon state and non-NPT member, has indigenously developed an advanced missile system. On the other hand, China, member of the NPT, has been repeatedly denied the membership of the elite club, due to the concerns regarding proliferation of missile technology to North Korea and Pakistan.[21]

RELEVANCE FOR CONTEMPORARY PROLIFERATION CASES

The decision of the United States to resume nuclear cooperation with India, a defacto nuclear weapon state, generated a storm of controversy regarding the implications of the deal on the nuclear nonproliferation regime. Critics argued that this deal generates the message that nuclear proliferation is rewarded, since India was offered the deal within seven years of crossing the nuclear threshold.

On the contrary, there are certain lessons that can be drawn from India's accommodation in the nuclear nonproliferation regime, such as: engagement strategies work better than alienation strategies, responsible nonproliferation behavior gets rewarded, pragmatic solutions are more effective than lofty ideals, and one size does not fit all.

Post-1974, India's peaceful nuclear test explosion, the United States alienated India and the latter was at the receiving end of technological embargoes. The Clinton administration with its strong advocacy for nonproliferation exerted pressure on India to sign the NPT and the CTBT. India continued its stance that the treaties were discriminatory and refused to accede to these. Rather, to the utter dismay of the United States, in 1998 India proceeded to test nuclear devices at Pokhran, Rajasthan. Earlier, the United States was complacent that India would not nuclearize, and would at some stage succumb to pressure to "cap and rollback." But, post-Pokhran, Washington realized that the policies of sanctions and coercive diplomacy proved to be ad hoc and reactionary. Post-1998, the Clinton administration initiated a sustained dialogue with India, yet due to several intervening factors, the nonproliferation objectives could not be achieved. Nonetheless, the Talbott-Singh dialogue helped to create intersubjective understanding and began a process of harmonization after decades of estrangement. Subsequently, the growing interaction and dialogue opened a path for incentives-based diplomacy to become effective. But, it was several years before a mutually agreed solution was reached. Previously for three decades, the United States had pursed a policy of alienation but in less than a decade of India's nuclearization, Washington changed its policy to engage India. Probably, if the United States had previously pursued engagement, India could have been prevented from conducting nuclear weapons tests.

Learning from the experience with India, Washington needs to engage other defacto nuclear weapon states, viz., Pakistan and Israel, "as partners in nuclear nonproliferation and arms control."[22] Quite understandably, without engaging in bilateral diplomacy, how can Washington expect to achieve its nuclear nonproliferation and foreign policy objectives?

Although universalization of the NPT is an ideal, for several decades Pakistan and Israel, like India, have been left out of the nuclear nonproliferation regime. In order to strengthen the nuclear nonproliferation regime and adapt it for a "challenging future" it is essential that the perspectives of the discontented states are accommodated to draw them within the regime.[23]

Pakistan is also interested in getting a nuclear deal, including an NSG waiver, similar to that of India. In this context, ElBaradei, the then director general of IAEA, remarked that support can be extended to Pakistan for a nuclear deal, if it shows responsible behavior with nuclear technology.

> Once you [Pakistan] put your nuclear activities in order—particularly in the aftermath of the AQ Khan network and all that—you should be able to get a similar deal and I would support a similar deal for Pakistan under appropriate circumstances because, again, Pakistan needs energy.[24]

As there is no one size that fits all, it is only through engagement in negotiations that state-specific solutions will emerge. As ElBaradei states, that with regard to nuclear weapons proliferation and arms control issues, "the fundamental problem is clear: Either we begin finding creative, outside-the-box solutions or the international nuclear safeguards regime will become obsolete."[25]

Furthermore, the critics vehemently argued that the U.S.-India nuclear deal sets a bad precedent for dealing with other challengers of the nuclear nonproliferation regime, including Iran and North Korea. I contend that it is fallacious to compare the case of India with those of Iran and North Korea. India chose to stay outside the Nuclear Nonproliferation Treaty; this is different from signing the treaty and then, violating the terms of the agreement. Moreover, even as a non-NPT member, India adhered to the norm of horizontal proliferation, therefore, it was recognized as a "responsible" state. Former IAEA director-general Mohammed ElBaradei echoed the sentiment of the Bush administration: "India has never joined the NPT; it has therefore not violated any legal commitment, and it has never encouraged nuclear weapons proliferation."[26]

Unlike India, Iran and North Korea joined the nuclear nonproliferation treaty, gained access to nuclear technology, and took undue advantage of the loopholes of the treaty. The NPT allows nonnuclear weapon state members to acquire the entire nuclear fuel cycle—from uranium mining to enrichment and reprocessing—as long as the nuclear materials and technology are placed under safeguards. Thus, signatories to the treaty can first acquire the advanced nuclear technologies and know-how and then, with six months' notice, withdraw from the treaty,[27] as North Korea did in 2003. After withdrawal, North Korea has conducted five nuclear tests (2006, 2009, 2013, and twice in 2016) and "now seeks recognition as a nuclear weapon state."[28] Since 2006, there were apprehensions that Iran would also follow North Korea, in its pursuit of developing nuclear weapons.

Consequently, this drew attention on the urgency to fix the drawbacks of the NPT, to prevent noncompliance and withdrawal issues in the future. These include: halting the sale of enrichment and reprocessing technologies to states; establishing international fuel banks, so that states do not need to reprocess nuclear fuel; and, making adherence to the additional protocol mandatory. Significantly, UNSCR 1887 emphasized the establishment of regulations that allow supplier states to seek return of nuclear technology and materials from states that are noncompliant with the treaty or threaten to withdraw from the treaty.[29]

U.S. policy regarding North Korea has been like a pendulum, swinging from one extreme—isolation, threats and sanctions—to another—engagement. To be effective, the dialogue has to be consistent and sustained. Surprisingly, while the United States often engaged North Korea, it never had bilateral negotiations with Iran since the overthrow of the Shah of Iran in 1979.[30] In 2000s, there were strong apprehensions, that Iran was on the verge of a nuclear breakout, that is, within a period of 2–3 months, Iran could gather enough fissile material to build a nuclear weapon. Moreover, Iran had refused the inspections by the International Atomic Energy Agency. In 2012, the United States imposed an economic embargo on Iran to curb its nuclear program, that restricted multinational trade with Iran.

A lesson that emerges from India's case is that nuclear diplomacy should not be based on lofty ideals of immediate rollback and elimination, as pursued by the Clinton administration prior to the nuclear tests. Rather the initial objective should be what is possible and achievable. As Ambassador Saeed suggested that in the case of Iran and North Korea, the United States should first insist upon a "nuclear pause," and then, through sustained dialogue, expand to broader terms of engagement. Saeed remarks, "securing nuclear materials and gaining access, oversight, monitoring, and transparency over facilities and programs [in Iran and North Korea], however imperfect, serves critical U.S. interests."[31]

Pursuing the path of engagement, the Obama administration, after intense negotiations of twenty-two months, was able to harness Iran in a nuclear deal. In July 2015, Iran signed the Joint Comprehensive Plan of Action (JCPOA) deal with the P5+1 (China, France, Germany, Russia, the United Kingdom, the United States, and European Union). As required, it came into effect on January 16, 2016 after the review by IAEA that Iran had implemented the key measures in the JCPOA. Now, it is perceived that it would take more than twelve months for Iran, to assemble a weapon, only if it is able to evade intensive monitoring, calling for unleashing of sanctions.[32] Based on the successful negotiations in the nuclear sector, the United States should pursue broad-based engagement of Iran to achieve several strategic objectives-ranging from terrorism to regional issues in mid-east as well as Afghanistan-Pakistan sector. This is so because the dialogue process creates space for realization of mutual interests and engagement.

Ambassador James Dobbins affirms,

> Engagement is a virtue in its own right. It may or may not lead to agreement but it will always lead to better information, and better information will lead to better policy. The more information a president and his administration have, the more soundly based their decisions are likely to be. And engagement always leads to information. It may not always lead to agreement.[33]

CONTRIBUTION TO THEORY AND PRAXIS

Since the signing of the NPT in 1968, the trajectory of the U.S.-India relationship was marked by significant estrangement regarding the nuclear nonproliferation regime. This book presents an interesting, probably unique, case study of how divergent perspectives regarding a particular regime can create friction between two states—especially, if one state is a leading advocate and the other is a nonparticipant. Despite burgeoning literature, theoretical work on nuclear nonproliferation regime, especially regime analysis, is scant. This book makes significant contribution to the regime theory literature in several respects. Furthermore, there was an unsettled debate whether the U.S.-India civilian nuclear agreement undermines or strengthens the nuclear nonproliferation regime. The literature review revealed not only absence of a comprehensive study but also little objective understanding of the issue. Consequently, in the absence of theoretical analysis and in-depth investigation there were considerable speculations and subjective opinions that could prove detrimental to the nuclear nonproliferation regime. To overcome these drawbacks, this book provides a comprehensive examination of the triadic relationship among the United States, India, and the nuclear nonproliferation regime. It conducts an in-depth analysis of the U.S.-India nuclear pact to assess its implications for the nonproliferation regime. The book concludes that the U.S.-India nuclear pact brings India—a nonsignatory of the Nuclear Nonproliferation Treaty and defacto nuclear weapon state—within the nuclear nonproliferation regime and under global nuclear governance.

Stephen Krasner, defines a regime is an array of "principles, norms, rules, and decision-making procedures." The NPT forms the core of the nuclear nonproliferation regime and is largely focused on the prevention of horizontal proliferation of nuclear technology and materials. A regime constrains the behavior of participant states but the relationship between the regime and nonparticipants is still a grey area. Especially, in a regime critical to international security, such as the nuclear nonproliferation regime, it is important to define the relationship between participants and nonparticipants. It is also important to define how to deal with states that oppose or challenge the regime. For instance, the NPT is silent on nuclear cooperation with non-signatories of the NPT. Furthermore, there seems to be an underlying assumption that there will be no nuclear crossovers, as such there is no provision for the dealing with states that choose to cross the nuclear threshold. Thus, when India and Pakistan exploded nuclear weapons in 1998, there was no coherent plan to deal with the defacto nuclear states. The Clinton administration imposed sanctions under the Glenn Amendment, but these were meant to be pre-proliferation measures and accordingly, to deal with the post-proliferation situations. This book highlights the lack of effective post-proliferation management of defacto nuclear states and emphasizes that there is a need to establish stringent post-proliferation measures to rein in other defacto nuclear weapon states as well as stall future nuclear crossovers. Thus, this book identifies a major loophole in the nuclear nonproliferation regime.

This book conducts a thorough investigation of the transition of the U.S. India nuclear estrangement evolving into nuclear cooperation, based on reciprocal obligations to ensure responsible handling of the nuclear technology. Thus, it analyzes the strategy of the United States to engage a recalcitrant state within the nuclear nonproliferation regime. This book highlights how a nonparticipant state, that refused to accede to a founding agreement of a regime, was accommodated within the context of the principles and norms of the regime. This book could be useful to other exceptional cases, especially where the interest of the international community lies in the universal acceptance of a regime.

Also, this book suggests that the example of bringing India within nuclear governance creates a pathway to deal with the other defacto nuclear states. For instance, how to deal with the issue of nuclear weapons in a fragile state, such as Pakistan, is a challenging question for the international community. This book emphasizes the need to go beyond the generic realist perceptions to determine the specific factors that shape the interests of individual states in relation to international regimes. In other words, the question needs to be raised, *why* does a specific state refuse to accede to a particular regime? Edward Luck points out that, "The relative neglect of the factors that make individual states unique, in favour of an assumption of generic motivations, values, and responses, has had distorting consequences for both the theory and practice of global governance."[34] Luck notes that considerable research is required to determine the motivations and intentions of states adhering to or dissenting from international agreements.[35] Therefore, this book suggests more state-specific studies; to make international relations (IR) theory more global, several scholars prescribe a focus on third world states.

Stephanie Neumann suggests, "Shifting our gaze from the few powerful actors in world affairs to the many who are less powerful may help us to revise and strengthen the conceptual foundations upon which IR theory is built, so that it better reflects what is happening today."[36] Moreover, in the contemporary globalized era characterized by "time-space distanciation," it has become crucial to understand the specific perspectives of the states. As Luck argues, "Until we fully understand and appreciate the essential building blocks—states—we are unlikely to make much progress toward a more secure and just international order or toward better global governance."[37]

The book explored the question of a developing country's quest for advanced nuclear technologies for the purpose of sustainable nuclear energy and economic growth. With the increasing stress on energy resources, more and more developing nations will be tempted to harness nuclear energy for development purposes. This impending nuclear renaissance could challenge the delicate, yet lopsided, balance of obligations of nuclear weapon states and nonnuclear weapon states enshrined in the NPT. This book stresses that the nuclear dilemma—between the promotion of nuclear energy and the threat of nuclear proliferation—has been managed to a great extent, but is not yet resolved. In the contemporary scenario, the rise of the third world, the increasing demand for nuclear energy, and the heightened potential of several states such as Iran, North Korea, and Syria to acquire advanced nuclear technology creates additional pressure on the nuclear nonproliferation regime. Besides, this book emphasizes the need for new approaches that enable equitable utilization of nuclear resources by NNWS as well as NWS, yet curtail the threat of nuclear proliferation. The expansion of restraints on the transfer of nuclear technology simultaneously could lead to a demand for equitable treatment; thereby, increasing pressure on the NWS to fulfill their obligations toward disarmament as enshrined in Article VI of the NWT. In the absence of concrete commitments by NWS, there is danger that the nuclear bargain may prove to be the fault line of the nuclear regime. Therefore, steps need to be taken to ensure more equitable nuclear order.

This author recognizes that regimes are dynamic and need to evolve to be able to respond to contemporary challenges. The NPT, framed in the late 1960s, seems incompetent to deal with the challenges of the post–9/11 era, especially nuclear trafficking and terrorism. Emanuel Adler affirms that crisis situations hasten a process of re-evaluation of policies and ignite change. He remarks,

> dramatic events such as war, depression, acute hunger, or a large environmental accident such as Chernobyl may have the effect of a "cognitive punch," making it apparent to political actors that existing institutions and types of political behavior have become dysfunctional and can no longer deal with the situation in the old ways. . . . It helps to show, in fact, that policies based on old analogies to the past are likely to have deleterious consequences."[38]

The 9/11 terrorist attacks and the radical changes perceived in international security, especially related to the global nuclear scenario, forced the United States to reassess the nuclear nonproliferation regime and introduce measures based on multilateral cooperation. Nonetheless, the Bush administration's emphasis on countering proliferation actively, with the introduction of measures such as Proliferation Security Initiative and the Container Security Initiative, were viewed with skepticism. In a similar vein, the critics viewed the new measures, including the U.S.-India nuclear cooperation as acts in utter disregard of the Nuclear Nonproliferation Treaty. On the contrary, this book argues that the Bush administration realized that there was a critical need to supplement the NPT-centric nuclear nonproliferation regime and thus, incorporated new measures to deal with the contemporary risks of proliferation of WMD. The nuclear nonproliferation regime is undergoing a reflexive adjustment to be better prepared to respond to contemporary challenges.

FUTURE DIRECTIONS FOR RESEARCH

The rich empirical data and analysis provided in this book lay a foundation for further research in several aspects:

First, the U.S.-India nuclear pact represents a bridging of the nuclear nonproliferation divide, but significant differences remain. India will continue to pursue its development objectives and attempt to retain its strategic autonomy. There is lot of scope for research on how India can be fully integrated in, or at least deepen its engagement with the nuclear nonproliferation regime.

Second, the book provides insight into the involvement of high level Bush administration officials in the unprecedented decision to lift the technological embargoes against India. Thus, the role of personality factors in foreign policy decision-making could be pursued in future studies.

Third, this book has focused on the change in U.S. nuclear nonproliferation policy in the context of the U.S.-India accord. It would be interesting to explore India's motivations to engage in nuclear cooperation with Washington. Did Indian decision makers realize that remaining outside the nuclear nonproliferation regime was not serving Indian interests any longer? What factors motivated India to accept the regulations of the nuclear nonproliferation regime contained in the U.S.-India nuclear pact? What role does India seek to play in the nuclear nonproliferation regime?

Fourth, this book has employed regime analysis to explore the significance of the U.S.-India nuclear pact. It would be interesting to explore, whether this change in U.S. nuclear nonproliferation policy can be considered as a paradigmatic shift or not? In this context, what can Kuhn's theory of paradigm, and paradigm shift, contribute to our understanding of this issue?

Fifth, this book reflects how the United States has dominated in the establishment and maintenance of the nuclear nonproliferation regime. The United States is not regarded as an economic hegemon any longer, but it is still a hegemon in the nuclear weapons arena. How can the hegemonic theory of stability help us understand U.S.-India nuclear cooperation?

Sixth, in the future studies, scholars can also examine the U.S.-India nuclear cooperation through a neo-Gramscian lens. After imposing technological embargoes for several decades, the United States has attempted to engage India in nuclear cooperation. Can it be argued that in view of the multitudinous challenges confronting the global nuclear order and the emerging demand for greater access to nuclear technology, the United States has co-opted India—a leading voice of counter-hegemonic ideas? In the increasing demand for nuclear technology, India's position as a resentful outsider could have added strength to counter-hegemonic ideas for a more equitable nuclear order. The hegemonic system survives with the consent and acquiescence of less powerful states, but it also has to prevent the emergence of counter-hegemonic ideas. Does the Gramscian concept of "*trasformismo*" help in understanding this nuclear cooperation?

Last but not the least, this book has highlighted the expansion in the functional scope of the nuclear nonproliferation regime. Yet, there is considerable space for indepth analysis of the evolution of the nuclear nonproliferation regime, especially with regard to the delicate balance of obligations enshrined in the NPT—Articles IV (nuclear energy) and VI (disarmament). What is the response of the nonnuclear weapon states with regard to the strengthening of the supplier restraints on the transfer of nuclear technology? How the nuclear nonproliferation regime can be further engineered to withstand the challenges of the impending nuclear renaissance?

NOTES

1. Donald J. Puchala and Raymond F. Hopkins, "International Regimes: Lessons from Inductive Analysis," *International Organization* 36, no. 2 (Spring 1982): 247.
2. Stephen D. Krasner, "Structural Causes and Regime Consequences: Regimes as Intervening Variables," *International Organization* 36, no. 2 (Spring 1982): 185–88.
3. Puchala and Hopkins, "Lessons from Inductive Analysis," 249.
4. Miller, "Nuclear Collisions," 3.
5. Andy Knight, *A Changing United Nations: Multilateral Evolution and the Quest for Global Governance*, (New York: Palgrave, 2000), 82.
6. Steven E. Miller, Wael Al-Assad, Jayantha Dhanapala, C. Raja Mohan and Ta Minh Tuan, *Nuclear Collisions: Discord, Reform and the Nuclear Nonproliferation Regime*, (Massachusetts: American Academy of Arts and Sciences, April 2012), 1.
7. Joseph F. Pilat, "The End of the Regime?" *International Affairs* 83, no. 3 (2007): 475.
8. Remarks of IAEA Director General, Mohammed ElBaradei, "IAEA Director General Reacts to U.S.-India Cooperation Agreement," IAEA Press Release, International Atomic Energy Agency, 20 July 2005. Available at http://www.iaea.org/newscenter/pressreleases/2005/prn200504.html.
9. Narayan Lakshman, "India will not apply for U.S. sanctions exemption on Iran," *The Hindu*, March 28, 2012.
10. Ibid.
11. Joint Statement by President Obama and Prime Minister Singh of India, White House, Office of the Press Secretary, November 8, 2010. Available at https://www.whitehouse.gov/the-press-office/2010/11/08/joint-statement-president-obama-and-prime-minister-singh-india.
12. Ibid.
13. A. Vinod Kumar, "Doctrine at Work," 212.
14. Shyam Saran, Special Envoy of Prime Minister (India) on Nuclear Issues, Speech at the Brookings Institution, Washington DC on *Indo-US Civil Nuclear Agreement: Expectations and Consequences*, March 23, 2009. Available at http://www.indianembassy.org/prdetail520/address-by-special-envoy-to-the-prime-minister-mr.-shyam-saran-at-the-brookings-institution-washington-dc-on-indo-us-civil-nuclear-agreement%3A-expectations-and-consequences (accessed March 18, 2012).
15. Carl Paddock, *Comprehensive Test Ban Treaty: Where Does India Stand?* (New Delhi: Epitome Books, 2010), 54.

16. Saran, "Indo-US Civil Nuclear Agreement."
17. Ibid., 52.
18. Kumar, "Doctrine at Work," 217.
19. Indrani Bagchi, "India Pitches for Membership of Global Non-proliferation Regimes," *The Times of India*, April 19, 2012. Available at http://articles.timesofindia.indiatimes.com/2012–04–19/india/31362088_1_top-non-proliferation-regimes-wassenaar-arrangement-control-regime.
20. Sandeep Dikshit, "NSG to Include India's Request for Membership as a Special Agenda Item," *The Hindu*, May 25, 2011.
21. The Missile Technology Control Regime at a Glance, Factsheets and Briefs, Arms Control Association, November 2015. Available at https://www.armscontrol.org/factsheets/mtcr.
22. Mohammed ElBaradei, "Rethinking Nuclear Safeguards," *The Washington Post*, June 14, 2006.
23. Miller et al., "Nuclear Collisions,"
24. ElBaradei, in an interview with Siddharth Varadarajan, "The Reality is India will Remain Outside the NPT," *The Hindu*, October 6, 2009.
25. Baradei, "Rethinking Nuclear Safeguards."
26. ElBaradei, "Rethinking Nuclear Safeguards."
27. Trevor Findlay, *Nuclear Energy and Global Governance: Ensuring Safety, Security and Non-proliferation*, (Routledge: New York, 2011), 142.
28. Ferial Ara Saeed, *Redefining Success: Applying Lessons in Nuclear Diplomacy from North Korea to Iran*, Strategic Perspectives, no. 1, Institute for National Strategic Studies (Washington D.C.: National Defense University, September 2010), 5.
29. Miller et al., "Nuclear Collisions," 29.
30. Saeed, "Redefining Success," 5.
31. Ibid., 7.
32. The Iran Nuclear Deal: What you Need to Know Historic Deal that Will Prevent Iran from Acquiring Nuclear Weapon, White House Briefing, Washington D.C. Available at https://www.whitehouse.gov/issues/foreign-policy/iran-deal
33. Ambassador James Dobbins, Remarks at the ACA Press Briefing, "Iran's Nuclear Challenge: Where to go from here?" Arms Control Association, Washington D.C., October 22, 2009.
34. Edward C. Luck, "Rediscovering the State," *Global Governance*, 8 (2002): 7–8.
35. Ibid., 9.
36. Stephanie G. Neumann, (ed) *International Relations Theory and the Third World*, (New York: St. Martin's Press, 1998), 17.
37. Luck "Rediscovering the State," 11.
38. Emanuel Adler, *Communitarian International Relations: The Epistemic Foundations of International Relations*, (Routledge: New York, 2005), 75.

Bibliography

Abe, Nobuyasu. "The Current Problems of the NPT: How to Strengthen the Non-proliferation Regime." *Strategic Analysis* 34, no. 2 (March 2010).

Abraham, Itty. *Making of the Atomic Bomb: Science, Secrecy, and the Postcolonial State.* London: Zed Books, November 1998.

Adhikari, Gautam. "India and America: Estranged No More." *Current History* (April 2004).

Adler, Emanuel. "Cognitive Evolution: A Dynamic Approach to the Study of International Relations and Their Progress" in *Progress in Postwar International Relations.* Edited by Emanuel Adler and Beverly Crawford. New York: Columbia University Press, 1991.

Albright, David. "The Shots Heard 'Round the World." *The Bulletin of Atomic Scientists* 54, no. 4 (July–August 1998).

Albright, Madeleine K. Interview by Wolf Blitzer, Late Edition, CNN, June 14, 1998, *Transcript: Secretary of State Albright's CNN Interview,* Office of the U.S. Spokesman, U.S. Department of State, June 15, 1998.

———. *Press Remarks on India and Pakistan,* Office of the Spokesman, U.S. Department of State, Washington D.C., June 3, 1998.

Allison, Graham. "Nuclear Disorder: Surveying Atomic Threats." *Foreign Affairs* 89, no. 1 (January/February 2010).

Arksey, Hilary and Peter Knight, *Interviewing for Social Scientists* (London: Sage Publications, 1999).

Asia Society. *Preventing Nuclear Proliferation in South Asia.* Report of the Study Group. Chaired by Arthur A. Hartman. New York: Asia Society, 1995.

Ayoob, Mohammed. "Subaltern Realism: International Relations Theory Meets the Third World," in *International Relations Theory and Third World.* Edited by Stephanie G. Neumann. New York: St. Martin's Press, 1998.

Bagchi, Indrani. "India Pitches for Membership of Global Non-proliferation Regimes." *The Times of India,* April 19, 2012.

Bagla, Pallava. "Washington Blocks 8 US Scientists from TIFR Physics Seminar." *Indian Express* (Mumbai), January 15, 1999.

Bajpai, Kanti. "India-U.S. Foreign Policy Concerns: Cooperation and Conflict," in *Engaging India: U.S. Strategic Relations with the World's Largest Democracy.* Edited by Gary K. Bertsch, Seema Gahlaut and Anupam Srivastava. New York: Routledge, 1999.

Baker, Howard and Lloyd Cutler, *A Report Card on the Department of Energy's Nonproliferation Programs with Russia.* The Secretary of Energy Advisory Board, U.S. Department of Energy, January 10, 2001. Accessed at http://www.seab.energy.gov/publications/rusrpt.pdf (accessed February 15, 2009).

Baruah, Amit. "Iraq Dominates PM's Talks with Leaders." *The Hindu,* June 1, 2003.

Bedi, Rahul. "Lifting of Sanctions a 'Sweetner' for Siding with U.S.," *The Telegraph,* September 24, 2001.

Bennet, James. "Nuclear Anxietiy: The President; Clinton Calls Tests a 'Terrible' Mistake and Announces Sanctions against India." *New York Times,* May 14, 1998.

Bhaskar, C. Uday. "Systemic Compulsions in India-U.S. Relations," in *India-U.S. Relations: Addressing the Challenges of the 21st Century,* edited by N.S Sisodia, Peter R. Lavoy, Cherian Samuel and Robin Walker. Delhi: Magnum Books, 2008.

Bhatia, Shyam. *India's Nuclear Bomb.* Sahibabad: Vikas Publishing, 1979.

Bhatia, Vandana. "Nonproliferation Policy of the Clinton Administration toward India: Shifting of Nuclear Goalposts?" *Comparative Strategy* 32, no. 3 (2013): 261–82.

———. "The US-India Nuclear Agreement: Revisiting the Debate." *Strategic Analysis* 36, no. 4 (July 2012).

———. "*Abandon the CD, Rescue the Treaty*," Paper written for the Graduate Research Award in Nuclear Nonproliferation, Arms Control and Disarmament, Submitted to the Simons Foundation, Vancouver, January 20, 2012.

———. "Toward a Comprehensive Test Ban." Paper presented at the Graduate Students Conference, University of Delhi, South Campus, 1996.

Bindon, George and Sitoo Mukherjee. "Canada-India Cooperation." *Research Policy* 7 (1978).

Blackwill, Robert D. "The India Imperative." *The National Interest* no. 80 (Summer 2005).

Bodansky, Daniel and Elliot Diringer, *The Evolution of Multilateral Regimes: Implications for Climate Change*. Prepared for the Pew Center on Global Climate Change, December 2010.

Boese, Wade. "US-India Discussing Arms Deals, Military Ties." *Arms Control Today* (December 2001). Available at http://www.armscontrol.org/act/2001_12/indarmsdec01 (accessed April 26, 2009).

Borman, Matthew S. "NSSP: U.S., India Interests in Action." *The Hindu*, October 2, 2004.

Borooah, Dev Kant. "Introduction," in *Atoms for Peace: An Exposition of India's Nuclear Policy*, edited by Balwant A. Desai. Bombay: All India Congress Committee, 1975.

Boutin, Kenneth. "93+10: Strengthened Nuclear Safeguards a Decade On." *Vertic Brief* no. 2 (April 2004).

Bouton, Marshall M. "Heed South Asia's Concerns." *Far Eastern Economic Review* 161, no. 26 (June 25, 1998).

Breitmeier, Helmut, Oran R.Young, and Michael Zurn. *Analyzing International Environmental Regimes: From Case-Study to Database*. Cambridge, MA: MIT Press, 2006.

Brown, David. *Palmerston and the Politics of Foreign Policy, 1846–1855*. Manchester: Manchester University Press, 2002.

Bruneau, Richard. "Engaging a Nuclear India: Punishment, Reward and the Politics of Non-proliferation." *Journal of Public and International Affairs* 17, (Spring 2006).

Budania, Rajpal. *India's National Security Dilemma: The Pakistan Factor and India's Policy Response*. New Delhi: Indus Publishing Company, 2001.

Burns, John F. "India rejects U.S. Bid for Nuclear Pact with Pakistan." *New York Times*, March 26, 1994.

———. "U.S. Ends A $4 Billion Visit to India." *The New York Times*, January 18, 1995.

Burns, Nicholas. "America's Strategic Opportunity with India." *Foreign Affairs* 86, no. 6, (November/ December 2007).

Carranza, Mario. "Can the NPT Survive? The Theory and Practice of U.S. Nuclear Nonproliferation Policy after September 11." *Contemporary Security Policy* 27, no. 3 (December 2006).

———. "From Non-Proliferation to Post-Proliferation: Explaining the U.S.-India Nuclear Deal." *Contemporary Security Policy* 28, no. 3 (2007).

Cerniello, Craig. "NMD Bill Clears Congress as Senate Re-examines ABM Treaty," *Arms Control Today*, April/May 1999. Available at http://www.armscontrol.org/act/1999_04–05/nmdam99 (accessed December 26, 2010).

Chari, P.R. "An Indian Reaction to U.S. Nonproliferation Policy." *International Security* 3, no. 2 (Autumn 1978).

Chellaney, Brahma. "Non-proliferation: An Indian Critique of U.S. Export Controls." *Orbis* (Summer 1994).

———. "India's U.S.-Influenced Decision to Shut Down Cirus Research Reactor," June 22, 2006. Available at http://chellaney.net/2008/06/22/indias-u-s-influenced-decision-to-shut-down-cirus-research-reactor/ (accessed April 12, 2012).

Chengappa, Raj. "Nuclear Dilemma." *India Today*, April 30, 1994.

———. "Say 'No' to Regional Capping." *India Today*, April 30, 1994.

———, and Saurabh Shukla. "Nuclear Showdown." *India Today*, March 7, 2008.

Chopra, A.K. *India's Policy on Disarmament*. New Delhi: ABC Publishers, 1984.

Choudhury, Geeta and Sheila Nair. *Power Post-colonialism and International Relations: Reading Race, Gender and Class*. Routledge: London and New York, 2002.

Christopher, Warren. "Strengthening U.S. Relations with South Asia." Speech by the U.S. Secretary of State to the South Asian Association for Regional Cooperation, New York City, September, 29, 1994, Bureau of Public Affairs, *U.S. Department of State Dispatch* 5, no. 40 (October 3, 1994).

Cirincione, Joseph. "Strategic Collapse: The Failure of the Bush Nuclear Doctrine." *Arms Control Today* (November, 2008).

———. "The US's Nuclear Cave-In," *Asia Times Online* (March 2006).

Clary, Christopher. "A.Q. Khan and the Limits of the Nonproliferation." *Disarmament Forum*, no. 4 (2004).

Cohen, Avner and Thomas Graham Jr. "An NPT for Non-Members." *Bulletin of Atomic Scientists*. May/June 2004.

Cohen, Stephen P. "1990: South Asia's Useful Crisis." Paper presented to the Annual Meeting of the American Association for the Advancement of Science, Chicago, February 6–7 1992.

———. *India: Emerging Power*. Washington D.C.: Brookings Institution Press, 2002.

———. *A Deal Too Far?* ORF-Brookings Paper. New Delhi: Observer Research Foundatin, 2006.

———. *A New Beginning for South Asia*. Policy Brief no. 55, Washington D.C.: Brookings Institution, January 2000.

Conley, Major Jerome M. *Indo-Russian Military and Nuclear Cooperation: Implications for U.S. Security Interests*. INSS Occasional Paper 31, Proliferation Series. Colorado: USAF Institute for National Security Studies, USAF Academy, February 2000.

Cox, Robert W. ed. "Introduction," in *The New Realism: Perspectives on Multilateralism and World Order*. New York: United Nations University Press, 1997.

———. *Approaches to World Order*. Cambridge: Cambridge University Press, 1996.

———. "Gramsci, Hegemony and International Relations: A Method," in *Gramsci, Historical Materialism and International Relations*. Edited by Stephen Gill. New York: Cambridge University Press, 1993.

———. "Crisis of the World Order and Problem of International Organisation in the 1980s." *International Journal* 35, no. 2 (Spring 1980).

Cronin, Richard P., and Barbara Leitch LePoer. *South Asia: U.S. Interests and Policy Issues*. CRS Report for Congress, no. 93–243. Washington D.C.: Congressional Research Service, updated February 12, 1993.

———. Barbara Leitch LePoer, Jonathan Medalia and Dianne Rennack. *India-Pakistan Nuclear Tests and U.S. Response*. CRS Report for Congress. Washington D.C.: Congressional Research Service, updated November 24, 1998.

Curtis, Lisa. "Nuclear Crunch for U.S.-India." *The Washington Times*, September 23, 2008.

———. "The Costs of a Failed U.S.-India Civil Nuclear Deal," Web Memo no. 1688. Washington, D.C.: The Heritage Foundation, 2007.

———. "New U.S. Alliance with India Forges Key Strategic Relationship," Commentary. Washington, D.C.: The Heritage Foundation, 2009.

———, and Baker Spring. *U.S. Nuclear Agreement with India: An Acceptable Deal for Major Strategic Gain*. Web Memo no. 1587, Washington D.C.: The Heritage Foundation, August 14, 2007.

Davis, Zachary S. and Mitchell Reiss. *U.S. Counterproliferation Doctrine: Issues for Congress*. CRS Report no. 94–734 ENR, Washington D.C.: Congressional Research Service, September 21, 1994.

Department of Atomic Energy. *Annual Report 1994–1995*. New Delhi: Government of India, 1995.

———. *Annual Report 1993–1994*. New Delhi: Government of India, 1994.

Diamond, Howard. "U.S. Waives Many Test-Related Sanctions on India, Pakistan," *Arms Control Today* (November/December 1998). Available at http://legacy.armscontrol.org/act/1998_11–12/ipnd98.asp (accessed March 8, 2009).

Dikshit, Sandeep. "NSG to include India's request for membership as a special agenda item." *The Hindu*, May 25, 2011.

Dillon, Dana R., and Baker Spring. "Nuclear India and the Nonproliferation Treaty." *Backgrounder*, no. 1935. Washington D.C.: The Heritage Foundation, May 18, 2006.

Director of National Intelligence. National Intelligence Council. *Mapping the Global Future: Report of the 2020 Project,* Washington D.C., December 2004.

Divine, Robert. *Blowing on the Wind: The Nuclear Test Ban Debate 1954–1960*. New York: Oxford University Press, 1978.

Dixit, J.N. "Indo-U.S. Relations: Delhi Dialogue and After." *Rediff News*, February 11, 1999. Available at www.rediff.com/news/1999feb/11dixit.htm (accessed March 10, 2009).

Dobbins, James. Remarks at the ACA Press Briefing, "*Iran's Nuclear Challenge: Where to go from here?*" Arms Control Association, Washington D.C., October 22, 2009.

Doty, Roxanne. "Foreign Policy as a Social Construction: A Post-Positivist Analysis of U.S. Counter-Insurgency Policy in the Philippines." *International Studies Quarterly* 37 (September 1993).

Doyle, Michael. "Kant, Liberal Legacies, and Foreign Affairs (I and II)." *Philosophy and Public Affairs* 12, no. 3 and 4 (Summer and Autumn 1983).

Dunn, Lewis. "Today's Global Proliferation Challenges: Some Thoughts on Potential Indo-U.S. Cooperation," in *India-U.S. Relations: Addressing the Challenges of the 21st Century*, edited by N.S Sisodia, Peter R. Lavoy, Cherian Samuel and Robin Walker. New Delhi: Magnum Books, September 2008.

Eckberg, Douglas Lee, and Lester Hill Jr. "The Paradigm Concept and Sociology: A Critical Review." *American Sociological Review* 44, no. 6 (December 1979).

Einhorn, Robert. "Should the US Sell the Technology to India? Part I." *Yale Global* (8 November, 2005). Available at http://yaleglobal.yale.edu/display.article?id=6474 (accessed March 8, 2009).

ElBaradei, Mohammed. 'Rethinking Nuclear Safeguards." *The Washington Post*, June 14, 2006.

Evans, Stephen. "US Attraction to Nuclear Power." BBC News, May 15 2001. Available at http://news.bbc.co.uk/2/hi/americas/1330256.stm (accessed March 26, 2009).

Fair, Christine. "Learning to Think the Unthinkable: Lessons from India's Nuclear Tests." *India Review* 4, no. 1 (January 2005).

———. "India and the U.S.: Embracing a New Paradigm," in *Indian Foreign Policy in a Unipolar World*. Edited by Harsh Pant. London: Routledge, 2009.

Findlay, Trevor. *Nuclear Energy and Global Governance: Ensuring Safety, Security and Non-proliferation.* New York: Routledge, 2011.

Finnemore, Martha. *National Interests in International Society*. Ithaca: Cornell University Press, 1996.

Frankel, Francine R., ed. "Preface," in *Bridging the Nonproliferation Divide: The United States and India.* Lanham, MD: University Press of America, 1995.

Frantz, Douglas and Catherine Collins. *The Nuclear Jihadist: The True Story of the Man Who Sold the World's Most Dangerous Secrets and How We Could Have Stopped Him.* New York: Twelve, 2007.

Fuhrmann, Matthew. "Spreading Temptation: Proliferation and Peaceful Nuclear Cooperation Agreements." *International Security* 34, no. 1 (Summer 2009).

Fukuyama, Francis. "Liberal Democracy as a Global Phenomenon." *Political Science and Politics* 24, no. 4 (1991).

Ganguly, Sumit. "Indo-Pakistani Nuclear Issues and the Stability/Instability Paradox." *Studies in Conflict and Terrorism* 18 (1995).

———. "India's Pathways to Pokhran II: The Prospects and Sources of New Delhi's Nuclear Weapons Program." *International Security* 23, no. 4 (Spring 1999).

Garver, John W. *China and Iran: Ancient Partners in a Post-Imperial World.* Seattle: University of Washington Press, 2006.

Geske, Mary. "Globalisation is What States Make of It: U.S. Foreign Economic Policy and the Economic Crisis." *International Politics* 37, no. 3 (2000).

Ghose, Arundhati. "Maintaining the Moratorium: A Defacto CTBT." *Disarmament Forum* 2, United Nations Institute for Disarmament Research, UNIDIR, Geneva (2006).

———. "Negotiating the CTBT: India's Security Concerns and Nuclear Disarmament." *Journal of International Affairs* 51, no. 1 (Summer 1997).

Gill, John H. "Regional Concerns, Global Ambitions," in *Strategic Asia 2003–2004: Fragility and Crisis.* Edited by Richard J. Ellings. Washington D.C.: National Bureau of Asian Research, 2003.

Gillette, Robert. "India: Into the Nuclear Club on Canada's Shoulders." *Science* 184, no. 4141 (June 7, 1974).

Glaser, Barney G. and Anselm L. Strauss. *The Discovery of Grounded Theory: Strategies for Qualitative Research.* New York: Aldine Transaction, 1967.

Gopalkrishnan, A. "Indo-U.S. Cooperation: A Non-Starter." *Economic and Political Weekly*, July 2, 2005.

———. "Assured Fuel Supply is a Mirage," *Deccan Chronicle*, August 5, 2007.

Graham Jr., Thomas. "South Asia and the Future of Nuclear Non-proliferation." *Arms Control Today* (May 28, 1998).

Grimmett, Jeanne. *Nuclear Sanctions: Section 102(b) of the Arms Control Export Act and Its Application to India and Pakistan.* CRS Report no. 98–486. Washington D.C.: Congressional Research Service, updated September 19, 2001.

Gupta, Amit. *The U.S.-India Relationship: Strategic Partnership or Complementary Interests?* Carlisle, PA: Strategic Studies Institute, 2005.

Gupta, Arvind. "NPT Review Conference 2010: Issues and Prospects." *Strategic Analysis* 34, no. 2 (March 2010).

Haass, Richard. Testimony before the Senate Task Force on Economic Sanctions. Senate, 105th Congress, 2nd Session, Washington D.C., September 9, 1998. Available at http://www.brookings.edu/testimony/1998/0909sanctions_haass.aspx?rssid=sanctions (accessed March 10, 2009).

———. *Economic Sanctions: Too Much of a Bad Thing*, Brookings Policy Brief Series, no. 34. Washington D.C.: Brookings Institution, June 1998. Available at http://www.brookings.edu/papers/1998/06sanctions_haass.aspx?rssid=sanctions (accessed March 10, 2009).

———. "The US Role in India's Nuclear Tests." *The Washington Times*, May 14, 1998.

Hagerty, Devin T. "The Power of Suggestion: Opaque Proliferation, Existential Deterrence, and the South Asian Nuclear Arms Competition." *Security Studies* 2, no. 3–4 (Spring-Summer 1993).

———. "Nuclear Deterrence in South Asia: The 1990 Indo-Pakistani Crisis." *International Security* 20, no. 3 (Winter 1995/96).

Halperin, Morton H. and Richard N. Haass. "Our Misguided South Asia Nuclear Policy." *The Washington Post*, September 13, 1998.

Haniffa, Aziz. "Sanctions Against India, Pakistan May be Lifted Simultaneously." *The Tribune* (Chandigarh) September 8, 2001.

Harrison, Selig S. "India's Muscle Flexing is Over. Let the Bargaining Begin." *The Washington Post*, May 17, 1998.

———. "Dialogue of the Deaf: Mutual Perceptions and Indo-American Relations." in *Conflicting Images*, edited by Sulochana Raghavan Glazer and Nathan Glazer. Glen Dale, MD: Riverdale, 1990.

Hasenclever, Andreas, Peter Mayer and Volker Rittberger, *Theories of International Regimes.* New York: Cambridge University Press, 2002.

Hassner, Pierre. "Who Killed Nuclear Enlightenment?" *International Affairs*, 83, no. 3 (2007).

Hathaway, Robert M. "Confrontation and Retreat: The U.S. Congress and the South Asian Nuclear Tests," *Arms Control Today* (January–February 2000). Available at http://www.armscontrol.org/act/2000_01–02/rhjf00 (accessed March 8, 2009).

Hayes, Jarrod. "Identity and Securitization in the Democratic Peace: The U.S. and the Divergence of Responses to India and Iran's Nuclear Program." *International Studies Quarterly* 53 (2009).

Hersh, Seymour. "On the Nuclear Edge." *New Yorker*, March 29, 1993.

Holloway, David. "The United States and the NPT 'Double Bargain,'" in *Nuclear Proliferation and International Order: Challenges to the NPT*, edited by Olav Njolstad. New York: Routledge, 2011.

Hosur, Prashant. "The Indo-U.S. Civilian Nuclear Agreement: What's the Big Deal?" *International Journal* (Spring 2010).

IAEA Director General Welcomes U.S. and India Nuclear Deal. Remarks of Mohammed El-Baradei, IAEA Press Release, Press Office, Division of Public Information, International Atomic Energy Agency, March 2, 2006. Available at www.iaea.org/newscenter/pressreleases/2006/prn200605.html (accessed March 18, 2012).

Implementation of the Treaty on the Non-Proliferation of Nuclear Weapons. Report submitted by Canada, 2010 Review Conference of the Parties to the Treaty on the Non-Proliferation of Nuclear Weapons, NPT/CONF.2010/9, (March 18, 2010). Available at http://daccess-dds-ny.un.org/doc/UNDOC/GEN/N10/279/58/PDF/N1027958.pdf?OpenElement (accessed March 10, 2012).

"Integrated Safeguards in the Non-Nuclear Weapon States of the European Union," Technical Sheets." *ESARDA Bulletin*, no. 41 (June 2009).

Iyengar, P. K. "123 Agreement is a Gilded Cage." *The Asian Age*, August 16, 2007.

———. "123 Agreement is a Gilded Cage," *The Asian Age*, August 16, 2007.

Jervis, Robert. "Security Regimes." *International Organisation* 36, no. 2 (Spring 1982).

Johnson, Rebecca. "Rethinking the NPT's Role in Security: 2010 and Beyond." *International Affairs* 86, no. 2 (March 2010).

Joint Statement, Third Meeting of the U.S.-India Defence Policy Group, December 3–4, 2001. Available at http://avalon.law.yale.edu/sept11/joint_010.asp (accessed February 15, 2009).

Joshi, Manoj. "Dousing the Fire: Indian Missile Program and the United States Nonproliferation Policy." *Strategic Analysis* 17, no. 5 (August 1994).

———. "Indo-Iran Ties May Hurt Good Friend, U.S." *Times of India* (New Delhi), February 22, 2004.

———. "Curbs on Missile Technology." *The Hindu*, November 1989.

Juster, Kenneth. "Stimulating High-Technology Cooperation with India." Speech at the 28th Annual Meeting of the US-India Business Council, New York, June 2, 2003.

———. "September 11 and U.S. Nonproliferation Policy." Speech at the Ninth Asian Export Control Seminar, Tokyo, Japan, February 26, 2002.

Kan, Shirley A. *China's Proliferation of Weapons of Mass Destruction: Current Policy Issues*. CRS Issue Brief for Congress, Washington D.C.: Congressional Research Service, May 16, 2001.

———. *China: Possible Missile Technology Transfers from U.S. Satellite Export Policy: Background and Chronology*. CRS Report for Congress no. 98–485F, Washington D.C.: Congressional Research Service, updated August 13, 1998.

Kapur, Ashok. "The Canada-India Nuclear Negotiations: Some Hypotheses and Lessons." *The World Today* 34, no. 8 (August 1978).

———. "India and the Atom." *The Bulletin of Atomic Scientists* 30, no. 7 (September 1974).

Kapur, K.D. *Nuclear Non-Proliferation Diplomacy: Nuclear Power Programmes in the Third World*. New Delhi: Lancers Books, 1993.

Karnad, Bharat. *Nuclear Weapons and Indian Security: The Realist Foundations of Strategy*. New Delhi: Macmillan, 2002.

——— "Nuclear Test is a Must." *The Asian Age*, 22 February 2008.

Katyal, Anita. "'No Freeze on N-Capability' US told." *The Times of India* (Mumbai) November 26, 1998.

Kazi, Reshmi. "Proliferation Security Initiative and India." *Peace and Conflict* 7, no. 7 (October 2004).

Keller, William W. *Arm in Arm: The Political Economy of the Global Arms Trade*. New York: Basic Books, 1995.

Kennan, George. "The Sources of Soviet Conduct." *Foreign Affairs* 25, no. 4 (July 1947).

Keohane, Robert. *International Institutions and State Power: Essays in International Relations*. Boulder, CO: Westview Press, 1989.

———, and Joseph Nye. "Power and Interdependence in the Information Age." *Foreign Affairs* 77, no. 5 (1998).

Kerr, Paul K. *U.S. Nuclear Cooperation with India: Issue for Congress*. CRS Report for Congress, 7–5700, RL-33016, Washington D.C.: Congressional Research Service, December 15, 2011.

Khurana, Gurpreet S. "India and the Container Security Initiative," *IDSA Strategic Comments* (July 17, 2007).

Kiesiel, T. "Paradigms," in *Contemporary Philosophy* edited by G. Floistad. Volume 2. Hague: Martinus Nijhoff Publishers, 1982.

Knight, W. Andy. *A Changing United Nations: Multilateral Evolution and the Quest for Global Governance*. New York: Palgrave, 2000.

Kraemer, Jay R. and Frank Aum, "The U.S.-India Nuclear Agreement: Progress Toward Nuclear Cooperation with India and a New Paradigm in Non-proliferation Policy," *International Journal of Nuclear Law* 1, no. 4 (2007).

Krasner, Stephen D. "Structural Causes and Regime Consequences: Regimes as Intervening Variables." *International Organisation* 36, no. 2 (Spring 1982).

Krause, Joachim. "Enlightenment and Nuclear Order." *International Affairs* 83, no. 3 (May 2007).

Krepon, Michael. "Engaging India." Review of *Engaging India: Diplomacy, Democracy and the Bomb*. Strobe Talbott. *Arms Control Today* 34 (September 2004). Available at www.armscontrol.org/act/2004–09/bookreviews (accessed March 10, 2009).

———. "Another Contentious Nuclear Issue." *The Hindu*, July 12, 2011.

Krishnaswami, Sridhar. "US, India Reach Common Ground." *The Hindu* (Chennai), November 27, 1998.

———. "Sanctions Strategy has not Worked: Blackwill." *The Hindu*, June 28, 2001.

———. "Trading Sanctions for Flexibility." *Frontline* 15, no. 16 (August 1–14, 1998).

Krishnaswamy, K. V. "Celeste Defends Demand on Deterrence." *The Hindu*, January 23, 1999.

Kugler, Jacek and A.F.K. Organski. "The Power Transition: A Retrospective and Prospective Evaluation," in *Handbook of War Studies*, edited by Manus I. Midlarsky (Boston: Unwin Hyman, 1988).

Kumar, Amit. *India and the U.S. led WMD Non-Proliferation Initiatives*. Pugwash India, March 29, 2008. Available at http://www.indianpugwashsociety.org/article_detail.asp?aid=62 (accessed on December 6, 2010).

Kumar, Vinod A. "Counterproliferation: India's New Imperatives and Options." *Strategic Analysis* (January–February 2007).

———. "A Doctrine at Work: Obama's Evolving Nuclear Policy and What it Bodes for India." *Strategic Analysis* 35, no. 2 (March 2011).

Kutchesfahani, Sara. "Case Study: The Khan Network," in *Nuclear Safeguards, Security and Nonproliferation: Achieving Security with Technology and Policy*, edited by James Doyle. Burlington, MA: Butterworth-Heinmann, July 2008.

Kux, Dennis. *India and the United States: Estranged Democracies, 1941–1991*. Thousand Oaks, CA: Sage Publications, 1994.

———. "U.S.-Pakistan Relations as the Twentieth Century Ends," in *Pakistan 2000*, edited by Charles H. Kennedy and Craig Baxter. Lanham, MD: Lexington Books, 2000.

Lakshman, Narayan. "India Will Not Apply for U.S. Sanctions Exemption on Iran." *The Hindu*, March 28, 2012.

Ledogar, Stephen J. "Concluding the Negotiations." *Disarmament* 18, no. 1 (1995).

Lemke, Douglas. "The Continuation of History: Power Transition Theory and the End of Cold War." *Journal of Peace Research* 34, no. 1 (February, 1997).

Levi, Michael A. and Charles D. Ferguson. *US-India Nuclear Cooperation: A Strategy for Moving Forward*. Council Special Report, no. 16, Council on Foreign Relations, June 2006.

Levy, Jack S. "Domestic Politics in War," in *The Origin and Prevention of Major Wars*, edited by Robert I. Rotberg and Theodore K. Rabb. New York: Cambridge University Press, 1989.

Levy, Marc A. Oran R. Young and Michael Zurn. "The Study of International Regimes." *European Journal of International Relations* 1, no. 3 (1995).

Limaye, Satu P. "US-India Relations: Stuck in Nuclear Narrative." *Comparative Connections* 3, no. 1 (April 2001).

Lincoln, Y.S. and E.G. Guba, *Naturalistic Enquiry*. Thousand Oaks, CA: Sage Publishers, 1985.

Lippman, Thomas W. "US Effort to Curb Nuclear Weapons in Peril as India Insists on Limits for China." *Washington Post*, July, 7 1994.

Lok Sabha Debates, Parliament of India, Third Series, no. 2, August 20, 1962.

Luck, Edward C. "Rediscovering the State," *Global Governance*, 8 (2002).

Malhotra, Vinay Kumar, ed. "U.S. Latest Initiatives on Nonproliferation in South Asia and Indo-U.S. Relations," in *Indo-U.S. Relations in the Nineties*. Delhi: Anmol Publications Pvt. Ltd, 1995.

Malik, Mohan J. "India's Response to the Gulf Crisis: Implications for Indian Foreign Policy." *Asian Survey* 31, no. 9 (September 1991).

Mansingh, Lalit. *Accomplishments and Challenges in the New Era of Cooperation*." Keynote address at the Sigur Centre for Asian Studies, The Elliot School of International Affairs, George Washington University, Washington D.C., April 1, 2004.

Masterman, Margaret. "The Nature of a Paradigm," in *Criticism and Growth of Knowledge: Proceedings of the International Colloquium in the Philosophy of Science*, edited by Imre Lakatos and Alan Musgrave. Cambridge: Cambridge University Press, 1970.

Mazarr, Michael J. "Clinton Foreign Policy R.I.P." *The Washington Quarterly* 21, no. 2 (Spring 1998).

McGoldrick, Fred. *The U.S.-UAE Peaceful Nuclear Cooperation Agreement: A Gold Standard or Fool's Gold?* Washington D.C.: Center for Strategic and International Studies, CSIS, November 30, 2010.

———, Harold Bengelsdorf and Lawrence Scheinman. "The US-India Nuclear Deal: Taking Stock," *Arms Control Today* (October, 2005). Available at www.armscontrol.org/act/2005_10/OCT-Cover (accessed March 26, 2008).

McGwire, Michael. "Shifting the Paradigm." *International Affairs* 78, no. 1 (January 2002).

Menon, Krishna. Remarks at the Eighteen Nations Committee on Disarmament, *Final Verbatim Record of the Conference of the Eighteen Nation Committee on Disarmament*, 5th Meeting (ENDC/PV5, United Nations General Assembly, March 20, 1962).

Merriam B., Sharan. *Qualitative Research and Case Study Applications in Education*. San Francisco, CA: Jossey-Bass Publishers. 1998.

Messari, Nizar. "Identity and Foreign Policy: The Case of Islam in US Foreign Policy," in *Foreign Policy in a Constructed World*, edited by Vendulka Kubalkova. New York: M. Sharpe Inc, 2001.

Milhollin, Gary. "The U.S.-India Nuclear Pact: Bad for Security." *Current History* (November 2006).

Miller, Steven E., Wael Al-Assad, Jayantha Dhanapala, C. Raja Mohan and Ta Minh Tuan. *Nuclear Collisions: Discord, Reform and the Nuclear Nonproliferation Regime.* Cambridge, MA: American Academy of Arts and Sciences, 2012.

Mirchandani, G.G. *India's Nuclear Dilemma*. New Delhi: Popular Book Service, 1968.

Miron, G. "Memorandum of Law: Did the ABM Treaty of 1972 Remain in Force After the USSR Ceased to Exist in December 1991 and Did it Become a Treaty Between the U.S. and the Russia Federation?" *American University International Law Review* 17, no. 2 (2002).

Mishra, Bhabani. "India-U.S. Relations: A Paradigm Shift." *Strategic Analysis* 29, no. 1 (January-March 2005).

Mishra, Brajesh. "India, United States and the New World Order: Prospects for Cooperation." Speech at the Council on Foreign Relations, New York. May 7, 2003. Available at http://mea.gov.in/speech/2003/05/07spc01.htm (accessed April 06, 2009).

Mistry, Dinshaw. "Diplomacy, Domestic Politics, and the U.S.-India Nuclear Agreement." *Asian Survey* 46, no. 5 (September/October 2006).

———, and Sumit Ganguly. "The U.S.-India Pact: A Good Deal." *Current History* (November 2006).

Mohan, C. Raja. "Early Solution to Nuclear Issues Will Help: Talbott." *The Hindu* (Chennai), January 14, 2000.

———. "The Paradigm Shift Toward South Asia." *The Washington Quarterly* 26, no. 1 (Winter 2002–2003).

———. "Lowering the Barriers?" *The Hindu*, November 20, 2003.

———. "Indo-US Relations: The Trend Lines," in *India-U.S. Relations: Addressing the Challenges of the 21st Century*. Edited by N.S Sisodia, Peter R. Lavoy, Cherian Samuel and Robin Walker. Delhi: Magnum Book, 2008.

———. "Vajpayee, Bush Explore Tie-up in Missile Defence." *The Hindu* (Chennai), September 23, 2003.

———. *Impossible Allies: Nuclear India, United States and the Global Order*. New Delhi: India Research Press, 2006.

———. "China Slams India's Nuclear Talks." *The Hindu*, January 18, 1999.

Monroe, Kristen Renwick. "Paradigm Shift: From Rational Choice to Perspective." *International Political Science Review* 22, no. 2 (2001).

Morring Jr., Frank and Neelam Matthews, "Third World Rising." *Aviation Week and Space Technology* 161, no. 20 (November 22, 2004).

Muni, S.D. "India and the Post-Cold War World." *Asian Survey* 31, no. 9 (September 1991).

Muralidharan, Sukumar. "On to the Next Round." *Frontline* 16, no. 3 (January 30–15 February 1999). Available at www.hindu.com/fline/fl1603/16030970. (accessed April 05, 2009).

Narula, Sunil, Ludwin Joseph, Ramananda Sengupta. "CTBT: In Isolation Ward Again." *Outlook India*, July 17, 1996.

National Security Council. The White House. *The National Security Strategy of the United States*, Washington D.C., 2002.

Nayan, Rajiv. "Integrating India with the Global Export Controls System: Challenges Ahead." *Strategic Analysis* 35, no. 3 (May 2011).

———. "The Global Nuclear Non-Proliferation Paradigm and India." *Strategic Analysis* 35, no. 4 (July 2011).

Nehru, Jawahar Lal. *India's Foreign Policy: Selected Speeches, September 1946–1961*. New Delhi: Ministry of Information and Broadcasting, 1961.

Nehru, R. K. Remarks in the Eighteen Nations Committee on Disarmament, *Final Verbatim Record of the Conference of the Eighteen Nation Committee on Disarmament*, 162nd Meeting,(ENDC/PV162, United Nations General Assembly, January 31, 1964).

Neumann, Stephanie G., ed. *International Relations Theory and the Third World*. New York: St. Martin's Press, 1998.

Norris, Robert Standish and Thomas B. Cochran. *U.S. Nuclear Tests July 1945 to December 1992*. Washington D.C: Natural Resources Defense Council, 1994.

Nuclear Information and Research Service. *NIRS Investigation Finds That "New" Browns Ferry-1 Reactor Still Doesn't Meet Fire Protection Regulations Its 1975 Fire Caused*, Press

Release, NIRS, June 20, 2007.Available at http://www.nirs.org/press/06–20–2007/1 (accessed April 06, 2009).

Nuclear Regulatory Commission. *Cable Fire at Brown's Ferry Nuclear Plant.* NRC Bulletin, BL-75–04A. Washington D.C., April 3, 1975.

Nuclear Security Summit National Progress Report: India. Prime Minister's Office, Press Information Bureau, Government of India, New Delhi, March 27, 2012. Available at http://pib.nic.in/newsite/erelease.aspx?relid=81755 (accessed March 16, 2012).

Nye, Joseph S. "New Approaches to Nuclear Proliferation Policy." *Science* 256 (May 29, 1992).

Obama, Barack. Speech in Prague, April 5, 2009. Available at www.cfr.org/proliferation/Obamas-speech-prague-april-2009/p20960 (accessed March 26, 2010).

Office of the Press Secretary. The White House, *Remarks by the President to the People of Poland,* Press Release, Washington D.C., 31 May, 2003.

———. *President Announces New Measures to Counter the Threat of WMD.* Fact Sheet. George W. Bush speech, National Defense University, Fort McNair, 11 February, 2004. Available at www.whitehouse.gov/news/releases/2004/02/20040211–4.html (accessed March 26, 2009).

———. "Remarks of the President to Students and Faculty at National Defence University." May 21, 2001. Available at www.whitehouse.gov/news/releases/2001/05/20010501–10.html (accessed March 15, 2009).

———. "Remarks by the President to the People of Poland." May 31, 2003.

———. *Proliferation Security Initiative: Statement of Interdiction Principles.* Fact Sheet. Washington D.C., September 4, 2003. Available at http://www.state.gov/t/isn/c27726.htm (accessed April 05, 2009).

———. *Promoting Energy Independence and Security.* Fact Sheet. Washington DC, April 27, 2005. Available at http://georgewbush-whitehouse.archives.gov/news/releases/2005/04/20050427–9.html (accessed April 01, 2009).

———. "President Discusses Energy at National Small Business Conference." Washington D.C., April 27, 2005; Available at www.whitehouse.gov/releases/2005/04/20050427–3.htm (accessed April 01, 2009).

Ogilvie-White, Tanya. "Is there a theory of Nuclear Proliferation? An Analysis of the Contemporary Debate?" *The Nonproliferation Review* (Fall 1996).

Ohajunwa, Emeka. *Disarmament and Nuclear Proliferation in India-U.S. Security Relations 1947–1990.* New Delhi: Chanakya Publications, 1992.

Oldenburg, Philip. "India and the United States: Accidental or Inevitable Antagonists?" *Asian Survey* 15, no. 4 (Winter 1988/89).

Ollapally, Deepa M. "Mixed Motives in India's Search for Nuclear Status." *Asian Survey,* 41, no. 60, (November/December 2001).

———. "*U.S.-India: Ties that Bind.*" The Sigur Centre Asia Papers. Washington D.C: Elliott School of International Affairs, George Washington University, 2005.

Organski, A.F.K. *World Politics.* New York: Alfred A. Knopf, 1958.

Pande, Savita. "Future of NPT and India–Any Options?" *Strategic Analysis* (July 1994).

———. *CTBT: India and the Nuclear Test Ban Treaty.* New Delhi: Siddhi Books, 1996.

Pant, Harsh V. "The U.S.-India Nuclear Pact and the Non-Proliferation Regime: Triumph of Politics over Institutions." Paper presented at the 48th Annual ISA Convention, Illinois, February 28–March 3, 2007.

———. "A Fine Balance: India walks a Tightrope between Iran and the United States." *Orbis* (Summer 2007).

———. "The U.S.-India Nuclear Deal: The Beginning of a Beautiful Relationship." *Cambridge Review of International Affairs* 20, no. 3, (September 2007).

Parlez, Jane. "U.S. Ready to End Sanctions on India to Build Alliance." *The New York Times,* August 27, 2001.

Parthasarthy, Malini. "India, U.S. Natural Allies: Vajpayee." *The Hindu,* September 9, 2000.

Pasricha, Anjana. *India, U.S. Resume Cooperation on Nuclear Safety*. Voice of America News, February 27, 2003. Available at http://www.voanews.com/english/archive/2003-02/a-2003-02-17-India.cfm?moddate=2003-02-27 (accessed, Feburary 19, 2009).

Patil, R. L. M. *India-Nuclear Weapons and International Politics*. Delhi: National Publishing House, 1969.

Patton, M. Q. *Qualitative Evaluation Methods*. Thousand Oaks, CA: Sage Publications, 1990.

Paul, T.V. "The US-India Nuclear Accord: Implications for the Nonproliferation Regime." *International Journal* (Autumn 2007).

———. *Power versus Prudence: Why Nations Forego Nuclear Weapons*. Montreal: McGill-Queens University Press, 2000.

———, and Mahesh Shankar, "Why the US-India Nuclear Accord is a Good Deal," *Survival* 49, no. 4 (2007).

Perkovich, George. "Faulty Promises: The US-India Nuclear Deal." *Policy Outlook* (September 2005).

———. "Global Implications of the U.S.-India Deal." *Daedalus* (Winter 2010).

———, Jessica T. Mathews, Joseph Circincione, Rose Gottemoeller and Jon B. Wolfsthal. *Universal Compliance: A Strategy for Nuclear Security*. Washington D.C.: Carnegie Endowment for International Peace, June 2007.

———. *India's Nuclear Bomb: The Impact on Global Proliferation*. Los Angeles: University of California Press, 2001.

———. *Democratic Bomb*. Policy Brief no. 49 (Washington D.C.: Carnegie Endowment for International Peace, November 2006).

———. "A Nuclear Third Way in South Asia." *Foreign Policy* 91 (Summer 1993).

Perry, Todd E. "The Growing Role of Customs Organisations in International Strategic Trade Controls," in *Nuclear Safeguards, Security and Nonproliferation: Achieving Security with Technology and Policy*, edited by James Doyle. Burlington, MA: Butterworth-Heinmann, 2008.

Polkinghorne, Donald. *Methodology for the Human Sciences: Systems of Inquiry*. (New York: State University of New York Press, 1983).

Potter, William C. "India and the New Look of U.S. Nonproliferation Policy." *Nonproliferation Review* 12, no. 2, (July 2005).

———, and Jayantha Dhanapala, "The Perils of Nonproliferation Amnesia." *The Hindu*, September 1, 2007.

Puchala, Donald J. and Raymond F. Hopkins, "International Regimes: Lessons from Inductive Analysis." *International Organisation* 36, no. 2 (Spring 1982).

Rajamohan, C. "Indo-US Relations: The Trend Lines," in *India-U.S. Relations: Addressing the Challenges of the 21st Century*, ed. N. S. Sisodia, Peter R. Lavoy, Cherian Samuel and Robin Walker. New Delhi: Magnum Book, 2008.

Rajaraman, R. "The India-US Nuclear Deal: The Perspective of a Non-governmental Nuclear Scientist," in *Canadian Policy on Nuclear Cooperation with India: Confronting New Dilemmas*, edited by Karthika Sasikumar and Wade L. Huntley. Vancouver: Simons Centre for Disarmament and Non-Proliferation Research, 2007.

Rajghatta, Chidanand. "American Sanctions Will Go Soon, Says Inderfurth." *The Indian Express (Mumbai)*, August 31, 1998.

Ramachandran, R. "Out of the Blacklist." *Frontline* 18, no. 21 (October 13–26, 2001).

———. "On Slippery Ground," *Frontline* 28, no. 16, July 30–August 12, 2011. Available at http://www.frontlineonnet.com/fl2816/stories/20110812281611900.htm (accessed March 18, 2012).

Rao, R. R. "India's Nuclear Progress: A Balance Sheet." *India Quarterly* 30 (October-December 1974).

Ravich, Samantha F. "Nuclear Nonproliferation and the Cases of Russia, China and India," in *The Challenge of Proliferation: A Report of the Aspen Strategy Group*, edited by Kurt Campbell. Washington D.C.: The Aspen Institute, 2005.

Reddy, Muralidhar. "India May Sign CTBT Next Year." *The Hindu* (Chennai), November 26, 1998.

Reforming the National Security System. Recommendations of the Group of Ministers, Cabinet Secretariat, Government of India, February 2001.

Reiss, Mitchell. *Bridled Ambition: Why Countries Constrain their Nuclear Capabilities.* Washington, DC: Woodrow Wilson Centre Press, 1995.

Rennack, Dianne E. "India-Pakistan: Current U.S. Economic Sanctions." CRS Report, Washington D.C.: Congressional Research Service, February 11, 2002.

Report on the International Control of Atomic Energy. Prepared for the Secretary of State's Committee on Atomic Energy. U.S. Department of State, Publication 2498, Washington D.C., March 16, 1946. p.4. Available at http://www.foia.cia.gov/cgi/1946/03%20-%20March%201946/Report_on_the_International_Control_of_Atomic_Energy_16_Mar_1946.PDF (accessed January 12, 2009)

Rice, Condoleezza. Prepared Statement of Secretary of State, *U.S.-India Global Partnership*, Hearing before the Committee on International Relations, House of Representatives, 109th Congress, Second Session, April 5, 2006. Available at http://commdocs.house.gov/committees/intlrel/hfa26905.000/hfa26905_0f.htm (accessed March 16, 2012).

———. Remarks of Secretary of State, U.S.-*India Atomic Energy Cooperation: The Indian Separation Plan and the Administration's Legislative Proposal*. Senate Foreign Relations Committee, U.S. Senate, 109th Congress, Second Session, April 5, 2006. Available at http://www.foreign.senate.gov/hearings/hearing/?id=d2fe308b-f34d-83ee-1e10–83b3d9e70f8e (accessed March 18, 2012).

Rothe, J.P. *Qualitative Research: A Practical Guide*. Ontario: RCI/PDE Publications, 1993.

Ruggie, John Gerard. "International Responses to Technology: Concepts and Trends." *International Organisation* 34 (Summer 1975).

Ruhle, Michael. "Enlightenment in the Second Nuclear Age." *International Affairs* 83, no. 3 (May 2007).

Rydell, Randy J. "Giving Nonproliferation Norms Teeth: Sanctions and the NNPA." *The Nonproliferation Review* 6, no. 2 (Winter 1999).

Sabherwal, O. P. "Real Hurdles in Indo-Pak Talks." *The Tribune* (Chandigarh), January 20, 1999.

Saeed, Ferial Ara. *Redefining Success: Applying Lessons in Nuclear Diplomacy from North Korea to Iran.* Strategic Perspectives no. 1. Washington D.C.: National Defense University, 2010.

Sakhuja, Vijay. "Container Security Initiative: Is India Serious About its Maritime Trade." IPCS article no. 1748. New Delhi: Institute of Peace and Conflict Studies, May 19, 2005.

Saksena, Jyotika and Suzzane Grillot. "The Emergence of Indo-U.S. Defence Cooperation: From Specific to Diffuse Reciprocity," in *Engaging India: U.S. Strategic Relations with the World's Largest Democracy*, edited by Gary Bertsch, Seema Gahlaut and Anupam Srivastava. New York: Routledge, 1999.

———. "Regime Design Matters: The CTBT and India's Nuclear Dilemma." *Comparative Strategy* 25 (2006).

Sasikumar, Karthika. "India's Emergence as a 'Responsible' Nuclear Power." *International Journal* (Summer 2007).

Saunders, Philip C. "New Approaches to Nonproliferation: Supplementing or Supplanting the Regime." *The Nonproliferation Review* (Fall-Winter 2001).

Schwartz, Stephen I. "Reconciling Indian Nuclear Cooperation and the International Proliferation Regime," in *Canadian Policy on Nuclear Cooperation with India: Confronting New Dilemmas*, edited by Karthika Sasikumar and Wade L. Huntley. Vancouver: Simons Centre for Disarmament and Non-Proliferation Research, 2007.

———, ed. *Atomic Audit: The Costs and Consequences of U.S. Nuclear Weapons Since 1948.* Washington D.C.: Brookings Institution Press, 1998.

Seaborg, Glenn T. and Benjamin S. Loeb. "Make the Partial Test Ban Comprehensive." *Bulletin of the Atomic Scientists* 4, no. 7 (May 1987).

———. *Kennedy, Krushchev and the Test Ban*. Berkeley: University of California Press, 1981.

Sethi, Manpreet. "NPT RevCon 2010: An Oppurtunity to Refocus Priorities." *Strategic Analysis* 34, no. 2 (March 2010).

Sharma, Ashok. *Indo-US Strategic Convergence: An Overview of Defence and Military Cooperation*. CLAWS Papers. New Delhi: Centre for Land Warfare Studies, November 2, 2008.

Shimp, Charles A. "Scientific Peer Review: A Case Study from Local to Global Analyses." *Journal of the Experimental Analysis of Behavior* 82, no. 1 (2004).

Shourie, Arun. "'Parity,' Did You Say?" *The Indian Express*, August 24, 2006.

———. "This is About Energy, Did You Say?" *The Indian Express*, August 23, 2006.

Shyam Saran, Speech at the Brookings Institution, Washington DC on *Indo-US Civil Nuclear Agreement: Expectations and Consequences*, March 23, 2009. Available at http://www.indianembassy.org/prdetail520/address-by-special-envoy-to-the-prime-minister,-mr.-shyam-saran-at-the-brookings-institution,-washington-dc-on-indo-us-civil-nuclear-agreement%3A-expectations-and-consequences (accessed March 18, 2012).

Sidhu, Waheguru Pal Singh. *Enhancing Indo-U.S. Strategic Cooperation*. Adelphi Paper no. 313. London: The International Institute for Strategic Studies, IISS, 1997.

Singh, Jasjit. "Prospects for Nuclear Proliferation," in *Nuclear Deterrence: Problems and Perspectives in the 1990s*, edited by Serge Sur. New York: UNIDIR, 1993.

Singh, Sandhya "US: A Civilisational Ally," *The Pioneer*, May 8, 2001.

Smith, Jonathon A. and Mike Osborn. "Interpretative Phenomenological Analysis," in *Qualitative Psychology: A Practical Guide to Research Methods*, edited by Jonathon A. Smith. London: Sage Publishers, 2003.

Smith, Roger K. "Explaining the Non-proliferation Regime: Anomalies for Contemporary International Relations Theory." *International Organisation* 41, no. 2 (Spring 1987).

Sokolski, Henry. "Implementing the DPRK Nuclear Deal: What U.S. Law Requires." *The Nonproliferation Review* (Fall-Winter 2000).

Spector, Leonard S. *Status of U.S. Sanctions Imposed on India and Pakistan*. Monterrey: James Martin Center for Nonproliferation Studies, 2001.

Squassoni, Sharon. *Proliferation Security Initiative*. CRS Report for Congress. Washington D.C.: Congressional Research Service, updated September 14, 2006.

———. "U.S.-Indian Deal and its Impact." *Arms Control Today* (July/August 2010). Available at http://www.armscontrol.org/act/2010_07–08/squassoni (accessed March 26, 2008).

Srivastava, Anupam and Seema Gahlaut. "India and The NPT: Separating Substantive Facts from Normative Fiction." *Strategic Analysis* 34, no. 2 (March, 2010).

———. "The Strategic Context of India's Economic Engagement with China." *Indian Journal of Economics and Business*, Special Issue on China and India (September 2006).

———. "NSG Waiver for India." *Pacnet*, no. 46 (September 8, 2008).

———. "India: Toward True Partnership." *Journal of International Security Affairs*, no. 11 (Fall 2006).

———. "Indo-U.S. Strategic Dialogue: From Sound Bytes to Sound Decisions." *Bharat Rakshak Monitor* 2, no. 4 (January–February 2000).

Statement of Principles for U.S.-India High Technology Commerce. Bureau of Industry and Security, U.S. Department of Commerce, Washington D.C., February 5, 2003. Available at http://www.bis.doc.gov/internationalprograms/statementprinciplesindia.htm (accessed March 15, 2009).

Subrahmanyam, K. "India's 'No' to Observer at the NPT Extension Conference." *Times of India*, January 25, 1995.

———. "India 'First' Country to Accede to Partial N-Test Ban Treaty." *The Times of India*, February 13, 1995.

———. "Indian Attitudes Towards NPT," in *Nuclear Proliferation Problems*, edited by Bhupendra Jasani. Stockholm: Almquist and Wiksell, 1974.

———. "Nuclear Policy Perspective." *World Focus* (January 1988).

———. *Self-Reliance and National Resilience: The Indian Nuclear Policy*. New Delhi: Abhinav Publishing, 1975.

———. "N-deal Reflects New World Reality: India Must Make Use of the Opportunity." *The Tribune*, July 30, 2007.

Subramaniam, C. "Science as an Instrument of Economic Progress," in *Science and Technology in India*, edited by Vadilal Dagli. New Delhi: S. Chand and Company, 1982.

Sullivan III, Michael J. "Indian Attitudes on International Atomic Energy Controls." *Pacific Affairs* 43, no. 3 (Fall 1970).

———. "Reorientation of Indian Arms Control Policy, 1969–1972." *Asian Survey* 13, no. 7 (July 1973).

Suryanarayana, P.S. "India Sees No Proxy War with Any Other Rising Nation." *The Hindu*, 1 June 2008.

Talbott, Strobe. "Dealing with the Bomb in South Asia." *Foreign Affairs* 78, no. 2 (March–April 1999).

———. *Engaging India: Diplomacy, Democracy and the Bomb*. Washington, D.C.: Brookings Institution Press, 2004.

———. Remarks at the Brookings Institution on South Asia, USIS Washington File, 12 November 1998.

———. "U.S. Diplomacy in South Asia: A Progress Report," Address at the Brookings Institution, Washington D.C., November 12, 1998.

Tate, Trevor McMorris. "Regime-Building in the Non-proliferation System." *Journal of Peace Research* 27, no. 4 (1990).

Technology Policy Statement 1983. Department of Science and Technology, Ministry of Science and Technology, Government of India, 1983. Available at http://www.dst.gov.in/stsysindia/sps1983.htm (accessed March 26, 2010).

Tellis, Ashley J. *India's Emerging Nuclear Doctrine: Exemplifying the Lessons of the Nuclear Revolution.* NBR Analysis. Seattle: National Bureau of Asian Research, 2001.

———. *Nuclear Posture: Between Recessed Deterrent and Ready Arsenal*. Santa Monica, CA: RAND, 2001.

———. *India as a Global Power: An Action Agenda for the United States*. Washington D.C.: Carnegie Endowment, 2005.

———. *The U.S.-India: Global Partnership: How Significant for American Interests?* Testimony before the House Committee on Interantional Relations, November 16, 2005.

———. "What Should We Expect From India as a Strategic Partner," in *Gauging U.S.-Indian Strategic Cooperation*, edited by Henry Sokolski. Carlisle: Strategic Studies Institute 2007.

———. *Behind India's Bomb: The Politics and Strategy of Nuclear Deterrence*. Santa Monica: RAND Corporation, 2001.

Text of the Anti-Ballistic Missile Treaty available at www.state.gov/www/global/arms/treaties/abm/abm2.html (accessed January 9, 2009).

Text of the Treaty on Nonproliferation of the Nuclear Weapons available at http://www.un.org/en/conf/npt/2005/npttreaty.html.

Text of the UN Resolution 1540, S/RES/1540. Adopted by the Security Council at its 4956th meeting, 28 April 2004, 3. Available at http://daccessdds.un.org/doc/UNDOC/GEN/N04/328/43/PDF/N0432843.pdf?OpenElement (accessed April 16, 2009).

Thomas, V.A. and P.S. Goel. "Indian Space Program and National Development." *Advances in Astronautical Sciences*, 117 (2004).

Trainor, Bernard E. "US Should not Deplore New Nuclear States: It Should Help them Curb Risks." *The Boston Globe*, June 4, 1998.

Trivedi, V.C. Remarks at the Eighteen Nations Committee on Disarmament, *Final Verbatim Record of the Conference of the Eighteen Nation Committee on Disarmament*. 298th Meeting. ENDC/PV298, United Nations General Assembly, May 23, 1967.

———. Remarks at the Eighteen Nation Disarmament Committee, *Final Verbatim Record of the Conference of the Eighteen Nation Committee on Disarmament*. 334th Meeting. ENDC/PV334, United Nations General Assembly, September 28, 1967.

U.S. Congress. *Congressional Record*. Senator Glenn, "Nuclear Weapons and Sanctions." 105th Congress, 2nd Session, 144, July 6, 1998.

———. House of Representatives. House Committee on International Relations. Subcommittee on Asia and the Pacific, 105th Congress, 2nd Session. Hearing on India-Pakistan Nuclear Proliferation. *Testimony of the Undersecretary of Commerce for International Trade*, Ambassador David L. Aaron, June 18, 1998.

———. Senate. Hearing before the Committee on Foreign Relations and the Subcommittee on International Operations of the U.S. Senate, 106th Congress, 1st Session. *Fiscal Year 2000 Budget and Embassy Security for a New Millennium.* Prepared statement by the Secretary of State, Madeline Albright. February 24, 1999.

———. Senate Foreign Relations Committee. Subcommittee on Near Eastern and South Asian Affairs. *The Crisis in South Asia*, Part II. Statement by William Schneider, *Policy Issues and Implications of Nuclear Testing by India and Pakistan*, 3 June 1998.

———. Senate. Senate Foreign Relations Committee, 106th Congress, 1st Session, 106–339. Written Testimony by Douglas J. Feith and George Miron. *Memorandum of Law: Did the ABM Treaty of 1972 Remain in Force After the USSR Ceased to Exist in December 1991 and Did it Become a Treaty Between the U.S. and the Russia Federation*, May 25, 1999.

———. Senate. Committee on Armed Services. Testimony of the Director, Wisconsin Project on Nuclear Arms Control, Gary Milhollin, July 9, 1998.

———. Senate. Committee on Energy and Natural Resources. Testimony of David J. Victor. *The India Nuclear Deal: Implications for Global Climate Change*. Washington D.C., July 18, 2006.

———. Senate. Senate Governmental Affairs Committee. Testimony of the Director of Central Intelligence Agency, James Woolsey. 103rd Congress, 1st Session, Washington DC, February 24, 1993.

———. Senate. Senate International Relations Committee. Subcommittee for Asia and the Pacific. Testimony of Karl Inderfurth, July 13, 1998.

U.S. Department of Energy, *United States Nuclear Tests: July 1945-September 1992*, DOE/NV-209-REV15. Las Vegas, Nevada: Nevada Operations Office, December 2000.

U.S. Department of State. Bureau of Public Affairs. Warren Christopher, "Strengthening U.S. Relations with South Asia," Speech by the U.S. Secretary of State to the South Asian Association for Regional Cooperation, New York City, September, 29, 1994., *U.S. Department of State Dispatch* 5, no. 40 (3 Oct, 1994).

U.S. Department of State. *Report to Congress on the Progress toward Regional Nuclear Nonproliferation*. Washington D.C.: Department of State, May 5, 1993.

Unclassified Report to Congress on the Acquisition of Technology Relating to Weapons of Mass Destruction and Advanced Conventional Munitions, July 1 through December 31, 2000.Washington DC: Office of the Director of Central Intelligence, 2000.

United Nations. Disarmament Commission. *Official Records: Supplement for January-December 1965*, Document DC/227, New York, 1966.

United Nations General Assembly Resolution 2028 (XX), *Non-Proliferation of Nuclear Weapons*, Twentieth Session of the United Nations General Assembly, 19 November, 1965.

Vajpayee, A. B. "Bilateral Talks with United States." Statement of the Prime Minister in the Parliament, December 15, 1998, in *Strategic Digest* 24, no. 1 (January 1999).

Valencia, Mark J. *The Proliferation Security Initiative: Making Waves in Asia*. Adelphi Paper no. 376. London: International Institute for Strategic Studies, 2005.

Varadarajan, Siddarth. "U.S. for Indian Hand in Proliferation Initiative." *Times of India*, March 18, 2005.

Victor, David J. "Nuclear Power for India is Good for Us All." *International Herald Tribune*, March 16, 2006.

Vohra, Ranbir. *The Making of India: A Historical Survey*. 2nd edition. New York: M.E. Sharpe, 2000.

Wagner, Alex. "Bush Waives Nuclear Related Sanctions on India, Pakistan." *Arms Control Today* (October 2001).

Walker, William. "Nuclear Enlightenment and Counter-Enlightenment." *International Affairs* 83, no. 3 (May 2007).

———. "Cut off the Source." *Bulletin of Atomic Scientists*, (March/April 2006).

Walt, Stephen M. "Two Cheers for Clinton's Foreign Policy." *Foreign Affairs* 79, no. 2 (March-April 2000).

The Weapons of Mass Destruction Commission. *Weapons of Terror: Freeing the World of Nuclear, Biological and Chemical Arms*. Stockholm, 2006.

Weeks, Jennifer. *Iran and North Korea: Two Tests for U.S. Nuclear Nonproliferation Policy*, Report for American Nuclear Society. La Grange Park, Il, August 30–September 2, 1999.. Available at http://belfercenter.ksg.harvard.edu/publication/2015/iran_and_north_korea.html (accessed March 12, 2012).

Weiss, Leonard. "India and the NPT." *Strategic Analysis* (March 2010).

———. "US-India Nuclear Cooperation: Better Later Than Sooner." *Nonproliferation Review* 14, no. 3 (November 2007).

———. "Atoms for Peace." *Bulletin of Atomic Scientists* 59, no. 6 (November 2003).

Weiss, Stanley A. "India Should Be at the Top of Washington's Contact List." *The International Herald Tribune*, November 16, 1998.

Wendt, Alexander. "Anarchy is What the States Make of It: The Social Construction of Power Politics." *International Organisation* 46 (1992).

———. "The Agent-Structure Problem in International Relations Theory." *International Organisation* (Summer 1987).

The White House. *National Strategy to Combat Weapons of Mass Destruction* (WMD). Homeland Security Presidential Directive 4. Washington D.C., December 2002.

Widmaier, Wesley W. "The Democratic Peace is What States make of it: A Constructivist Analysis of the U.S.-Indian 'Near-Miss' in the 1971 South Asian Crisis." *European Journal of International Relations* 11, no. 3 (2005).

———, Mark Blyth, and Leonard Seabrooke. "Exogenous Shocks or Endogenous Constructions? The Meanings of Wars and Crises." *International Studies Quarterly* (2007).

Wolfsthal, Jon. "The Next Nuclear Wave." *Foreign Affairs* (January-February 2005). Available at http://www.foreignaffairs.com/articles/60452/jon-b-wolfsthal/the-next-nuclear-wave?page=show

Wood, Randall S. *Non-proliferation Strategies for India and Pakistan in the Aftermath of the May 1998 Tests.* (December 2004), 18. Available at http://therandymon.com/papers/nonproliferation.pdf (accessed March 18, 2012).

Woods, Matthew. "Inventing Proliferation: The Creation and Preservation of the Inevitable Spread of Weapons." *The Review of International Affairs* (Spring 2004), 416.

Yim, Man-Sung "Nuclear Nonproliferation and the Future Expansion of Nuclear Power," *Progress in Nuclear Energy* 48 (2006).

Yost, David S. "Analysing International Nuclear Order." *International Affairs* 83, no. 3 (May 2007)

Young, Oran R. "Regime Dynamics: The Rise and Fall of International Regimes." *Critical Concepts in Political Science.* Volume 2. Edited by Andrew Linklater. New York: Routledge, 2000.

———. "International Regimes: Toward a New Theory of Institutions." *World Politics.* (1986).

Zartman, I. William. "Negotiating the Rapids: The Dynamics of Regime Formation." in *Post-Agreement Negotiation and International Regimes.* Edited by Bertram I. Spector and I. William Zartman. Washington D.C.: United States Institute of Peace, 2003.

Index

About the Author

Vandana Bhatia is a former lecturer at University of Houston, Houston, Texas. She earned her PhD in political science from University of Alberta, Edmonton, Canada. Her research expertise is in issues of international security, with a special focus on South Asia. She has taught courses ranging from U.S. national defense policy, international security, international organization, Asian politics, comparative politics, and India's foreign policy. Previously, she taught as assistant professor at Kalindi College, University of Delhi, Delhi, India.